Teaching Primary Mathematics

Education at SAGE

SAGE is a leading international publisher of journals, books, and electronic media for academic, educational, and professional markets.

Our education publishing includes:

- accessible and comprehensive texts for aspiring education professionals and practitioners looking to further their careers through continuing professional development

- inspirational advice and guidance for the classroom

- authoritative state of the art reference from the leading authors in the field

Find out more at: **www.sagepub.co.uk/education**

Sylvia Turner

Teaching Primary Mathematics

Illustrations and diagrams
Luke Turner

Los Angeles | London | New Delhi
Singapore | Washington DC

Los Angeles | London | New Delhi
Singapore | Washington DC

SAGE Publications Ltd
1 Oliver's Yard
55 City Road
London EC1Y 1SP

SAGE Publications Inc.
2455 Teller Road
Thousand Oaks, California 91320

SAGE Publications India Pvt Ltd
B 1/I 1 Mohan Cooperative Industrial Area
Mathura Road
New Delhi 110 044

SAGE Publications Asia-Pacific Pte Ltd
3 Church Street
#10-04 Samsung Hub
Singapore 049483

Commissioning editor: James Clark
Project manager: Bill Antrobus
Assistant editor: Monira Begum
Assistant production editor: Nicola Marshall
Copyeditor: Peter Williams
Proofreader: Caroline Stock
Marketing manager: Catherine Slinn
Cover design: Wendy Scott
Typeset by Kestrel Data, Exeter, Devon
Printed in India at Replika Press, Pvt Ltd

© Sylvia Turner 2013

First published 2013

Library of Congress Control Number: 2011946184

British Library Cataloguing in Publication data

A catalogue record for this book is available from the British Library

ISBN 978-0-85702-879-2
ISBN 978-0-85702-880-8 (pbk)

MIX
Paper from
responsible sources
FSC
www.fsc.org FSC® C013604

To John, Luke and Jane

CONTENTS

ABOUT THE AUTHOR

Sylvia Turner is a Senior Lecturer in the Faculty of Education, Health and Social Care at the University of Winchester where she works with student teachers and teaching assistants in the Early Years and Primary sectors of education. Her areas of teaching and research are mathematics education, Early Years and career progression for support staff. She has also worked as a school partnership coordinator engaging in staff liaison and preparing student teachers for experience in school.

ACKNOWLEDGEMENTS

I have worked with many student teachers and teaching assistants and they have been the inspiration for this book. I would like to thank particularly Rebecca Kemp, Vicki Blakemore and Amy Empson for their contributions from perspectives as student teachers and practising teachers.

The book owes much to those who enabled me to observe and discuss practice in Europe. Particular thanks are due to Carmen Sotelino, Joana Francis Marriott, Barbara Chatwin, Piero Cedrati, Aimee McAllister Linehan, Leo Frost and Nicola Murray for their various roles in enabling access to schools, providing translation when needed and giving background information.

Thank you also to Luke Turner, my son, for providing illustrations and diagrams and Jane Turner, my daughter, for her valuable insights as a practising teacher.

Thank you to James Clark and Monira Begum at Sage for editorial input and excellent support.

Finally, thank you to mathematics team colleagues past and present, Laura Clarke, Judith McCullouch, Claire Morse, Jackie Nicholson, Clare Tope, Reg Wrathmell and Mick Yates. Our discussions and their comments have been invaluable.

Publisher's Acknowledgements

Sage gratefully acknowledges the contributions of the following reviewers who read the proposal and draft chapters along the way:

Carol Murphy, Senior Lecturer, School of Education,
University of Exeter, UK

Sian Howie, Module co-ordinator for PGCE Primary Mathematics,
University of Chichester, UK

Caroline Rickard, Lecturer, School of Education,
University of Chichester, UK

Sandy Pepperell, Lecturer, School of Education,
University of Roehampton, UK

Additional thanks go to:

Askew, M., Hodge, J., Hossain, S. and Bretscher, N. (2010) *Values and variables: Mathematics education in high-performing countries*. London: Nuffield Foundation.

LIST OF ABBREVIATIONS

ACER	Australian Council for Educational Research
ACME	Advisory Committee on Mathematics Education
AfL	Assessment for Learning
BEAM	Be A Mathematician Project
Becta	British Educational Communications and Technology Agency
BEE UK	The Best Evidence Encyclopaedia UK (website)
BERA	British Educational Research Association
BSL	British Sign Language
CATE	Council for the Accreditation of Teacher Education
CERC	Comparative Education Research Centre, Hong Kong
CL	Communication and Language
CLL	Community Language Learning
CPD	Continuing Professional Development
DCFS	Department for Family, Schools and Children
DES	Department of Education and Science
DfE	Department for Education
DfEE	Department for Education and Employment
ERS	'European Research Study'
ESRC	Economic and Social Research Council
EYFS	Early Years Foundation Stage
EYFSP	Early Years Foundation Stage Profile
EYP	Early Years Practitioner

GCSE	General Certificate of Secondary Education
GTP	Graduate Teacher Programme
ICT	Information and Communications Technology
IEE	Institute for Effective Education
INCA	International Review of Curriculum and Assessment
ITE	Initial Teacher Education
KUW	Knowledge and Understanding of the World
LA	Local Authority
MaST	Mathematics Specialist Teacher
NACCCE	National Advisory Committee on Creative and Cultural Education
NAEP	National Assessment of Educational Progress
NCES	National Center for Education Statistics
NCETM	National Centre for Excellence in Teaching Mathematics
NFER	National Foundation for Educational Research
NNP	National Numeracy Project
NNS	National Numeracy Strategy
NQT	Newly Qualified Teacher
OECD	Organisation for Economic Cooperation and Development
Ofsted	Office for Standards in Education, Childen's Services and Skills
PCK	Pedagogical Content Knowledge
PD	Personal Development
PGCE	Postgraduate Certificate in Education
PISA	Programme for International Student Assessment
PNS	Primary National Strategy
PPA	Planning, Preparation and Assessment
ProfGCE	Professional Graduate Certificate in Education
PSE	Personal, Social and Emotional Development
PSHE	Person, Social and Health Education
PSRN	Problem Solving, Reasoning and Numeracy
QCA	Qualifications and Curriculum Authority
QCDA	Qualifications and Curriculum Development Agency
QTS	Qualified Teacher Status
SATs	Standard Attainment Tests
SCAA	Schools Curriculum and Assessment Authority
SCITT	School-Based Initial Teacher Training
SRMO	Sage Research Methods Online
STEM	Science, Technology, Engineering and Mathematics
TDA	Training and Development Agency
TIMSS	Trends in International Mathematics and Science Study
TLRP	Teaching and Learning Research Programme
TTA	Teacher Training Agency
UCAS	Universities and Colleges Admissions Service
VAK	Visual, Auditory or Kinaesthetic
VARK	Visual, Auditory, Reading/Writing and Kinaesthetic

INTRODUCTION

The Primary Curriculum has been considered by the Rose Review (2009), the Cambridge Primary Review (2009) and the Commons Select Committee inquiry into the National Curriculum (2009). The independent review of mathematics teaching in early years and primary school settings by Sir Peter Williams (2008) has begun to be implemented with the Mathematics Specialist Teacher (MaST) programme. A new curriculum based on the recommendations of the Rose Review was due to start in schools from September 2010. Indeed, it had been published on the Qualifications and Curriculum Development Agency (QCDA) website. However, QCDA is being closed as part of the Coalition government's wider education reforms. The Schools White Paper *The Importance of Teaching* published in November 2010 contains contrasting messages from the government about schools having 'greater freedom over the curriculum' yet being 'properly accountable'. While these aims are not necessarily conflicting, over the past two decades there has been a tension between the primary school curriculum and the associated national tests. Although comparison of the final reports shows agreement as well as difference, whatever statutory primary curriculum is in place, it would seem significant changes are set to take place.

Since the Education Reform Act of 1988 and the introduction of a national curriculum in schools, the role of the teacher in curriculum design and pedagogy has been significantly marginalised by central prescription and regulation. The role I took on in the mid-1970s bears little relationship to the role for which I am preparing my current student teachers. They could truly have become 'trainees' in the jargon of the Teaching and Development Agency, being trained to teach in a certain way unless providers of teaching enable them to be educated to teach.

I believe this centralised intervention in both the statutory education system and that of teacher training has left a significant void. Skills that would have been common place for teachers before the introduction of the National Curriculum in 1988, such as planning the content of the curriculum from first principles and writing schemes of work, are no longer evident. If the way forward for the primary curriculum that is now evident allows schools, and particularly class teachers, more autonomy in what and how they are teaching, then arguably they need preparation and support in developing skills to devise this curriculum.

The success or not of a new curriculum for primary schools will rest on whether teachers are empowered to work in a new way, a factor acknowledged by the Commons Select Committee (2009). Mathematics is constantly under scrutiny in terms of performance in league tables both nationally and internationally, so the subject is even more vulnerable to change. *Teaching Primary Mathematics* is a book for either a student on an initial teacher education (ITE) programme or a practising teacher. The principle aim is to empower teachers so that they can make sense of recent initiatives associated with the curriculum, particularly the mathematics curriculum. Such empowerment should enable teachers to take ownership of what they are teaching and why it should be taught, within the obvious constraints of national, local and school legislation, directives and policies.

Starting from a personal viewpoint, teachers would be encouraged to think what has made them the teachers they are, what may need to change and what is positive about their current practice. The nature of mathematics would be considered. What is mathematics about and how did it evolve into the subject we know today? Learning mathematics will be discussed by suggesting how decisions can be made in terms of what children really need to learn and why. Teachers' knowledge will be explored by considering the generalist role of the teacher and what types of knowledge are required to teach mathematics. The teaching process will be explored by considering the choices teachers make in their approach, the resources they use and how assessment and planning are dependent upon the expectations and needs of children, their families and society as a whole. The final chapters of the book will consider the next steps from the perspective of the teacher, whether a student or teacher practising in school. Practice in a sample of European countries will be discussed and how this practice can support the teaching and learning of the subject within the constraints of a local or national curriculum and agenda.

Confidence would appear key to supporting teachers and therefore children in their learning. Teachers seem constantly under scrutiny whether it is in school through appraisal, inspection by local authority or by Ofsted. I believe the balance has shifted adversely so many primary teachers have no clear opinion on what and how they are teaching and this is detrimental to the quality of teaching in primary schools today.

Each of the chapters follows the same format of beginning with aims and finishing with summaries, review questions and conclusions. There will be activities to help you engage with the ideas being developed in the text. These will be identified by the following icon:

Reflection will be encouraged by the review questions. The term 'reflection' can have a negative reaction among some people as they think of it as a form of self-analysis for which they do not have the skills. The term 'reflect' means looking back in some way. You could be considering an experience, an object or an idea but revising the 'image' through further experience, reading or discussion. Sometimes the activity of reflection is aided by the use of questions and/or formats. You will find further guidance in Appendix 2.

Here are some final notes to clarify some terminology used in the book. I have tried to avoid the term 'trainee'. It is hard to avoid this term as it is the word used by the Teaching and Development Agency (TDA) to denote a student on any initial teaching programme. However, education is a process, not a product. The idea that someone can be *trained* to teach defies research and good practice. For example, I can be trained to use a new software program but I cannot be trained to read children a story. Teaching strategies to perform this task may be similar such as demonstrating and breaking the task down into achievable goals but the difference is that the range of factors and variables determining success will increase as the task moves from working with an inanimate to an animate object. In the case of reading a story, there is the children's reaction and the dialogue between the adult and children. As far as teaching is concerned, consideration of and response to such variables in terms of knowledge skills and understanding is the essence of teacher education.

The last ten years or so have seen a significant change in the expectations of education below the statutory school age so expectations now relate from 0 rather than 5 years. The terms *primary teacher* and *primary mathematics* relate to the 0–11 age range in terms of personnel and curricular guidance in a formal setting outside the family home. Education policy in the United Kingdom is not identical in each of its countries, England, Northern Ireland, Scotland and Wales. Unless stated otherwise education policy discussed relates to England only.

References

Alexander, R. (ed.) (2009) *Children, Their World, Their Education: Final Report and Recommendations of the Cambridge Primary Review*. London: Routledge.

House of Commons, Children, Schools and Families Committee (2009) *The Fourth Report of Session 2008–9 Concerning the National Curriculum of the House of Commons, Children, Schools and Families Committee*. London: HMSO.

Rose, J. (ed.) (2009) *The Independent Review of the National Curriculum: Final Report*. London: DCSF.

Williams, Sir P. (2008) *Mathematics Teaching in Early Years Setting and Primary Schools*. London: DCFS.

THE 2012 TEACHING STANDARDS

Standards for Teachers (Department for Education) 2012

Qualified Teacher Status (QTS) is required in England and Wales to become a teacher of children in the state and special education sectors. Similar statuses exist in Scotland and Northern Ireland but an undergraduate degree and some form of teacher training is compulsory for those wishing to teach. As of September 2012, all graduates have to have a minimum lower second-class Honours degree. The ways for a graduate to gain QTS status are by taking:

- a one-year university or other higher education institution-based Postgraduate Certificate in Education (PGCE) or Professional Graduate Certificate in Education (ProfGCE). The programme includes a significant period of time on teaching practice in a school. The PGCE carries credits towards a master's degree;
- a school-based initial teacher training (SCITT) programme based in a school. Some SCITT programmes also award a PGCE qualification. It is available in England only;
- a Graduate Teacher Programme (GTP) while working as an unqualified teacher in a school;

- Teaching Schools' training which is a new initiative launched in 2011 using a variety of models but generally involves clusters of high-performing schools working with partners including a university;
- a Leadership Development Programme through Teach First which is an independent charity. Its aim is to change the lives of children from all backgrounds by recruiting highly motivated graduates to teach and lead in challenging schools across the United Kingdom. As with the Teaching Schools initiative, candidates are trained with the support of schools, businesses and universities. The programme takes two years with successful participants graduating to become Teach First Ambassadors at which time they continue in leadership in school or elsewhere. The scheme operates in specific regions and participants must have in addition to standard graduate requirements:
  - o a 2:1 degree or above 300 UCAS points (or equivalent, excluding general studies);
  - o degree or A-levels that satisfy the teaching subject requirements.

Those wishing to become teachers who do not have a degree can enrol on a three- or four-year undergraduate qualification. Again, this programme includes a significant period of time on teaching practice in school.

Regardless of all higher-level qualifications student teachers must have GCSEs at grade C or above or their equivalents in English and mathematics and, for those wishing to become primary teachers, in science. Additionally, potential students must have prior experience in school before starting a teacher training programme.

Any teacher training programme leading to QTS must equip students to teach across at least two key consecutive age ranges between the seven age bands between the ages of 3 and 19 years.

QTS is technically recognised only in the country it was awarded (England or Wales), but teachers can normally apply for QTS in the other country. QTS is also recognised by many other countries. Teachers trained outside England and Wales must also apply to be awarded QTS if they wish to teach in England and Wales.

After completion of a recognised teachers' training programme participants must pass a period of induction of three consecutive school terms. Until induction has been completed successfully teachers are referred to as Newly Qualified Teachers (NQTs).

Whatever teacher training programme a potential teacher undertakes in England and Wales, it must support the completion of Professional Standards. In Wales, the Standards were revised and came into effect in 2011 (Welsh Government, 2011). The Standards in England were also recently revised in 2011 and come into effect in September 2012 (DfE, 2011).

The Standards identify statutory requirements. They have been reviewed at regular intervals since their introduction by the Council for the Accreditation of Teacher Education (CATE), established in 1983 to set standards for initial teacher training courses. Until that time teachers' entry to the profession was based upon successful completion of an accredited teacher training programme. Subsequent versions of the Standards have been produced at regular intervals by whatever government body was given responsibility at the time. The 1998 version of the Standards, commonly referred to by their Department for Education and Employment (DfEE) designation '4/98', was the most detailed coming at a time when the Literacy and Numeracy Strategies were introduced. Many publications were launched to support meeting the 4/98 Standards such as the series by Learning Matters. However, since the 1998 Standards, subsequent versions have been less specific in their detail until in 2007 they related only to those teachers entering the profession. The 2007 version of the Standards included teachers other than those seeking to gain Qualified Teacher Status and gave Standards for different stages in a teacher's career, QTS, Core, Post-threshold, Excellent and Advanced.

The 2012 version of the Standards (DfE, 2011) relates to *all* teachers. In line with government policy of devolving more responsibility to schools, headteachers will be responsible for arranging assessment of qualified teachers in school against the standards to a level related to their career stage. No specific guidance has yet been given as to how the Standards will be interpreted at different career stages other than by the use of 'professional judgement'.

The Teachers' Standards (DfE, 2011) are divided into two parts: teaching, which is subdivided into eight parts, and personal and professional conduct (see below).

One of the challenges of assessing Standards is that they can be phrased in general terms in order to meet all contexts. As more specificity is added, so they can become more numerous and assessed by using a 'tick box' approach to make the task manageable. The previous Standards have been criticised for their 'vagueness' (DfE, 2011) but interpretation of Standards still remains an issue as they are open to subjectivity on the part of the assessor's preconceptions, particularly when comparative adjectives are not defined and intangible verbs are used, for example: *Set high expectations which inspire, motivate and challenge pupils* (DfE, 2011). High on what scale and inspirational to whom? Significant work has to be carried out so such Standards can be quantified in some way such as by their outcome so that they have a shared meaning. Additionally, as significant assessment is now to be devolved to schools, the vast differences in interpretation as well as context could lead to significant variance in the assessment of teachers unless some form of national or regional benchmarking is introduced.

The Standards apply to whatever route is taken into teaching, whether it is school-based or university-based training. There is the issue that school-based routes give the necessary practice and experience yet have the potential to be devoid of theoretical underpinning whereas the reverse can be true of university-based routes unless clear links are made between theory and practice in the classroom. As they stand, the 2012 Standards refer to teaching in terms of personal attributes and expectations of children, progression in learning, subject and curriculum knowledge, planning, differentiation and behaviour as well as wider school responsibilities. Evidence for meeting Standards can be demonstrated by the observation of lessons, planning documentation and tracking children's progress. There is implicit reference to a broad knowledge base in terms of subject knowledge and reflective practice in terms of the personal terms of 'self-criticality' and professionalism but such evidence is less tangible and cannot be directly demonstrated.

Students embarking on teacher training programmes will need to develop a shared understanding of the Standards with their tutors whether they are in school or university. Identifying how they can work towards meeting the Standards other than by observation and documentation will enhance their understanding. Such opportunities as engaging in discussion with their peers to debate issues, develop resources and disseminate information to colleagues will allow students to develop the depth of knowledge to become effective teachers.

Standards for Teachers*

Preamble

Teachers make the education of their pupils their first concern, and are accountable for achieving the highest possible standards in work and conduct. Teachers act with honesty and integrity; have strong subject knowledge, keep their knowledge and skills as teachers up-to-date and are self-critical; forge positive professional relationships; and work with parents in the best interests of their pupils.

*Reproduced under the terms of the Open Government Licence.

Part One: Teaching

A teacher must:

1 Set high expectations which inspire, motivate and challenge pupils
- establish a safe and stimulating environment for pupils, rooted in mutual respect
- set goals that stretch and challenge pupils of all backgrounds, abilities and dispositions
- demonstrate consistently the positive attitudes, values and behaviour which are expected of pupils.

2 Promote good progress and outcomes by pupils
- be accountable for pupils' attainment, progress and outcomes
- plan teaching to build on pupils' capabilities and prior knowledge
- guide pupils to reflect on the progress they have made and their emerging needs
- demonstrate knowledge and understanding of how pupils learn and how this impacts on teaching
- encourage pupils to take a responsible and conscientious attitude to their own work and study.

3 Demonstrate good subject and curriculum knowledge
- have a secure knowledge of the relevant subject(s) and curriculum areas, foster and maintain pupils' interest in the subject, and address misunderstandings
- demonstrate a critical understanding of developments in the subject and curriculum areas, and promote the value of scholarship
- demonstrate an understanding of and take responsibility for promoting high standards of literacy, articulacy and the correct use of standard English, whatever the teacher's specialist subject
- if teaching early reading, demonstrate a clear understanding of systematic synthetic phonics
- if teaching early mathematics, demonstrate a clear understanding of appropriate teaching strategies.

4 Plan and teach well structured lessons
- impart knowledge and develop understanding through effective use of lesson time
- promote a love of learning and children's intellectual curiosity
- set homework and plan other out-of-class activities to consolidate and extend the knowledge and understanding pupils have acquired

- reflect systematically on the effectiveness of lessons and approaches to teaching
- contribute to the design and provision of an engaging curriculum within the relevant subject area(s).

5 Adapt teaching to respond to the strengths and needs of all pupils
- know when and how to differentiate appropriately, using approaches which enable pupils to be taught effectively
- have a secure understanding of how a range of factors can inhibit pupils' ability to learn, and how best to overcome these
- demonstrate an awareness of the physical, social and intellectual development of children, and know how to adapt teaching to support pupils' education at different stages of development
- have a clear understanding of the needs of all pupils, including those with special educational needs; those of high ability; those with English as an additional language; those with disabilities; and be able to use and evaluate distinctive teaching approaches to engage and support them.

6 Make accurate and productive use of assessment
- know and understand how to assess the relevant subject and curriculum areas, including statutory assessment requirements
- make use of formative and summative assessment to secure pupils' progress
- use relevant data to monitor progress, set targets, and plan subsequent lessons
- give pupils regular feedback, both orally and through accurate marking, and encourage pupils to respond to the feedback.

7 Manage behaviour effectively to ensure a good and safe learning environment
- have clear rules and routines for behaviour in classrooms, and take responsibility for promoting good and courteous behaviour both in classrooms and around the school, in accordance with the school's behaviour policy
- have high expectations of behaviour, and establish a framework for discipline with a range of strategies, using praise, sanctions and rewards consistently and fairly
- manage classes effectively, using approaches which are appropriate to pupils' needs in order to involve and motivate them
- maintain good relationships with pupils, exercise appropriate authority, and act decisively when necessary.

8 Fulfil wider professional responsibilities
- make a positive contribution to the wider life and ethos of the school
- develop effective professional relationships with colleagues, knowing how and when to draw on advice and specialist support
- deploy support staff effectively
- take responsibility for improving teaching through appropriate professional development, responding to advice and feedback from colleagues
- communicate effectively with parents with regard to pupils' achievements and well-being.

Part Two: Personal and professional conduct

A teacher is expected to demonstrate consistently high standards of personal and professional conduct. The following statements define the behaviour and attitudes which set the required standard for conduct throughout a teacher's career.

- Teachers uphold public trust in the profession and maintain high standards of ethics and behaviour, within and outside school, by:
  - treating pupils with dignity, building relationships rooted in mutual respect, and at all times observing proper boundaries appropriate to a teacher's professional position
  - having regard for the need to safeguard pupils' well-being, in accordance with statutory provisions
  - showing tolerance of and respect for the rights of others
  - not undermining fundamental British values, including democracy, the rule of law, individual liberty and mutual respect and tolerance of those with different faiths and beliefs
  - ensuring that personal beliefs are not expressed in ways which exploit pupils' vulnerability or might lead them to break the law.
  - Teachers must have proper and professional regard for the ethos, policies and practices of the school in which they teach, and maintain high standards in their own attendance and punctuality.
- Teachers must have an understanding of, and always act within, the statutory frameworks which set out their professional duties and responsibilities.

The following table cross-references the Teaching Standards across the chapters in this book.

Chapter	Relevant 2012 Teaching Standards 'Teaching'	In terms of:
1 Teachers as mathematicians	1 Set high expectations which inspire, motivate and challenge pupils	– demonstrate consistently positive attitudes, values and behaviour which are expected of pupil
	3 Demonstrate good subject and curriculum knowledge	– critical understanding of developments in the subject and curriculum areas
	8 Fulfil wider professional responsibilities	– take responsibility for improving teaching through appropriate professional development, responding to advice and feedback from colleagues
2 The nature and language of mathematics	3 Demonstrate good subject and curriculum knowledge	– critical understanding of developments in the subject and curriculum areas
3 What do children really need to know and why?	1 Set high expectations which inspire, motivate and challenge pupils	– set goals that stretch and challenge pupils of all backgrounds, abilities and dispositions
	2 Promote good progress and outcomes by pupils	– demonstrate knowledge and understanding of how pupils learn and how this impacts on teaching
	3 Demonstrate good subject and curriculum knowledge	– critical understanding of developments in the subject and curriculum areas
	4 Plan and teach well structured lessons	– promote a love of learning and children's intellectual curiosity
4 What should teachers know and why?	1 Set high expectations which inspire, motivate and challenge pupils	– set goals that stretch and challenge pupils of all backgrounds, abilities and dispositions
	2 Promote good progress and outcomes by pupils	– demonstrate knowledge and understanding of how pupils learn and how this impacts on teaching
	3 Demonstrate good subject and curriculum knowledge	– demonstrate a critical understanding of developments in the subject and curriculum areas – have a secure knowledge of the relevant subject(s) and curriculum areas, and promote scholarship

	5 Adapt teaching to respond to the strengths and needs of all pupils	– *have a secure understanding of how a range of factors can inhibit pupils' ability to learn, and how best to overcome these* – *demonstrate an awareness of the physical, social and intellectual development of children, and know how to adapt teaching to support pupils' education at different stages of development* – *have a clear understanding of the needs of all pupils, including those with special educational needs, those of high ability, those with English as an additional language and those with disabilities, and be able to use and evaluate distinctive teaching approaches to engage and support them*
	6 Make accurate and productive use of assessment	– *know and understand how to assess the relevant subject and curriculum areas, including statutory assessment requirements*
	8 Fulfil wider professional responsibilities	– *make a positive contribution to the wider life and ethos of the school*
5 Teaching approaches	2 Promote good progress and outcomes by pupils	– *plan teaching to build on pupils' capabilities and prior knowledge* – *guide pupils to reflect on the progress they have made and their emerging needs*
	4 Plan and teach well structured lessons	– *set homework and plan other out-of-class activities to consolidate and extend the knowledge and understanding*
	5 Adapt teaching to respond to the strengths and needs of all pupils	– *if teaching early mathematics, demonstrate a clear understanding of appropriate teaching strategies*
	7 Manage behaviour effectively to ensure a good and safe learning environment	– *manage classes effectively, using approaches which are appropriate to pupils' needs in order to involve and motivate them*
	8 Promote good progress and outcomes by pupils	– *communicate effectively with parents with regard to pupils' achievements and well-being*

6 Assessment and planning in mathematics	1 Set high expectations which inspire, motivate and challenge	– set goals that stretch and challenge pupils of all backgrounds, abilities and dispositions
	2 Promote good progress and outcomes for children	– be accountable for pupils' attainment, progress and outcomes – plan teaching to build on pupils' capabilities and prior knowledge – encourage pupils to take a responsible and conscientious attitude to their work and study
	4 Plan and teach well structured lessons	– impart knowledge and develop understanding through effective use of lesson time
	5 Adapt teaching to respond to the strengths and needs of all pupils	– reflect systematically on the effectiveness of lessons and approaches to learning
	6 Make accurate and productive use of assessment	– know when and how to differentiate appropriately, using approaches which enable pupils to be taught effectively – make use of formative and summative assessment to secure pupils' progress – use relevant data to monitor progress, set targets and plan subsequent lessons – give pupils regular feedback, both orally and through accurate marking, and encourage pupils to respond to the feedback
	8 Fulfil wider professional responsibilities	– communicate effectively with parents with regard to pupils' achievements and well-being
7 Resources for mathematics	1 Set high expectations which inspire, motivate and challenge	– establish a safe and stimulating environment for pupils rooted in mutual respect
	4 Plan and teach well structured lessons	– impart knowledge and develop understanding through effective use of lesson time
	5 Adapt teaching to respond to the strengths and needs of all pupils	– know when and how to differentiate appropriately, using approaches which enable pupils to be taught effectively
	8 Fulfil wider professional responsibilities	– deploy support staff effectively

8 What can we learn from other countries?	3 Demonstrate good subject and curriculum knowledge	– demonstrate critical understanding of developments in the subject and curriculum areas
	4 Plan and teach well structured lessons	– contribute to the design and provision of an engaging curriculum within the relevant subject area(s)
	8 Fulfil wider professional responsibilities	– make a positive contribution to the wider life and ethos of the school – develop effective professional relationships with colleagues, knowing how and when to draw on advice and specialist support – take responsibility for improving teaching through appropriate professional development, responding to advice and feedback from colleagues – communicate effectively with parents with regard to pupils' achievements and well-being
9 Researching mathematics education – a case study	3 Demonstrate good subject and curriculum knowledge	– demonstrate a critical understanding of developments in the subject and curriculum areas
	3 Plan and teach well-structured lessons	– contribute to the design and provision of an engaging curriculum within the relevant subject area(s)
	8 Fulfil wider professional responsibilities	– make a positive contribution to the wider life and ethos of the school – develop effective professional relationships with colleagues, knowing how and when to draw on advice and specialist support – take responsibility for improving teaching through appropriate professional development, responding to advice and feedback from colleagues

10 Conclusion	3 Demonstrate good subject and curriculum knowledge	– *critical understanding of developments in the subject and curriculum areas*
	4 Plan and teach well structured lessons	– *contribute to the design and provision of an engaging curriculum within the relevant subject area(s)*
	8 Fulfil wider professional responsibilities	– *make a positive contribution to the wider life and ethos of the school* – *develop effective professional relationships with colleagues, knowing how and when to draw on advice and specialist support* – *take responsibility for improving teaching through appropriate professional development, responding to advice and feedback from colleagues*

References

DfE (2011) *Teachers' Standards*. London: DfE. Available online at: https://www.education.gov.uk/publications/eOrderingDownload/DFE-00066-2011.pdf (accessed 14 March 2012).

Welsh Government (2011) *Revised Professional Standards for Education Practitioners in Wales*. Cardiff: Welsh Government.

CHAPTER 1

TEACHERS AS MATHEMATICIANS

Aims

By the end of this chapter you should:

- be aware of factors that are specific to effective mathematics teaching;
- become aware of factors that may affect your teaching of mathematics;
- have identified your response to mathematics;
- have identified incidents and experiences in your autobiography that may have affected your response to mathematics.

Introduction

In the United Kingdom state school teachers are expected to teach the full curriculum for children up to age 11. There arc some exceptions such as in those areas that operate a 'middle' school system for children from the age of 8 or 9 years, where some specialist teaching takes place. Some schools have an element of specialist teaching but it tends to be for Foundation subjects such as music and Physical Education in which it is standard to acknowledge some teachers may lack sufficient subject knowledge. However, in core subjects such as mathematics such a view would appear not to be acceptable for someone with Qualified Teacher Status (QTS). Just as we would not assume that teachers are artists or have specialist skills to teach art, so we assume that those teaching in the primary age range do not require specialist skills to teach mathematics. The generalist nature of teaching in the first years of education has many benefits for children and teachers in terms of pastoral care of children and opportunities to make links between subjects. In recent years, however, these general assumptions have been questioned in terms of the challenges faced by the generalist in subject knowledge, curriculum organisation and delivery.

Particular concern has focused on mathematics and its falling ranking in relation to international comparisons. Data from the Trends in International Mathematics and Science Study (TIMSS) and, more recently, in the Programme for International Student Assessment PISA study by the Organisation for Economic Cooperation and Development (OECD) indicates that the UK does not compare favourably with other countries.

Beliefs and their effect on learning and teaching mathematics

Where would you consider you are on the following scale in terms of your feelings about mathematics? Is it a subject you love or hate, or maybe your feelings are not so extreme and fall somewhere midway?

10 0

Mike Askew led a research project by King's College, London that was sponsored by the Teacher Training Agency (TTA) (Askew et al., 1997). The aim was to investigate the distinctive characteristics of effective teachers of numeracy. Effectiveness was measured in a test administered to the pupils of the teachers in the sample at the beginning of the Autumn term and the end of the Spring term and the average gain calculated. This produced an indicator of teacher effectiveness.

Using data from case studies it emerged that teachers held certain individual sets of beliefs about mathematics. Such beliefs were found to be fundamental in influencing the way in which they taught. The beliefs were categorised in the following way.

- *Connectionist* – beliefs based around valuing pupils' methods and teaching strategies with an emphasis on establishing connections within mathematics.
- *Transmission* – beliefs based around the primacy of teaching and a view of mathematics as a collection of separate routines and procedures.
- *Discovery* – beliefs clustered around the primacy of learning and a view of mathematics as being discovered by pupils.

(Askew et al., 1997)

One of the key findings was that effective teachers had connectionist beliefs. They made connections between different ideas and knew how to select and use effective and efficient strategies for calculation. They believed that their pupils could become numerate and that pupils develop strategies and connections between ideas or networks by being challenged to think by use of explanation, listening and problem-solving. There was little correlation between the effective teachers in the sample and their qualifications. However, there was evidence that they had undertaken mathematics professional development over an extended time.

Apart from the research led by Mike Askew, there has been considerable research carried out concerning beliefs about mathematics in both the adult population as a whole and more specifically in teachers of mathematics. In the UK alone there is a large body of evidence drawn from research over the last thirty years ranging from government reports, most significantly Cockcroft (1982) and Williams (2008), to research with teachers and those involved with education such as Buxton (1981), Haylock (2010), Jackson (2008), Boaler (2009) and Swan and Swain (2010). A brief overview of the research carried out may give you a sense of the significance of beliefs in the teaching of primary mathematics.

Over thirty years ago, Laurie Buxton, a mathematics adviser for the now defunct Inner London Education Authority, carried out research to investigate the aversion to mathematics that he was encountering among those involved with education. This group included a significant percentage of teachers who were otherwise high achievers and successful in their chosen career. The result was a series of detailed case studies based on individual interviews, group work and discussions that still have resonance today. Although the research was carried out with a small sample of nine adults, the fact that Buxton was seconded for a year enabled him to have time to work with the group in depth. He found that their emotional response was very important to learning mathematics and using it in an educational context.

Participants spoke of mathematics in terms of terror. When asked about their feelings towards mathematics phrases used ranged from worried to panic to the extent that one participant stated '. . . whenever I think back to it [mathematics], it's always that dreadful numbing panic' (Buxton, 1981). Buxton worked closely with Richard Skemp, a mathematician, educator and psychologist. He designed mathematics workshops to enable participants to develop confidence, which he believed to be fundamental to learning. Basic to the strategies Buxton used was the interaction of the individual's emotions with mathematics. He found common feelings about mathematics among the group such as a belief that mathematics was a collection of incomprehensible rules and facts to be remembered that mainly involved computation. He acknowledged the validity of these perceptions as they came from the individuals' experience. He believed that the *experience* of learning mathematics had to be changed if mathematics was to be seen as a comprehensible subject with interconnecting relationships.

The effect of emotion on mathematics was confirmed in the Cockcroft Report (1982) by surveys it commissioned. While acknowledging that many people coped with the demands of mathematics, it was found that among the adult population, mathematics induced feelings of anxiety, helplessness, fear and even guilt among interviewees and 'No connection was found between the extent to which those interviewed used mathematics and the level of their educational qualifications . . .' (Cockcroft, 1982: para. 2.20).

Despite the detailed recommendations of Cockcroft to address the problem in the intervening years, Ian Thompson found, when working with teachers on mathematical activity, they responded similarly to those cited in Cockcroft (1982) with the same feelings of panic, anxiety and guilt (Thompson, 2003). Similarly, Derek Haylock has considered the emotional response to mathematics with teaching students. In the fourth edition of his book *Mathematics Explained for Primary Teachers* (Haylock, 2010) he states 'Even well-qualified graduates feel insecure and uncertain about much of the mathematics they have to teach' (Haylock, 2010: xii).

Elizabeth Jackson carried out a literature review of mathematics anxiety and subsequently investigated the situation among primary teacher trainees

(2008). She suggests that mathematical anxiety exists to the degree that the ability to do mathematics is strongly influenced by people's attitudes rather than their cognitive skill.

Jo Boaler has carried out extensive research into mathematics teaching and learning in the USA and UK. Having completed longitudinal studies she has identified what she believes is wrong in classrooms today in terms of children's mathematical experiences. She found that belief was significant in forming ideas about mathematics. Some teachers believed that success in mathematics was a sign of general intelligence and that it was a subject that some people can do and others cannot. Such ideas have the potential to be harmful to children as it makes them feel 'helpless and stupid' (Boaler, 2009: 1–2).

More recently, Malcolm Swan (Swan and Swain, 2010) has undertaken a number of research projects into the professional development of numeracy teachers with post-16 learners. Although relating to teaching those beyond statutory education the focus still relates to mathematics teachers. Teachers investigated eight research-based principles for teaching:

1. Build on the knowledge that learners bring to the session.
2. Expose and discuss common misconceptions.
3. Develop effective questioning.
4. Use cooperative small-group work.
5. Emphasise methods rather than answers.
6. Use rich mathematical tasks.
7. Create connections between mathematical topics.
8. Use technology in appropriate ways.

Existing beliefs and practices were recognised and alternative practices were offered and considered. The teachers were encouraged to adopt new practices and reflect on their experiences and beliefs. Results suggested that many of the teachers' practices and beliefs were significantly affected. Their practice became less transmission-oriented and teachers began to create collaborative learning environments where students were challenged to confront difficulties and take on more active classroom roles.

Assessing your beliefs

Initially, the findings of the research cited above may seem somewhat negative in terms of teachers and the teaching of mathematics. However, it does give an insight into four key issues that can be identified from the research.

- *The subject of mathematics can be seen to hold a level of mystique for a significant number of the adult population, including teachers.*

Mystique is a characteristic that can mean charm and magic to some yet a level of impenetrability to others. It would seem that the teacher's role is to enable children to engage in the subject and so find the magic it can yield.

- *Adult mathematics qualifications and cognitive ability do not necessarily correlate with effective mathematics teaching.*

Such findings may seem surprising but consideration of teaching you have received in the past may help clarify this point. You may remember being taught a subject or a skill by someone who was obviously an expert in their field but could not impart their knowledge in a way that made it accessible to you. Conversely, you may remember being in a similar situation but with someone who enabled you but was not an expert in their field. Awareness of how you were enabled can act as a starting point to making sense of generic teaching skills and lead on to relating and developing these skills in mathematics.

- *Beliefs about mathematics are fundamental to engagement and enjoyment with the subject.*

Feelings towards mathematics will come from a wide spectrum of possible responses from a complete lack of confidence in the subject in terms of personal understanding and teaching, to having strong confidence in the subject. How you feel about a subject can be affected by a range of factors. If you think back to your childhood, your feelings towards subjects may have been influenced by achievement, your teacher, fellow classmates, the setting or a combination of such factors. Some factors can be less direct such as health or family issues that can lead to children finding it hard to concentrate or are unwilling to risk failure. As a teacher of mathematics, a positive feeling towards the subject is likely to enhance its teaching. Indeed, enjoyment of the subject was seen as a required competency in one of the earlier versions of the TDA Standards for Qualified Teacher Status (QTS): 'enjoy mathematics so that they can teach it with enthusiasm' (DfEE, 1998: Section C of Annex D). Enjoyment was found to be a factor in teaching judged as 'excellent' by Askew and his team when they carried out research (Askew et al., 1997).

- *Assessment of beliefs leading to active intervention can yield positive results for the teacher, their teaching and learning of children.*

One of the heartening findings of the research discussed, is that active intervention through mathematics courses in teacher training programmes and Continuing Professional Development (CPD) can enable teachers to understand why mathematics holds a mystical quality and how teachers can enable a new generation to access its power. Teachers have the opportunity to become learners again. However, it is not the same as returning to childhood experiences of learning, although the experience may evoke memory of such experience. The difference is that in this new role of acquiring knowledge about mathematics, the learner will have the experience of past learning and teaching to call upon. All teachers have the potential to improve their teaching but often making a change is hard as there is a move from the familiar to the unknown. Additionally, making a change can initially have a negative effect on teaching as the mechanics of the change may feel unnatural. For example, if the aim is to develop a more interactive style of teaching to elicit children's prior understanding, you may decide to develop your questioning skills. Initially, this change may make you feel self-conscious and children may not immediately respond to the change in your questions. It is only when the different questioning mechanisms are performed with fluency that the benefits of the change are likely to be seen.

The body of knowledge to make a change is broad. It is not simply gaining a deeper knowledge of mathematics and a repertoire of teaching 'tips'. As can be seen from the discussion about beliefs, subject knowledge in relation to teaching mathematics is more than having mathematics qualifications. What is meant by the term will be explored now.

Subject knowledge

The term subject knowledge is used widely in teacher training programmes. It is used directly and indirectly throughout the Teachers' Standards which are effective from 1 September 2012 (DfE, 2011b). Students are to:

- have 'strong subject knowledge'
- 'demonstrate good subject and curriculum knowledge'
- 'have a secure knowledge of the relevant subject(s) and curriculum areas'
- 'demonstrate a critical understanding of developments in the subject and curriculum areas'

- 'impart knowledge'
- 'foster and maintain pupils' interest in the subject'.

It is hard to categorise aspects of mathematics subject knowledge as they are interrelated but three broad areas will be used.

1. *Curricular knowledge* – the mathematical content to be taught and learnt by children.
2. *Background knowledge* – the knowledge teachers require, mathematical skills and understanding, the underpinning values and philosophy.
3. *Pedagogical knowledge* – as defined as the art of teaching, *how* mathematics is taught or learned, approaches to teaching and learning.

Over the last ten years much of the pedagogical as well as the curricular knowledge has been based on national initiatives (National Numeracy Strategy (NNS) (DfEE, 1999a) and the Primary National Strategy (PNS) (DfES, 2006)). Although the status of such documents is only advisory, they were adopted in the majority of schools. While their aims of improving teaching and learning of the core subjects were laudable, they have taken many decisions regarding how to teach mathematics away from teachers. Such disempowerment has been alluded to in recent government statements about the future National Curriculum. For example, in the Schools White Paper *The Importance of Teaching* (DfE, 2011a), it is stated that the paper sets out 'school-led school improvement replacing top-down initiatives'.

As can be seen from Askew's research (Askew et al., 1997), effective teachers tended to be those who were able to make connections. The ability to make connections comes beyond the knowledge of the curriculum requirements as identified in the National Curriculum (DfEE, 1999b). It requires personal background knowledge of these connections as well as teaching and learning strategies that support making connections such as the choice of examples and knowledge of common misconceptions.

Pedagogical knowledge starts on teaching programmes in relation to school-based work. Ideas are introduced and trialled and adapted to suit the context with increasing skill. Pedagogical knowledge develops over time leading to an increasing repertoire of experience from which to draw in terms of activities and strategies as well as contexts. As a result, background understanding of mathematics evolves and knowledge deepens. Askew's research cited earlier was with experienced teachers. It is unlikely that someone in their Newly Qualified Teacher (NQT) year is going to be a highly effective teacher of mathematics but it is possible that such a person can have a vision of where they might like to be at a certain stage in the future.

Some people enter teaching with *background* mathematics knowledge but, as can be seen from the research, many believe they do not. Teaching programmes are aimed at equipping teachers with *pedagogical* and *curricular* knowledge. Problems occur when teachers do not have sufficient background knowledge to understand or question what they are being taught. It is at this point that negative experiences and beliefs can re-emerge, often long hidden. Having knowledge without understanding is a significant factor if this knowledge is to be used to help children understand.

You may like to think about the three types of subject knowledge – curricular, background and pedagogical – and judge where your understanding lies. Sometimes it is helpful to view development as part of a continuum – where you are now, where you hope to be next year, e.g. at the beginning of your NQT year or in two years' time. You need to consider *curricular* knowledge in terms of what is taught and how it fits into the whole curriculum. *Background* subject knowledge relates to your ability in mathematics in terms of doing *and* understanding what you are doing. It involves your beliefs and attitude towards mathematics and your ability to enthuse children in their engagement with the subject. *Pedagogical* knowledge can be seen as relating to using a range of teaching and learning strategies specific to mathematics, planning suitable activities and making connections between mathematical topics.

Summary

This chapter has discussed research related to effective teaching in mathematics. It has outlined the importance of a teacher's beliefs in becoming an effective teacher of mathematics. An overview of the knowledge that a teacher requires to teach effectively has been outlined briefly in terms of three broad categories:

- curricular
- background
- pedagogical.

Conclusion

It would seem that mathematics teaching is now at a crossroads. The findings of the Williams Report (2008) strongly echo those of previous research.

Twenty-six years on from the Cockcroft Report, and despite a range of initiatives such as the implementation of the National Numeracy Strategy in 1998, little has changed. Maybe this is because the emphasis has been on curriculum content (*curricular subject knowledge*) and teaching methods (*pedagogical subject knowledge*) without addressing the more difficult and sensitive issues of teacher confidence, competence and philosophical perspective (*background subject knowledge*), as well as national inertia. As Williams states:

> . . . the United Kingdom is still one of the few advanced nations where it is socially acceptable . . . to profess an inability to cope with the subject. (Williams, 2008: 3)

Although resolving such a self-perpetuating attitude is not the sole responsibility of initial teacher education, teachers all play a fundamental part in changing such negative attitudes, not just for their own learning and practice but for future generations.

This chapter has introduced a number of issues that will be explored in later chapters. The generalist nature of teaching and subject knowledge will be discussed in Chapter 4 concerning what teachers should know. International comparisons will be discussed in detail in Chapter 8 which focuses on what can be learnt from other countries. The next chapter explores the subject of mathematics and how it has evolved into the subject being taught in schools today.

Review questions

Earlier in this chapter you were asked to consider your feelings about mathematics. It may be useful now to think about your initial reaction in order to understand the relationship between how you scored yourself on the scale at the beginning of this chapter and your beliefs about mathematics and from where they arose. You may want to categorise them under the following areas:

- Your immediate reaction to mathematics.
- Possible reasons for your response.
- The implications of your reaction to your role as a teacher of primary aged children.
- Using your response to drafting an action plan with the aim of becoming an effective teacher of mathematics.

Try to be honest with yourself and write down what you believe rather than what you think you ought to believe.

Models can be a helpful starting point in the process of reflection. Here is an example in response to the issues above but you may prefer a more discursive or diagrammatic style when you have read Appendix 2 on 'reflection'.

Journal entry 1

I love maths. I always enjoyed it at school more than English as I felt I knew if it was right or wrong. I used to try really hard writing stories and poems but never really got good marks, just comments like a 'good attempt' or 'try to write more descriptively'. I thought I had! At least with maths you know if you could do it or not.

Probably I like maths because I never saw it as a problem subject. My mother liked arithmetic. I can't remember her teaching me but she used it a lot when she was a school secretary. My father was a salesman and he would often get me to add up his sales in the evening. I do remember him showing me a quick way by making up to ten as I added. My grandmother taught me card games like 'Sevens'.

When I went to sixth form I did not choose to take maths A level because it was a time when you either chose to do sciences or arts. I didn't like the sciences that much so I chose arts subjects. However, when I trained to teach I chose to study sociology as it was different to work I had done at school. As a second subject I had to take one that could be taught in the age range I had chosen. As this was 5–11 I chose maths. The maths course was very practical – use of lots of resources with the emphasis on teaching children to understand rather than learn by rote – very different to the way I had been taught at primary school.

My interest in maths has continued throughout my time as a teacher. I have attended maths courses and I have been a maths coordinator in a number of schools. Maths is still something I do outside work. For example I often find myself estimating and calculating my time when I am swimming and I like planning mathematical designs for patchwork.

Another factor that can contribute to confidence and competence in mathematics can be the use and practice of mathematical skills on a day-to-day basis. The fact that you are reading this book means that you are likely to read, talk and write in some form on a daily basis but this may not be the situation for the complementary mathematical skills. Use and application are essential if skills are to be retained effectively. Skills can get lost when they have not been fully understood and, without use and application, this understanding can become more confused. Skills can usually be broken down into three categories

- those that you have used recently and of which you have secure understanding;
- those that you have not used recently but of which you have secure understanding;
- those you have been exposed to but do not really remember or understand.

Carry out the following activity to identify how frequently you use your mathematical skills. Note how your use of mathematical skills relates to your beliefs about mathematics.

Write down when you used any form of mathematics in

- the last 24 hours?
- the last week?

Write down when you used English in

- the last 24 hours?
- the last week?

References

Askew, M., Brown, M., Rhodes, V., Wiliam, D. and Johnson, D. (1997) *Effective Teachers of Numeracy: Report of a Study Carried Out for the Teacher Training Agency.* London: TTA.

Boaler, J. (2009) *The Elephant in the Classroom. Helping Children Learn and Love Maths.* London: Souvenir Press.

Buxton, J. (1981) *Do You Panic About Maths? Coping with Maths Anxiety.* London: Heinemann Educational.

Cockcroft, W. H. (1982) *Mathematics Counts: Report of the Committee of Inquiry into the Teaching of Mathematics in Schools under the Chairmanship of Dr W. H. Cockcroft.* London: HMSO. Available online at: http://www.educationengland. org.uk/index.html.

DfE (2011a) *The Importance of Teaching: Schools White Paper.* London: DfE.

DfE (2011b) *Teachers' Standards Effective from 1 September.* London: DfE.

DfEE (1998) *Teaching: High Status, High Standards. Requirements for Courses in Initial Teacher Training.* London: DfEE.

DfEE (1999a) *The National Numeracy Strategy.* Sudbury: DfEE.

DfEE (1999b) *The National Curriculum Handbook for Primary Teachers in England Key Stages 1 and 2.* London: HMSO.

DfES (2006) *Primary National Strategy. Primary Framework for Literacy and Mathematics.* Nottingham: DfES Publications.

Haylock, D. (2010) *Mathematics Explained for Primary Teachers*, 4th edn. London: Sage.

Jackson, E. (2008) 'Mathematics anxiety in student teachers', *Practitioner Research in Higher Education*, 2 (1): 36–42.

Skemp, R. (1991) *Mathematics in the Primary School.* London: Taylor & Francis.

Swan, M. and Swain J. (2010) 'The impact of a professional development programme on the practices and beliefs of Numeracy teachers', *Journal of Further and Higher Education*, 34 (2): 165–77.

Thompson, I. (2003) *Enhancing Primary Mathematics Teaching.* Maidenhead: OUP.

Williams, P. (2008) *Independent Review of Mathematics Teaching in Early Years Settings and Primary Schools.* London: DCFS. (Also available online.)

Websites

OECD Programme for International Student Assessment (PISA): http://www.pisa. oecd.org.

Trends in International Mathematics and Science Study (TIMSS): http://timss. bc.edu/timss2007/index.html.

Further reading

You may want to develop your understanding of mathematics anxiety. Here are some references to explore further.

Goulding, M., Rowland, T. and Barber, T. (2002) 'Does it matter? Primary teacher trainees' subject knowledge in mathematics', *British Educational Research Journal*, 28: 689–704.

Newstead, K. (1998) 'Aspects of children's mathematics anxiety', *Educational Studies in Mathematics*, 36 (1): 53–71.

Richardson, F. C. and Suinn, R. M. (1972) 'The mathematics anxiety rating scale', *Journal of Counseling Psychology*, 19: 551–4.

CHAPTER 2

THE NATURE AND LANGUAGE OF MATHEMATICS

Aims

By the end of this chapter you should:

- understand the origins of mathematics as a subject of study;
- understand the development of mathematics within the primary curriculum;
- have awareness of the value of historical knowledge of mathematics and how it can enhance the primary curriculum;
- understand the significance of the term 'mathematical language';
- understand the importance of structure, law and rules in understanding mathematics;
- understand the relevance of the hierarchical nature of learning and teaching mathematics.

Introduction

This chapter will introduce a broad vision of mathematics by considering its intrinsic value and broader dimensions than those currently related to the primary mathematics curriculum. Mathematics is often defined by its content, for example the Cambridge English Dictionary (2011) defines mathematics as 'the study of numbers, shapes and space using reason and usually a special system of symbols and rules for organizing them' and a mathematician as 'someone who studies teaches or is an expert in mathematics'. However, it is rare for teachers to see themselves as mathematicians and the term tends to be confined to those seen as 'experts'. In recent years there have been initiatives to bring artists and authors into school education to inspire children to see themselves as artists and writers. In Australia such initiatives have included mathematics and science. A project funded by the Australian Government 'Mathematicians in Schools' (Australian Government, 2009) is aimed at supporting professional partnerships between practising mathematicians and schools to help children appreciate the beauty and power of mathematics and its significance in all our lives. This wider interpretation of mathematics and mathematicians may seem far removed from the current mathematics curriculum but it may serve to broaden the view of what could be included within the curriculum and develop a more positive image of the subject.

Mathematics in the school curriculum

Mathematics is practised for both practical purposes and intrinsic interest. For those who love mathematics, it is a subject of beauty and challenge. Others value mathematics in terms of its application to science, engineering and everyday life. Unfortunately, there are those who view mathematics as an unpleasant necessity or try to avoid it altogether. What can make people have such different perceptions of a subject and what can be done to avoid these negative perceptions arising? Initially, it is teachers who need to be convinced of the diverse and fascinating nature of the subject before they become responsible for mathematics teaching as part of their role. A positive outcome is more likely when teachers are able to provide engaging yet challenging experiences and have belief in children's potential for success.

If children and adults experienced being taught English by just learning grammar and spelling, then it is probable that they would have the same feeling about English as some do about mathematics. Without literature they would miss out on making sense of their world by seeing into the lives and thoughts of others and, in so doing, become more aware and empathetic. They can access and engage in literature by talking, listening and participating in drama as well as reading and writing. As teachers, your personal experience of learning subjects can support the provision of positive learning experiences for children.

Read the following examples of the experiences written by teachers while on an undergraduate teacher training programme.

I remember the art room at secondary school really well. It was a place that looked so different to everywhere else. It was colourful and more informal with tables rather than desks and large displays. Everyone seemed to like going there and there was a more relaxed atmosphere. However, for me, it was not a place I looked forward to going. Initially I liked it but when we started to get marks for our work and mine were low, negative feelings set in. I just didn't see how you could give marks for art. Sometimes I thought my work was OK but I could see that the work of others was better yet what were they doing that I was not and how did their success seem to come so easily? They did not seem to be trying that hard but I was. The teacher did teach but not in a way that enabled me to improve what I did whether it was charcoal sketching, using paint or clay. I talked about my lack of success with my parents but they said it didn't matter as art was not important and you could do it or you couldn't.

When I was in primary school I didn't like English. I could read well and write without many errors. I was told I had to make my stories more imaginative and interesting. The problem was I liked them the way they were. My mother was advised to encourage me to read more. I did read a lot. I liked books about girls going to boarding schools or Just William books by Richmal Crompton but I did not like the books recommended such as books by Rudyard Kipling or Anna Sewell. I arrived at secondary school with an idea I was not good at English. However, I was successful in work related to grammar and liked the books we studied. I remember reading Jane Eyre and this led me on to reading other books by the Brontë sisters. No one said I wasn't imaginative and I did well in my exams.

These descriptions show a number of factors about the individual as a learner and also identify factors that affected their learning. In the first example there seemed to be confusion that what appeared to be an enjoyable, relaxed experience was *judged* and judged according to criteria that were not understood and which did not support improvement. Additionally the lack of success was not seen as important. In the second example, the learner understood some elements of the subject but when the content was less prescriptive such as in 'imaginative writing', the criteria by which it was judged were not understood. In this example, the *content* of what was being taught affected the enjoyment in the subject.

Judgement relates to assessment and *content* to the curriculum – two key components in teaching and learning. Reading of these experiences may trigger your own memories of being taught – including what you were taught and how it was assessed – and may include other elements. Groups of teaching students discussed learning experiences and agreed on these key factors. Look at the following grid and consider other factors that could contribute to the success or failure of learning experiences. You may find it useful to work with colleagues.

Factors that affect learning experiences

Positive learning experience	Negative learning experience
Teachers who make learning interesting	When you don't understand
Teachers who are good at explaining	When you don't see the point in what you are doing
Teachers who seem to like what they are teaching	When you are not interested
When you want to learn	When you are uncomfortable

Understanding the purpose of what you are doing, being interested in the content, knowing how your work is assessed and knowing how to improve seem key elements in developing a positive perception about a subject. 'Assessment for learning' which was part of the government's Excellence and Enjoyment Primary Strategy (DfES, 2003) was meant to support such elements of successful learning. A question emerges about how such strategies apply to different subjects. Look at the list you have devised and relate it to your teaching of mathematics and one other subject. Are you able to offer a positive experience to children across both subjects? What does this tell you about your teaching of mathematics in terms of your understanding?

Historical overview

A brief overview of the history of mathematics education may help inform your understanding of mathematics teaching at primary level. A substantial element of teaching mathematics has centred on the equivalent 'grammar and spelling' elements of the subject – the mechanics of calculation. The inception of compulsory state education in England and Wales in 1870 brought in the curriculum, commonly known as the 3Rs – reading, writing and arithmetic or reckoning. The purpose of arithmetic was to equip workers with the skills to support everyday life such as calculating measurements. Over time, as there have been changes in what was considered important to teach children in terms of its intrinsic value, so the curriculum has widened to include mathematics beyond arithmetic. The 1955 Mathematics Association Report advocated the teaching of mathematics rather than arithmetic, acknowledging the fact that this may be seen as 'pretentious' in association with primary schooling (Mathematics Association, 1955).

Prior to decimalisation in 1971, children were taught other place values than just base 10. They learnt to calculate in base 12 and 20 as there were 12 pence in a shilling and 20 shillings in a pound, and they acquired knowledge of other bases used in the imperial system of measurement. Additionally, as computers stored information in the binary system, the rise in this technology led to base 2 being taught.

	£*	s.	d.	
	3	4	6	(three pounds, four shillings and six pence)
+	2	16	9	(two pounds, sixteen shillings and nine pence)
	6	1	3	(six pounds, one shilling and three pence)

*Note: pounds sterling

Try the following calculation using multiple bases:*

	st	lbs	ozs	
	9	8	5	(six stone, eight pounds and five ounces)
+	10	10	11	(ten stone, eight pounds and eleven ounces)

*Note: 16 ounces (ozs) = 1 pound (lb)
          14 pounds (lbs) = 1 stone (st)

Decimalisation stimulated change. It gave time for schools to refocus on a broader mathematics curriculum beyond calculation methods. Two government reports, *Mathematics 5–11* (DES, 1979) and the Cockcroft Report *Mathematics Counts* (DES, 1982), recommended both changes in content and pedagogy. Teachers planned content as they saw fit, producing schemes of work rather like the long-term plans schools have today. Many schemes of work were commercial and were supported by textbooks and workcards or books. A range of pedagogical practice ensued from children working at their own pace through a series of workcards supported by the teacher to whole-class lessons based upon the relevant page in the textbook.

The advent of the National Curriculum in 1989 called for more emphasis on conceptual understanding and problem-solving that was informed by a constructivist approach to how children learn. However, the introduction of the National Numeracy Strategy (NNS) in 1999 saw renewed emphasis on calculation methods following concerns about falling standards.

The shift in emphasis within the mathematics curriculum raises a number of questions. Superficially it could be viewed as a failure of the curriculum of the 1980s and 1990s which broadened the scope of mathematics beyond calculation. However, although numeracy levels have improved, expectations have changed in terms of globalisation and technology. The problem-solving required of the international TIMSS and OECD PISA surveys is different to the expectations of the Primary National Strategy (PNS) (DfES, 2006). Mathematics tends to be taught from a 'content' rather learning perspective in order to find solutions to problems. It is true that in order to solve problems involving numbers, numerical skills are needed. However, symbiosis between numerical skills, problem-solving and investigative skills is frequently lacking. The process requires a sense of imagination and curiosity as well as knowledge of number skills. The legacy of the NNS and its successor, PNS, is that emphasis is still based on skills and procedures rather than problem-solving skills. Being able to transfer knowledge to changing situations will be significant in coping with a fast-changing world.

Consider the mathematics you teach. How does it support children in their application of mathematics to solving problems? You may want to give examples rather than explanations e.g. number games, cross-curricular planning that supports use of mathematical skills. Try to share your ideas with colleagues.

The origins of mathematics

Mathematics spans a wide body of knowledge that is constantly evolving. It has a core but it is a subject that, with imagination, can develop relationships and connections by making sense of newly acquired knowledge and applying it to the ever-changing world in which we live. Consequently, it relates to all areas of the curriculum and beyond. At worst, mathematics can be seen as tasks to be performed and procedures learnt for extrinsic purposes such as gaining entry to a career or further study. To bridge the gap between these extremes in interpretations of the subject it helps to explore the origins of mathematics. Children of all ages can gain from exposure to a rich interpretation of the subject.

Try this activity to illustrate how mathematics evolved and how it relates to the branches of mathematics we use in school today.

Look at the image below and try to describe it.

This task is not as simple as it seems. It is difficult as you cannot see the tree in relation to anything else. You could comment on its *shape or form* in that the tree is as high as it is wide as you are able to compare the two dimensions of the tree. You can state it stands alone to denote the *number* of trees present but it is not possible to comment on its *size or magnitude* as there is nothing with which to compare it.

Now look at the following image.

You can now describe the tree by relating it to its surroundings and other similar images in terms of its proximity and how it compares to them in terms of form and magnitude. In the second image you can also make a statement about quantity. If it could identify the view depicted at different times of the year you would be able to comment on change, another fundamental element of mathematics.

Since the earliest times humanity has sought to make sense of the world in terms of describing and seeking explanations for natural phenomena such as the changes in the position of the Sun and the Moon and the seasons. Making sense of the world and survival are inextricably linked so necessary nomadic activities of finding shelter and farming could be planned. Mathematics first arose from the practical need to measure time and to count. As a result all cultures have developed mathematics. In some cases, this mathematics has spread from one culture to another. Now there is one predominant international form of mathematics. Archaeologists have discovered artefacts that show sophisticated counting instruments in notched bones and scored pieces of wood and stone, some of which relate to the cycles of the Moon and sequences of prime numbers. Egyptian pyramids reveal evidence of a fundamental knowledge of surveying and geometry as early as 2900 BC.

Mathematics is believed to have originated in ancient Egypt and then developed in Babylonia, now part of present day Iraq. The Babylonian basis of mathematics was inherited by the Greeks and independent development by the Greeks began around 450 BC. Major Greek progress in mathematics took place from 300 BC to AD 200. After this time, progress continued in Islamic counties, particularly in those regions now named Iran, Syria and

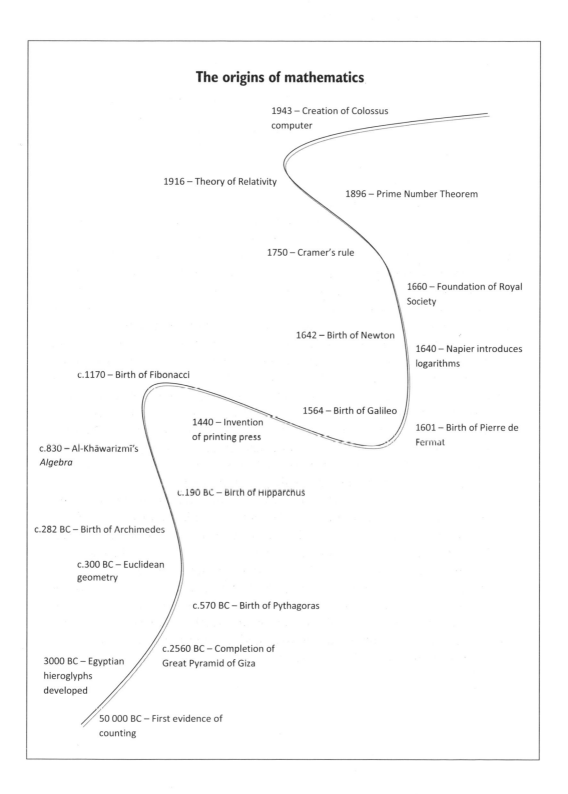

The origins of mathematics

1943 – Creation of Colossus computer

1916 – Theory of Relativity

1896 – Prime Number Theorem

1750 – Cramer's rule

1660 – Foundation of Royal Society

1642 – Birth of Newton

1640 – Napier introduces logarithms

c.1170 – Birth of Fibonacci

1440 – Invention of printing press

1564 – Birth of Galileo

1601 – Birth of Pierre de Fermat

c.830 – Al-Khāwarizmī's *Algebra*

c.190 BC – Birth of Hipparchus

c.282 BC – Birth of Archimedes

c.300 BC – Euclidean geometry

c.570 BC – Birth of Pythagoras

c.2560 BC – Completion of Great Pyramid of Giza

3000 BC – Egyptian hieroglyphs developed

50 000 BC – First evidence of counting

India. Mathematics written in ancient Greek was translated into Arabic so preserving Greek mathematics. About the same time some mathematics from India was translated into Arabic. From about the eleventh century Fibonacci of Pisa (now in Italy) brought Islamic mathematics and its knowledge of Greek mathematics into Europe. It is from these origins that the Hindu-Arabic numeral system emerged that is used today. China and Japan developed significant mathematics independently but have had less influence on what has become internationally understood western mathematics partly due to their geographical location.

Most definitions of mathematics include it being the science of quantity, form and magnitude. Quantity, form and magnitude can be translated roughly into the terms used in the current primary mathematics curriculum of number, shape, space and measures. As such it involves identifying change and pattern. The word 'mathematics' is derived from the Greek word 'manthanein' which means to learn. It came to have a more defined meaning during the ancient Greek civilisation. Mathematics related to the natural world but the Greeks pioneered its intrinsic value by exploring abstract ideas and developing generalised mathematical theories and proofs that depended upon logic and creativity. Mathematicians focus on solving problems that originate from the real world. They search for patterns and relationships and use techniques similar to those used by those who engage in more abstract work. However, work in abstract mathematics often has practical applications and, conversely, mathematics arising from practical situations can explain abstract theories. In this way both pure and applied branches of mathematics are mutually interdependent.

The fact that mathematics has a rich and exciting history means there is a body of knowledge which can be used to enthuse children in its study. There are a number of relevant connections to historical aspects of mathematics which relate not just to mathematics but to other curricular subjects.

It is not the purpose here either to make tenuous links or to include an exhaustive list but the following ideas may give you some inspiration of the possible connections that could be explored in more detail and incorporated into the curriculum. Such an approach can broaden the vision of mathematics as a subject which may lead to an enhanced outlook on its interest to both teachers and children.

Cross-curricular approaches to mathematics in the primary curriculum

The history of mathematics

Prior to there being a National Curriculum a number of historical aspects of mathematics were taught. Some related to topics such as the Romans and were seen as a form of general knowledge. Children learnt about Roman numbers, explored shapes through tessellations based on Roman tiling and used arbitrary objects to make measurements along the lines of Roman measurements based on the body such as spans and cubits. The value of the history of mathematics has not been evident in recent years but not only does it bring different cultures, histories and significant people into the classroom, it helps pupils make networks of connections between aspects of mathematical knowledge. Derek Haylock believes the history of mathematics numeration system to be 'a fascinating topic with considerable potential for cross curriculum work in school' (Haylock, 2006: 10). Here are some examples organised by subject to guide you in further exploration.

Mathematics

Science

History

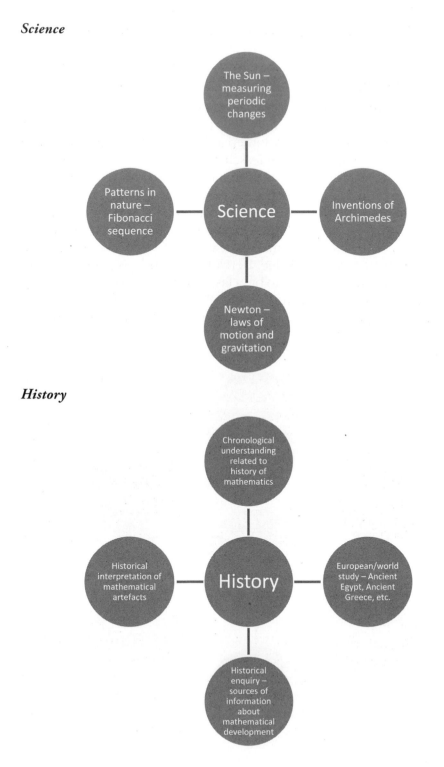

Cross-curricular connections

You can probably identify or have used connections to other subjects in terms of reference to a mathematical element within subjects. For example, you may be working on tessellations in mathematics and making connections to art and design and the work of craftsmen in Roman times.

Another way of considering the relationship of the history of mathematics to the curriculum is by taking a thematic approach to the curriculum. For example, the theme could be:

- the Sun
- buildings
- inventors.

The list is boundless. The more you look at the curriculum the more connections you will find. Historical aspects of mathematics can help make connections and explore them at both a child's and teacher's level when devising a school curriculum.

Supporting PSHE

The rise in international terrorism in the last few years has left a negative image not just of minority ethnic groups but of some entire countries in the eyes of many pupils. Afghanistan, Iran, Iraq and Pakistan frequently have such associations. Consideration of the legacy of knowledge arising from such countries can help foster a broader, positive image. For example, the mathematician Al-Khwārizmī of Persia, the former name of Iran, was the founder of a number of branches of mathematics and his book entitled *Al-Jabr wa-al-Muqabilah* was the origin of the word algebra. Additionally, children who have begun their education in different countries are influenced by different cultures at home and can contribute alternative methods such as calculating beyond ten using the fingers on their hands, a common stratedy in a number of countries such as Korea.

Enriching learning

Ofsted (2009) raised concerns about provision for meeting the needs of gifted and talented pupils. There are numerous websites that provide help for teachers, but providing appropriate activities alone is not sufficient as it is the support and questioning that is used by the teacher and the way that children are encouraged to actively engage in the task that provide its value.

There is a range of historical mathematics examples that can be used with children. For example, they can consider the different methods of multiplication and how they work. Teachers need to be prepared to acquire the knowledge such children require beyond the curricular knowledge they would normally need to teach their chosen age groups.

The NRICH Project is published by Cambridge University. It aims to enrich the mathematical experiences of all learners. The project includes support for professional development as well as free problems and games that can be used for 5–19 year olds. The aim is the development of subject knowledge and problem-solving and mathematical skills. It is an evolving resource bank and new material appears on the first day of each month. Looking at the NRICH website (see Further reading) will give you a wealth of information and ideas including the history of numbers, symbols, calendars, money and measurement.

Use of problem-solving tasks should not be just the preserve of children identified as gifted or talented. As Steve Hewson explains on the NRICH website:

Current research evidence indicates that students who are given opportunities to work on their problem-solving skills enjoy the subject more. (Online at: http://nrich.maths.org)

Museums and exhibitions

There are a number of artefacts and exhibitions relating to the history of mathematics. Examples are the Science Museum and Greenwich Observatory in London, and Eureka! The National Children's Museum in Halifax.

Engaging mathematicians

It has become quite common in recent years in the field of the arts to engage the support of experts in schools to inspire and develop children's work. Various websites have emerged to facilitate this process, for example http://www.dramateachers.co.uk/, http://www.schoolsmusic.org.uk/, http://www.artistsinschools.co.uk. As mentioned at the beginning of this chapter, the same opportunity relates to mathematicians in Australia. Although there is no specific organisation to support such work in this country, teachers can engage with the community to find those who use mathematics as part of their everyday work. Obviously care would need to be taken that such a visitor was able to relate to the children effectively. Most schools have significant contacts through multi-professional agencies as well as parents and governors. For example, policemen are frequent visitors to school and may be prepared to talk about how they use mathematics in their work.

Language, structure and notation

It is one thing to enthuse children to find out about a particularly fascinating figure in mathematical history but it is another to maintain that enthusiasm. Partly, this is down to how the subject is taught but there is a potential problem in the language of mathematics. Just as there are problems of alienation and frustration in not being able to understand a language which is not a mother tongue, so mathematics can cause similar feelings in this specific area alone.

Mathematics can be viewed as a language in itself. This may seem surprising but consideration of mathematics as a language should provide some understanding of the problems it can cause. Language may be defined as a form of communication which is not necessarily verbal but is shared by a community of people and has a vocabulary, a grammar in the form of its structure and a notation in the form of the symbols used. There are other examples of languages that fit this definition, such as British Sign Language (BSL) and music. By considering mathematics in a similar way to BSL and music, mathematics can be viewed as a language.

BSL is a visual means of communicating using gestures, facial expression and body language. It is used by a community of people who are deaf or have hearing impairments as well as their friends, relatives and colleagues. BSL has its own vocabulary and grammatical structure. As a language it is not dependent nor is it strongly related to spoken English.

Similarly, music is a form of communication that is shared across a community of people on a global scale. It has a vocabulary in recorded notation but is expressed through sound. There are defined conventions in terms of structure using such devices as rhythm, grouping and phrasing.

Now consider mathematics. It is used by all who engage in mathematics and has its own vocabulary. The vocabulary is made from notation that is understood on a global scale and words that have a specific meaning, which is often different from their meaning outside the context of mathematics. As such it is dependent on but not identical in meaning to everyday written and spoken language.

It is this specific vocabulary, notation and structure that can set up barriers for some people. It can make them feel unable to communicate in this 'foreign' language along with other negative feelings such alienation can cause. If you consider other subjects within the primary curriculum, they are generally accessible once the appropriate level of language has been taught and understood.

The 'richness' of the English language is cited in Chapter 1 in relation to the confusion that can occur in teaching and learning mathematics. Turner and McCullouch (2004) discuss 'richness' as a source of confusion as mathematics has an extensive vocabulary derived from a wide range of influences on its development. Although such 'richness' means that thoughts and ideas can be expressed showing nuances of meaning, it does not support the precision required for many elements of mathematics and can be particularly confusing for children whose first language is not English. Broadly there are four aspects of vocabulary which children can confuse in terms of

- words of instruction used in a mathematical context, e.g. *find the difference between*;
- mathematical words, e.g. *subtract*;
- words that have different everyday meanings in English, e.g. *table*;
- words that have a similar meaning to their everyday use but a more precise mathematical meaning, e.g. *area*.

Recently, the issue of mathematical language was raised by the Williams Review (2008) which stressed the importance of using accurate mathematical language. The review reinforced the idea that mathematics can be seen as a new language and identified the particular challenges faced by children for whom English is an additional language in relation to the differences between technical language and social language.

Language does not merely cause problems in understanding and accessing mathematical knowledge. It is particularly important in the formation of concepts. Skemp (1991) identified that the connection between spoken words is stronger than between thoughts and their written or symbolic representation. It is therefore particularly important that children are introduced to correct mathematical terminology at the beginning of their education. Such accuracy relies on teachers themselves having an accurate understanding of mathematical terminology.

You may find a mathematics vocabulary book useful for this activity. Consider the language associated with adding and subtracting. Do you know the difference between asking children to *add* 2 + 3 *together* and what 3 *more than* 2 will be? Initially, such words may seem simple to understand and result in the same answer but when used mathematically they relate to different mathematical structures. Asking children to add 2 + 3 together is aggregation: 2 and 3 are being combined as a single quantity to find the total. Asking children to find what 3 more than two will be is augmentation as a quantity of 2 is increased by 3 and the new quantity is being found. Just as there are grammatical structures in English, so mathematics has structures in terms of the number operations of addition, subtraction, multiplication and division and the commutative, associative and distributive laws relating to each of these operations.

Laws of arithmetic

Laws of arithmetic	Description	Examples	
Commutative law (relates to addition and multiplication)	When you add two numbers you can reverse the order of the numbers. When multiplying two numbers you can reverse the order of the two numbers.	$2 + 3 = 3 + 2$ $2 \times 3 = 3 \times 2$	
Associative law (relates to addition and multiplication)	When you add three or more numbers you can add them in any order. When you multiply three or more numbers, you can multiply them in any order.	$2 + 4 + 6 =$ $(2 + 4) + 6$ $(4 + 2) + 6$ $(4 + 6) + 2$ $(6 + 4) + 2$ $(2 + 6) + 4$ $(6 + 2) + 4$	$2 \times 4 \times 6 =$ $(2 \times 4) \times 6$ $(4 \times 2) \times 6$ $(4 \times 6) \times 2$ $(6 \times 4) \times 2$ $(2 \times 6) \times 4$ $(6 \times 2) \times 4$
Distributive laws (relates to multiplication and division over addition and subtraction)	When a sum or difference is being multiplied by a number, each number in the sum or difference can be multiplied by the number first and the products can then be used to find the sum or difference. When a sum or difference is being divided by a number, each number in the sum or difference can be divided by the number first and the dividends can then be used to find the sum or difference.	$12 \times 7 =$ $(10 + 2) \times 7 = (10 \times 7) + (2 \times 7)$ $8 \times 7 =$ $(10 - 2) \times 7 = (10 \times 7) - (2 \times 7)$ *and* $46 \div 2 =$ $(40 + 6) \div 2 = (40 \div 2) + (6 \div 2)$ $27 \div 3 =$ $(30 - 3) \div 3 = (30 \div 3) - (3 \div 3)$	

Rules of calculation

Computations that involve more than one calculation must be carried out in a particular order. The order is often referred to by the acronym BODMAS or BIDMAS.

1. **B**rackets – work out the calculation in the bracket
2. **O**rders/**I**ndices – calculate their value next, e.g. 2^3

Then complete the calculation using the operations in the following order:

3. **D**ivision
4. **M**ultiplication
5. **A**ddition
6. **S**ubtraction

Structure, laws and rules should not be confused with algorithms which are no more than a set methods for finding solutions to calculation problems. Knowledge of structure, laws and rules is fundamental to making sense of mathematics and, without such knowledge, understanding can be inhibited, in the same way that lack of knowledge of grammatical structure can inhibit understanding of a foreign language. Such knowledge empowers the learner to find different ways of solving calculation problems, depending on prior mathematical knowledge and the particular numbers involved. For example, if the problem was to find how many places there were in a school of 11 classes that had 24 in each class, a solution would be $(10 \times 24) + (1 \times 24)$, a calculation which probably could be carried out mentally using knowledge of the *distributive* law. However, if there were 17 classes and 24 in each class a solution could be $(10 \times 24) + (7 \times 20) + (7 \times 4)$ which could be completed mentally but may involve some jotting, or a decision could be made to carry out a standard algorithm: using the column method, first multiply by units and then by 10s, then add the results together.

$$\begin{array}{r} 17 \\ \times 24 \\ \hline 168 \\ {}^{2} \\ +340 \\ \hline 408 \end{array}$$

Structure in mathematics relates to associated symbolic representation and is fundamental in understanding mathematical language. Representation through symbols that make up mathematical notation is a form of vocabulary as it denotes a meaning, e.g. 3 is the symbol for the cardinal number three and = is the symbol for equals, the result when two or more quantities are added together. Thus 3 and = are forms of internationally accepted shorthand. This concision is part of the splendour of mathematics but such concision can make it inaccessible to many if it is not understood. Take a familiar example, Pythagoras' theorem. If you have a right-angled triangle with sides a, b and c, with c being the hypotenuse, then $a^2 + b^2 = c^2$. It can be proved geometrically as well as numerically by calculating the area but in order to generalise it, i.e. find a rule which works across other examples of right-angled triangles, algebraic symbols are used – a, b and c. Use of symbolic representation is a powerful tool in making sense of mathematics and supporting the process of making connections between different aspects of mathematics.

The hierarchical nature of mathematics

Stating that mathematics is hierarchical can suggest a linear approach to acquiring knowledge, skills and understanding. However, mathematics is made up of a number of branches that are interconnected. Rather than a linear image it would be more accurate to think of a network in the form of plant roots. Initially, there are just one or two roots but as they start to grow incrementally so a complex network of interconnections develop.

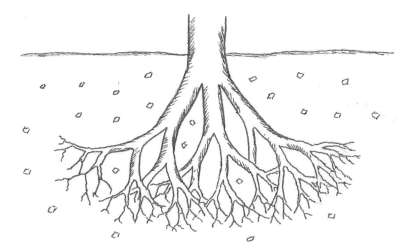

Similarly in mathematics, children acquire mathematical knowledge starting with basic or lower-order skills such as an understanding that the ordinal number 2 is the number after 1 and before 3, but as they are exposed to more knowledge they adjust or accommodate this new knowledge to develop higher order skills, e.g. 2 relates to pairing and even numbers and can operate on another number causing an increase (+), decrease (−), doubling (×) or halving (÷), and 2 can be used to denote 'squaring' a number causing the number to be multiplied by itself. Used in different places, it can have different values depending on location and the base used, e.g. base ten 0.2 would mean two-tenths. Unlike other curriculum subjects, it is difficult to engage in mathematical activity at a certain level without sufficient knowledge of preceding levels. As such mathematics requires a level of procedural knowledge.

Cardinal, ordinal, and nominal numbers	
Cardinal numbers	Numbers used to represent a set of things.
Ordinal numbers	Numbers used to represent a point on a number line, i.e. its order.
Nominal numbers	Numbers used as names or to identify something, e.g. a number 6 bus or a mobile phone number.

Using a food preparation analogy that children may encounter, consider the following. To follow a recipe to make a jelly, an understanding of vocabulary would be needed at a minimum as well as a sense of what the end product would look like. However, unless the prior knowledge is secure, confusion could arise when attempting the task. In recent years, there has been an almost pseudo-liberal attitude developing towards mathematics which implies that mathematics is not about right and wrong answers. *Calculation* is! No doubt this is in response to the negative attitudes people have towards mathematics and an attempt to try to make the subject 'user-friendly'. Ways of finding solutions are not confined or absolute and usually involve estimation and approximation, but the very nature of mathematics is about precision and using this precision in creative ways. To allude to mathematics being otherwise is a disservice to the subject and unhelpful to those who study it.

Summary

This chapter has explored the nature of mathematics both as a subject and in terms of its unique nature within the school curriculum. A number of issues have been raised with regard to teaching mathematics in terms of its language, structure, notation and hierarchy. The history of the subject from its origin to its inclusion in the school curriculum has been discussed and ways suggested to enhance the image of mathematics and support children in understanding it as part of a body of knowledge rather than in isolation.

Conclusion

The discipline of mathematics has been explored and has provided the context from which primary mathematics teaching today takes place. The next three chapters will develop ideas about the nature of mathematics and how it relates to the teaching and learning process.

Review questions

1. Consider your response to the activities relating to positive learning experiences in relation to mathematics and how they may explain your beliefs regarding learning and teaching the subject.
2. How does your understanding of mathematics relate to its history in the school curriculum and its language, structure, notation, hierarchy and associated laws and rules?
3. What issues do you wish to explore further? Use the guidance in the bibliography at the end of this chapter to aid in further investigation.

References

Australian Government (2009) 'Mathematicians in Schools'. Available online at: http://www.mathematiciansinschools.edu.au/ (accessed 8 January 2011).

Cambridge English Dictionary Online (2011) Available online at: http://dictionary.cambridge.org/ (accessed 6 June 2011)

DES (1979) *Mathematics 5–11: Handbook of Suggestions for Teachers*. London: HMSO.

DES (1982) *Mathematics Counts. Report of the Committee of Inquiry into Teaching of Mathematics in Schools*. London: HMSO.

DfEE/QCA (1999) *The National Curriculum: Handbook for Primary Teachers in England*. London: HMSO.

DfES (2003) *Excellence and Enjoyment: A National Strategy for Primary Schools*. London: DfES.

DfES (2006) *Primary National Strategy. Primary Framework for Primary Teachers in England Key Stages 1 and 2*. Nottingham: DfES Publications.

Haylock, D. (2006) *Mathematics Explained for Primary School Teachers*. London: Sage.

Mathematics Association (1955) *The Teaching of Mathematics in Primary Schools*. Leicester: Mathematical Association.

Mooney, C., Ferne, L., Fox, S., Hansen, A. and Wrathmell, R. (2009) *Primary Mathematics, Knowledge and Understanding*, 4th edn. Exeter: Learning Matters.

Skemp, R. (1991) *Mathematics in the Primary School*. London: Routledge.

Turner, S. and McCullouch, J. (2004) *Making Connections in Primary Mathematics*. London: David Fulton.

Williams, Sir P. (2008) *Independent Review of Mathematics Teaching in Early Years Settings and Primary Schools*. London: DCFS.

Website

NRICH, Cambridge University: http://nrich.maths.org/6013 (accessed 7 February 2011).

Further reading

Fauvel, J. (eds) (1990) *History in the Mathematics Classroom*. Leicester: Mathematical Association.

Mathematics Association (1955) *The Teaching of Mathematics in Primary Schools*. Leicester: Mathematical Association.

History

Joseph, G. G. (1992) *The Crest of the Peacock: Non-European Roots of Mathematics*. London: Penguin.

Language

Higgins, S. (2003) 'Parlez-vous mathematics?', in I. Thompson (ed.), *Enhancing Primary Mathematics Teaching*. Maidenhead: Open University Press.

Turner, S. and McCullouch, J. (2004) *Making Connections in Primary Mathematics*. London: David Fulton.

Hierarchy

Ernest, P. (1996) *Constructing Mathematical Knowledge: Epistemology and Mathematics Education*. London: Falmer Press.

CHAPTER 3

WHAT DO CHILDREN REALLY NEED TO LEARN AND WHY?

Aims

By the end of this chapter you should:

- understand what is meant by the primary mathematics curriculum;
- consider how a curriculum can meet the learning needs of all children;
- know and understand how different ideas about learning affect what children are taught;
- consider how the hierarchical nature of mathematics can affect the mathematics curriculum;
- consider the purpose of the mathematics curriculum in its design;
- begin to develop a vision of a mathematics curriculum and identify individual development needs.

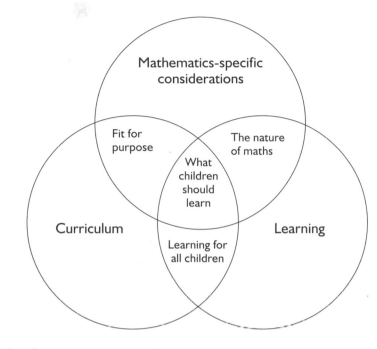

Introduction

At the time of writing (July 2011) the Education Act is yet to be published although the original White Paper *The Importance of Teaching* was launched in November 2010. Nevertheless, there are strong indications of its direction. For example, the DfE website states 'The new National Curriculum will set out only the essential knowledge that all children should acquire, and give schools and teachers more freedom to decide how to teach this most effectively and to design a wider school curriculum that best meets the needs of their pupils.' (DfE, 2011). Additionally, the Tickell Review of the Early Years Foundation Stage (EYFS) has reported (March, 2011). There are very clear messages about reducing the number of early learning goals by which children are assessed and prioritising personal and social development, communication and language, and physical development. Literacy, mathematics, expressive arts and design, and understanding of the world will take a more secondary role.

As a result, what to teach children is now possibly open to debate more than it has been for the last thirty years. The focus of this chapter will be to consider not only curriculum content but learning, its purpose and professional development in the light of the issues raised in Chapters 1 and 2 concerning the importance of beliefs and the nature of mathematics.

Curriculum

The National Curriculum, introduced in England in 1989, standardised the content of *what* was taught across schools. From the mid-1990s, with falling standards in schools compared to their international counterparts, there was a shift away from just prescribing *what* was to be taught to children to include *how* it was to be taught. The resulting National Numeracy Project (NNP) was lauded by Ofsted for raising standards and evolved into the National Numeracy Strategy (NNS, 1998) and later became part of the Primary National Strategy (PNS, 2006). It included guidance on *what* to teach and *how* to teach it.

However, reports concerning statutory education (Advisory Committee on Mathematics Education (ACME), 2006; House of Commons, Public Accounts Committee, 2009) raised concerns over attainment, curriculum planning, pedagogy and CPD, particularly noting that the Trends in International Mathematics and Science Study (TIMSS) surveys demonstrated that even though pupil attainment increased between 1995 and 2003, pupils' attitudes became significantly less positive. Did this relate to *what* was taught, *how* it was taught or a combination of these factors? It is hard to draw firm conclusions as content has changed at the same time as pedagogy.

The introduction of a Foundation Stage prior to statutory education brought another dimension into the curriculum. It marked a significant change in education policy in terms of provision, curriculum and pedagogy. In 1996, the government introduced a framework for a pre-school curriculum: *Desirable Outcomes for Children's Learning on Entering Compulsory Education* (SCAA, 1996), later revised as *Curriculum Guidance for the Foundation Stage* (QCA, 2000). This framework identified a large number of learning goals to be achieved by children. Chris Woodhead, Chief Inspector of Schools at the time, stated that adults working with 3- and 4-year-old children need to use a formal approach and direct teaching, an approach he believed should be used with every other age (Woodhead, 1999: 10). In 2003 *Birth to Three Matters* (DfES) was published giving the principles for early years' provision based on the importance of play and active learning, a contrast to the principles of the guidance for the 3–5 age range. The Early Years Foundation Stage (EYFS) (2008) brought guidance together for the 0–5 age range, and promoted the continuance of a child-centred play-based approach for the full age range. Tickell (2011) has advocated the continuance of a play-based approach to teaching and learning. The learning goals have been rationalised with the number being reduced from 69 to 17 with areas of learning being divided into two types: prime or specific.

Early Years Foundation Stage Framework (2008)	Early Years Foundation Stage Review Recommendations (2011)	
6 areas of learning and development:	7 areas	
• Personal, Social and Emotional Development (PSE) • Communication, Language and Literacy • Problem Solving, Reasoning and Numeracy (PSRN) • Knowledge and Understanding of the World (KUW) • Physical Development (PD) • Creative Development (CD)	**Prime:** • Personal, Social and Emotional Development (PSE) • Physical Development (PD) • Communication and Language (CL)	*Time-sensitive. If not securely in place by the age of 5, they will be more difficult to acquire and their absence may hold the child back in other areas of learning.* *Characterised by their universality: they occur in all socio-cultural contexts.* *Not dependent on the specific areas of learning, although the specific areas of learning provide the context for their development.*
	Specific: • Literacy • Mathematics • Understanding the World • Expressive Arts and Design	*Less time-sensitive. Specific areas of learning reflect cultural knowledge and accumulated understanding. It is possible to acquire these bodies of knowledge at various stages through life.* *Skills and knowledge which are specific to priorities within socio-cultural contexts.* *Dependent on learning in the prime areas – the specific learning cannot easily take place without the prime.*

Any curriculum from compulsory school age will need to acknowledge the revised EYFS in terms of curriculum content and approaches to teaching and learning.

A case could be made that the primary mathematics curriculum has become too broad and primary schools should be concentrating on enabling children to be numerate and developing basic mathematical concepts securely. In an interview with the BBC (20 January 2011) (online) Michael Gove, the Secretary of State for Education, indicated that the curriculum will be cut down with more emphasis on facts, but the challenge comes when trying to match content with pedagogy as they are inextricably linked. The didactic model of the 1960s was primarily based upon arithmetic which relates to the calculation aspect of number. Although the NNS did not revert to a didactic model it did expect a teacher-led approach, as demonstrated by the teaching strategies suggested such as modelling and demonstrating and a revision to a curriculum based on number – indeed the strategy was the National *Numeracy* Strategy not National *Mathematics* Strategy. Confusion arises when comparing teaching content and styles as didactic models of teaching do not necessarily mean that content is restricted, and similarly child-centred education does not always equate to the curriculum being expanded. It is highly unlikely that schools will be left alone to devise the curriculum but taking ownership of a core curriculum by agreeing basic principles is fundamental to its success within a school.

Although school curricula prior to the National Strategies were frequently based on commercial schemes of work, the easy availability of curriculum plans through web-based sources of information has meant that teachers now have even less experience of planning the curriculum from first principles. As a consequence, it can be challenging to consider the curriculum other than in its current form. Look at the following diagrams. The first is taken from the book *Lines of Development in Primary Mathematics* by Mary Deboys and Eunice Pitt, first published in 1979 with the latest edition in 2007. It was adopted as a set text by the Open University for primary PGCE programmes so has had significant influence on many teachers. It gives an example of how the primary curriculum was devised. The second diagram is taken from the BEAM (**Be a M**athematician) Project (1992) devised by Lynda Maple and Anita Straker which was supported by Islington Council in London after the ILEA was disbanded in 1990. Its aim was to provide mathematical materials and in-service support for schools in London and the UK. BEAM is still active today supporting Early Years and Primary mathematics education. This diagram gives an example of a curriculum post the first National Curriculum (1989).

Deboys and Pitt (1979) summary	National Numeracy Strategy (1998)	National Curriculum (1999)	Primary Framework – mathematics (2006)
10 topics organised at 3 levels relating roughly to KS1, lower KS2 and upper KS2 – belief that primary mathematics does not follow fixed, linear, hierarchical structure but is cumulative rather than sequential Teachers advised to work horizontally across topics as well as vertically through them	5 strands	4 attainment targets (ATs) in KS1 and 5 ATs in KS 2 (AT Handling data part of AT for Number (Ma2) in KS1 AT 1 Using and applying mathematics is subsumed within the other ATs)	7 strands divided into 5 blocks for planning purposes
NUMBER			
Sets Sorting, partitioning, combining, properties, basic set theory, classification of numbers, etc.	1. Number and the number system	Ma2 Number including Ma1 using and applying number	1. Using and applying mathematics
Number – concepts such as conservation, calculation including laws of arithmetic, fractional quantities, probability, historical number systems, patterns	2. Calculations		2. Counting and understanding number
Pictorial representation Pictorial representation of number, graphs, co-ordinates	3. Solving problems		3. Knowing and using number facts
			4. Calculating
SHAPE, SPACE AND MEASURES			
Shape – classifying, building nets • 3D Classifying, tessellating, finding symmetry, translating, enlarging • 2D	4. Measures, shape and space	Ma3 Shapes, space and measures including Ma1 using and applying shapes, space and measures	5. Understanding shape
Measurement – comparison, conservation • Capacity/Volume • Area • Length • Weight • Time • Money			6. Measuring
HANDLING DATA			
Pictorial representation Designated in third position	5. Handling data	Ma4 (KS2) Handling data including using and applying handling data	7. Handling data

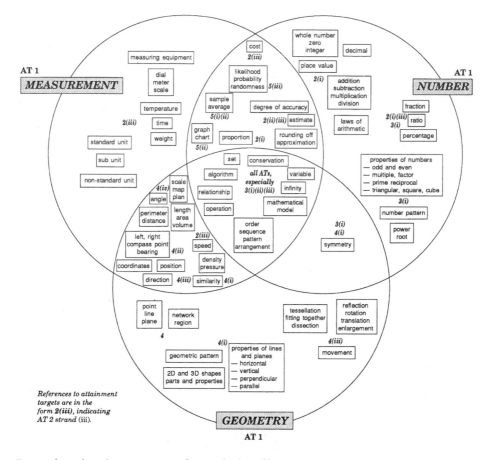

Reproduced with permission from Blackstaff Press

You can see that in the grid by Deboys and Pitt the core coverage of number including handling data, shape, space and measures is not so different to the current curriculum. However, there is a clear focus on concepts that span more than one aspect of mathematics, e.g. conservation. Also, there is reference to the history and nature of mathematics. The BEAM diagram shows similar coverage to the current curriculum with the inclusion of the concept of conservation, the laws of arithmetic and the relationship between branches of primary mathematics.

One area of the mathematics curriculum that is not evident in the examples given is information and communication technology (ICT). The speed at which technology has overtaken our lives is easily forgotten but ease of access to information and communication has fundamentally changed the way the majority of the population communicate on a local, national and global scale. As far as teaching and learning is concerned, there is an increasing emphasis on teaching *through* ICT rather than *about* ICT. ICT has transformed the availability of education for those who have problems accessing learning through logistic, physical or learning needs, enabling participation and communication that previously would not have been possible. However, there is a tension in the role played by technology within the curriculum. Is ICT just a powerful resource preparing children for the twenty-first century *if* the curriculum and the approach to teaching and learning are fundamentally based upon a pre-ICT world? As a resource it has huge power as both a teaching and learning tool. However, should ICT radically change what is included in the curriculum at the primary phase?

Discuss this issue with colleagues.

(Note: ICT is discussed further in Chapters 8, 9 and 10.)

Learning for all children

The curriculum should be accessible for all learners but learners do not come from the same starting points. They will be influenced by individual factors such as health and well-being and neurological factors as well as those that relate to the social context of learning such as their families, social relationships and the learning culture in the classroom. However, this opens up the dilemma of whether children's needs in mathematics – or indeed any subject – can be met within a prescribed time or whether the curriculum needs to be modified in relation to the child's needs. One of the challenges that primary education has to face is the time-bound feature of learning. In the Early Years it is accepted that children learn at different rates. Although this idea is not rejected through later education it is implicitly ignored as there are targets for achievement at specific stages which do not relate to the developmental stage or even a child's chronological age within a year. As the academic year runs between the first day of September and the last day of August, the same expectations are in place for year 6 children even though some can be almost a year different in age depending where in the year their birthday falls. It is interesting to note that reading tests such as Salford take account of the chronological age but these are rarely used with children beyond year 3. Although GCSEs do not have to be taken at a specific age, secondary schools are judged on the basis of GCSE results at the end of statutory education.

Nevertheless, there is an imperative to ensure that children do achieve their optimum before the statutory age for compulsory education is reached and this unavoidable fact is bound to impact on children in the primary phase. Additionally, there will always be a responsibility to make the transition into Key Stage 3 a smooth process for children, the content of the primary curriculum having prepared them for that of the secondary curriculum. What is debateable is whether the curriculum should be so directly related to age ranges and not development, and whether it is realistic to expect that achievement is inevitably diverse if a prescribed time is given for formal assessment.

In recent years, the government has set targets for achievement based on attainment assessed by national standard attainment tests (SATs). Additionally, Ofsted expects all children to progress based upon levels that do not always identify small steps in development. Although it is to be expected that there is a focus on children achieving their full potential, such targets and expectations can lead to an approach to teaching whereby expediency in meeting curriculum coverage can overshadow giving time to ensure that children fully understand what they are being taught.

The key question to consider here is how individual learning by children can be met within a curriculum. In the past various strategies have been tried:

- *Children working at their own pace through a set curriculum.* This form of organisation led to a number of challenges such as ineffective use of the teacher's time in supporting individuals or small groups and a reduction in collaborative learning.
- *Organisation of the curriculum by attainment.* Children did not always stay with their chronological age group but remained behind or were advanced a year depending on their attainment. There are still some versions of organisation by attainment such as streaming and setting. Such strategies are criticised on the basis that they have negative social and emotional implications and can lead to lowered self-esteem that can compound low attainment. For example, Boaler believes that to label children in these ways is one of the biggest problems with mathematics teaching in England (2009: 32–4).

Learning

Learning is a process within the individual which we cannot necessarily observe, nor of which are we immediately aware. In an educational sense it is usually seen as involving knowledge, skills and understanding. How would you define the terms knowledge, skills and understanding in relation to mathematics?

Record your initial thoughts in your learning journal.

Defining the difference between knowledge, skills and understanding can be perplexing. You may have found that your definitions include use of the other terminology you are trying to define!

Learning was not explicitly discussed in the National Curriculum (1999); the curriculum was expressed in terms of knowledge, skills and understanding. The debate around the acquisition *of* and the relationship *between* knowledge, skills and understanding is both multifaceted and controversial. Knowledge, skill and understanding were terms taken directly from the Education Act 1996, section 353a. They were again echoed in the terminology used in the National Strategies in the term 'to know, understand and can do'. Standard definitions often confuse the issue. Promoting the term understanding may be due to concern that children may not be learning with understanding, advocated so much since the Cockcroft Report (1982). Cockcroft defined the term *understanding* in mathematics by stating it 'implies an ability to recognise and make use of a mathematical concept in a variety of settings, including some which are not immediately familiar' (1982: 68). Haylock defined *understanding* in mathematics by stating 'to understand something means to make connections' (1982: 54) in terms of concrete situations, pictures, symbols and mathematical language.

The Early Years Foundation Stage Framework (DCFS, 2008) takes a different stance on the curriculum. In fact the term curriculum is not used at all but the document is described as 'a comprehensive framework which sets the standards for learning, development and care of children from birth to 5'. Implicit in its content is a clear theoretical perspective on learning although no model is explicitly identified. There is an emphasis on children constructing their own knowledge by integrating new concepts into existing mental structures in a supportive learning environment.

One way to consider the difference between knowledge, skills and understanding is to consider an example:

The sign × is usually interpreted as 'sets of', 'lots of' or 'groups of' but in fact means you have the first number the number of times of the second number, e.g. 4 × 3 means four, three times, that is 4 + 4 + 4, rather than four sets of three, i.e. 3 + 3 + 3 + 3. (See Haylock (2006: 71–2) for a full explanation.)

$3 \times 4 = 12$

I *KNOW* this statement as a knowledge fact.

I have *SKILLS* in applying this knowledge to mental calculations and everyday problems such as working out how many wheels are needed for three toy cars.

I *UNDERSTAND* multiplication as repeated addition and in the form of arrays such as

```
* * * *
* * * *
* * * *
```

I *UNDERSTAND* the inverse relationship between multiplication and division in terms of grouping. Therefore I *KNOW* more number facts e.g. $4 \times 3 = 12$, $12 \div 4 = 3$, $12 \div 3 = 4$.

I have SKILLS in applying this knowledge to mental calculations and everyday problems such as working out how many chocolates three children could each receive if a box held 12 chocolates.

It can be seen from this model that knowledge builds on understanding to form new knowledge and increases application skills. Of course, it is possible to know number facts purely by rote but such an approach does not foster making connections between the facts and limits understanding. For example, I could learn

$$3 \times 4 \quad = 12$$
$$4 \times 3 \quad = 12$$
$$12 \div 4 = 3$$
$$12 \div 3 = 4$$

as separate facts but if I forgot one of these facts, I would not necessarily have the understanding of the connections between the facts to find a solution to the fact I had forgotten. Richard Skemp discussed the concept of understanding in his seminal paper 'Relational Understanding and Instrumental Understanding' first published in 1979. He believed that *understanding* had two meanings and that the confusion between the meanings was the basis of many difficulties in mathematics education. Skemp had worked with Stieg Mellin-Olsen, a Norwegian mathematician and lecturer in education. He worked on qualitative methods in educational research and had analysed the concept of instrumentalism. Using the terminology of Mellin-Olsen, Skemp distinguished the two meanings by the terms relational and instrumental. Relational understanding is knowing what to do and why and instrumental understanding is knowing what to do but *not* why, usually through a process of applying rules.

A classic example of rote learning teachers remember is how to multiply fractions. They may have learnt by rote, a form of instrumental understanding, or they may have learnt it as quick way to solve multiplying fractions based on deeper or relational understanding, e.g.

$$\tfrac{2}{3} \times \tfrac{3}{4}$$

The rule people remember is that the top and bottom numbers need to be multiplied and the result 'cancelled' down:

$$2 \times 3 = 6$$
$$3 \times 4 = 12$$

$$\tfrac{6}{12}$$

Cancel down if there is a multiple of both the top and bottom numbers:

$$\frac{6 \div 6 = 1}{12 \div 6 = 2}$$

Therefore $\tfrac{2}{3} \times \tfrac{3}{4} = \tfrac{1}{2}$

If the rule could not be remembered then someone with relational understanding could consider relating the calculation to other mathematics they understood. For example:

1. Knowledge of the meaning of the symbol × as 'of' and application to an everyday situation:

   ⅔ of ¾

   e.g. two-thirds of three-quarters of a rectangular pizza.

Visualisation may work, possibly supported by a drawing. This may lead on to:

2. Finding the area of a shape:

   ⅔ of ¾ of the shape = ⁶⁄₁₂ or ½ of the shape

¾

⅔ × ¾

Look at the following example of a word problem and the possible solutions provided, though you may think of more. Try to work with colleagues. You may think the solution depends on the age and experience of the child and that the solutions below are not appropriate for just any child. However, it can be easy to assume that using resources is a strategy for just young children. You may be surprised by the range of strategies you and your colleagues use to solve what may appear quite simple problems.

I have 15p. How many pencils costing 4p each can I buy from the school shop?

1. $4 \times 3 = 12$ *(known fact)*

   $4 \times 4 = 16$ *(known fact)*

   15 is between 12 and 16 (known fact)

   As I have less than 16 pence I can only buy 3 pencils.

2. *Grouping on a number line:*

   $$+4 \ +4 \ +4 \ +4$$

   0 4 8   12 16

   3 lots but as I have only 15 I have not got enough for 4 lots so I can only buy 3 pencils

3. *Use pencils and pence, their replicas, or their representations in a drawing. Allocate 'pence' to pencils until there until there is not enough to buy another pencil.*

4. $4 \,\overline{)15}$

   3 remainder 3 or 3¾

   so I can buy 3 pencils (may lead to problem of answer being 3¾ pencils).

5. *1 pencil costs 4p (given fact)*

   2 pencils cost $4 \times 2 = 8$ (known fact or doubling given fact)

   3 (1 + 2) pencils cost 4p + 8p =12p

   4 pencils cost $8 \times 2 =16$ (knowledge of doubling derived fact but more than 15)

   Therefore only 3 pencils can be bought.

This is not an exhaustive list of solutions and the strategies relate to each other. However, the aim is to give guidance on the types of strategies that could be used. Now try the following examples.

- My bedroom has an area of 20 square metres and is a rectangle. I know one wall is 2½ metres long but want to know if a bed I want to buy will fit next to my desk. How long is the adjacent wall?

- I decide to buy a bacon roll to eat but can buy two bacon rolls for the same price as one. I offer to share the rolls with two friends. How much do we get each?

- A game requires reaching a target number by multiplying the result of throwing two dice. I am not doing well and want to find out how many pairs I could make so I could work out the odds of being successful. How many different pairs could I throw without reaching the target number of 12?

Record your responses and consider how the solutions supported learning in the types of understanding they required.

Teaching approaches that promote a particular style of learning, for example the use of repetition to encourage memorisation leading to rote learning, are not theories but the manifestation of approaches *based* on theories of how children learn. Look at the simple overview of theoretical approaches to learning in the grid below. Can you identify where you fall on the spectrum in terms of your teaching style? At this stage what is important is that you are aware of how you teach, how you expect children to learn and how this affects what you include in the content of the mathematics curriculum. For example, to the left of the spectrum the teacher is in control and content is set whereas to the right of the spectrum content is fluid and unpredictable as what is learnt evolves from the child, with the teacher acting more as a facilitator of learning. Also, consider whether the way you teach changes across the duration of a lesson and why this may be so.

Overview of how learning theories can relate to teaching styles

Learning theory		
⇐ Behaviourist	Cognitivist	Constructivist ⇒

Teaching style		
⇐		⇒
Didactic		*Child-centred*
Characteristics: *– leaning by transmitting knowledge, telling information, giving instructions to the learner* *– teacher controlled*	*Use of a range of styles that stimulate more senses and forms of communication than hearing, i.e. speaking, using visual aids, demonstrating, etc.* *Children assess their own performance against criteria*	*Characteristics:* *– investigative approach to learning, reflecting on actions to make generalisations* *– teacher acting as facilitator* *– teacher- and child-controlled guided discovery*

If possible work with colleagues to share your ideas.

You may find that there is variation depending upon the age of the children with whom you work or the aspect of mathematics you are teaching. Maybe the challenge is deciding whether understanding is easier once basic rules and procedures have been learnt. Lower-order mathematical knowledge such as number facts may be better taught in an instrumental way and, as children's knowledge increases and they become able to think more abstractly, they may be able to relate their knowledge to different areas of mathematics. Such an approach relies on the teacher having conceptual understanding and so knowing the connections between different aspects of mathematics.

When children are taught to read do they engage in instrumental or relational understanding? The novice reader must learn the connections between the approximately 44 sounds of spoken English (the phonemes) and the 26 letters of the alphabet. Whatever approach is taken in teaching and learning to read, it requires children recognising letters which, when combined in various ways, make words and these words have meaning. At first it may seem it is relational understanding as children learn to recognise these letters in an increasing range of contexts. However, knowing these letters and combinations is not negotiable in terms of reading. Rules and exceptions to those rules are taught. Is this a form of 'rote' learning? If a child were expected to explore the relationship between sounds and letters, learning to read could be a very time-consuming and potentially frustrating business.

It can be seen that the curriculum is influenced not only by what is to be taught but by ideas of how it is to be learnt. There are three key questions for consideration in devising a curriculum.

- How do you believe children learn mathematics?
- How will teaching support this learning process?
- How would you expect learning and teaching to evolve through the primary phase?

The nature of mathematics

The hierarchical nature of mathematics can add to these challenges of designing and teaching a curriculum. All human knowledge can be seen as hierarchical in that the higher-level concepts such as interpreting written information are dependent on lower-order skills such decoding words and understanding their meanings individually and collectively. Mathematics, has developed an extensive hierarchy or network of concepts, each more abstract than, and dependent upon, those supplied to it. The hierarchical nature of mathematics was referred to in Chapter 2 as a possible reason why people find it hard to understand or engage with mathematics. Hierarchy can be taken to refer to a logical sequence in the subject matter whereby the higher orders of the sequence are independent of lower orders of the sequence. However, hierarchy can mean the chosen teaching sequence or the learning sequence which is within the learner. If you think of an everyday example of learning such as how to use household equipment or learning a sport, learning rarely occurs after one session. You may think you can perform the task or understand what is being taught but once you return to it you may not have been accurate in your assessment. You may surprise yourself and do well or you may feel you have forgotten what you had learnt. Mathematics is no different. It involves coming to know by 'doing' mathematics.

It can be seen how decisions about what is taught have to be in tune with *both* the learning needs of the individual and the chosen teaching sequence influenced by the curriculum. In many ways this summarises the challenge of teaching! This leads to two key questions.

- How will the curriculum be structured?
- How can it be assessed?

Fitness for purpose

Mick Walters, former director of curriculum at the Qualifications and Curriculum Agency (QCA), emphasised the importance of the learning experience if any curriculum was to be successful. His view of the curriculum as 'the big picture' is based on 'what are we trying to achieve in learning, how are we going to organise that learning and how do we know if we're being successful?' (Waters, 2007).

The phrase 'what are we trying to achieve in learning' can be interpreted as the purpose of the learning. Identifying purpose is fundamental to deciding what children should learn. There is no moral justification of what to include in a curriculum. UK society has changed substantially since the 1980s in terms of cultural diversity and technology; the same cannot be said for the National Curriculum when it was first introduced. The rate of change is such that we cannot anticipate the world for which we are preparing children. In terms of mathematics resources alone, the range of technology we have available today was unknown in the 1980s. The key question here is what are the aims of the mathematics curriculum and how will they be evaluated?

Developing a vision

The following grid gives a brief overview of the decisions that could be made when deciding what children should learn.

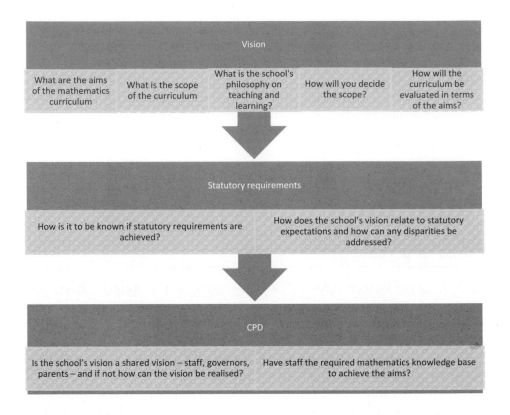

Summary

The aim of this chapter was not to prescribe a curriculum but to support teachers in planning the content of the mathematics curriculum. It has outlined the five key factors to address when deciding what mathematics should be taught and learnt.

- What is to be included in the scope of the mathematics curriculum?
- How will the curriculum meet the learning needs of all children?
- How will the vision of teaching and learning influence the mathematics curriculum?
- How will the mathematics curriculum be structured?
- How will we know if we have been successful?

Conclusion

What children should learn must be in balance with what teachers must know in order to teach effectively. The next chapter will explore the nature of teacher subject knowledge and how it relates to generic theories of learning and to mathematics as a distinct subject.

Review questions

Refer back to the activities in this chapter and the questions at the end of each section.

* Can you identify action that you could take in response to what children should learn?

References

ACME (2006) *Making Mathematics Count – Two Years On*. London: Royal Society.

Askew, M. and Brown, M. (2001) *Teaching and Learning Primary Numeracy: Policy, Practice and Effectiveness*. Southwell: BERA.

Askew, M., Brown, M., Rhodes, V. and Wiliam, D. (1997) *Effective Teachers of Numeracy: Report of a Study Carried Out for the Teacher Training Agency*. London: TTA.

BBC Online (2011) Interview with Michael Gove, Secretary of State for Education, 20 January. Available online at: http://www.bbc.co.uk/news/education-12227491 (accessed 5 August 2011).

Boaler, J. (2009) *The Elephant in the Classroom. Helping Children Learn and Love Maths*. London: Souvenir Press.

Cockcroft, W. H. (1982) *Mathematics Counts: Report of the Committee of Inquiry into the Teaching of Mathematics in Schools under the Chairmanship of Dr W. H. Cockcroft*. London: HMSO. Available online at: http://www.educationengland. org.uk/index.html.

Deboys, M. and Pitt, E. (1995) *Lines of Development in Primary Mathematics*. Belfast: Blackstaff Press.

DCSF (2008) *Practice Guidance for the Early Years Foundation Stage*. Nottingham: DCSF.

DfE (2011) *Teaching the Curriculum*. London: DfE.

DfEE (1999) *National Numeracy Strategy*. London: DfEE.

DfEE/QCA (1999) *The National Curriculum: Handbook for Primary Teachers in England*. London: HMSO.

DfEE/QCA (2000) *Curriculum Guidance for the Foundation Stage*. London: DfEE.

DfES (2003) *Birth to Three Matters*. London: DfES Publications.

Haylock, D. W. (1982) 'Understanding in mathematics: making connections', *Mathematics Teaching*, Association of Teachers of Mathematics Publication No. 98. Cheltenham: Nelson, pp. 54–6.

Haylock, D. (2006) *Mathematics Explained for Primary Teachers*. London: Sage.

House of Commons Children, Schools and Families Committee (2009) *The Fourth Report of Session 2008–9 Concerning the National Curriculum of the House of Commons, Children, Schools and Families Committee*. London: HMSO.

QCA (2000) *Curriculum Guidance for the Foundation Stage*. London: QCA.

SCAA (1996) *Nursery Education: Desirable Outcomes for Children's Learning on Entering Compulsory Education*. London: SCAA and DfEE.

Skemp, R. (1979) 'Relational understanding and instrumental understanding', in *The Psychology of Mathematics*. Harmondsworth: Penguin.

Tickell, C. (2011) *The Early Years: Foundations for Life, Health and Learning. An Independent Report on the Early Years Foundation Stage to Her Majesty's Government*. London: DfE.

Waters, M. (2007) *Big Picture*. London: QCDA. Available online at: http://www.teachfind.com/national-strategies/seal-secondary-schools (accessed June 2011).

Woodhead, C. (1999) 'Is the formal approach better?', *Early Years Educator*, 1 (6): 10–11.

Further reading

Ball, D. and Bass, H. (2000) 'Interweaving context and pedagogy in teaching and learning to teach: knowing and using mathematics', in J. Boaler (ed.), *Multiple Perspectives on Teaching and Learning Mathematics*. Westport, CT: Ablex, pp. 83–104.

BEAM (Be A Mathematician Project): http://www.beam.co.uk/.

Cotton, T. (2010) *Understanding and Teaching Primary Mathematics*. Harlow: Pearson Education.

Hansen, A. (2008) *Extending Knowledge in Practice: Primary Mathematics*. Exeter: Learning Matters.

Haylock, D. W. (1982) 'Understanding in mathematics: making connections', in *Mathematics Teaching*, Association of Teachers of Mathematics Publications, No. 98. Cheltenham: Nelson.

Haylock, D. (2010) *Mathematics Explained for Primary Teachers*, 4th edn. London: Sage.

Haylock, D. and Cockburn, A. (2008) *Understanding Mathematics in the Lower Primary Years*, 3rd edn. London: Sage.

Haylock, D. and Thangata, F. (2007) *Key Concepts in Teaching Primary Mathematics*. London: Sage.

Hiebert, J. and Lefevre, P. (1986) 'Conceptual and procedural knowledge in mathematics: an introductory analysis', in J. Hiebert (ed.), *Conceptual and Procedural Knowledge: The Case of Mathematics*. Hillsdale, NJ: Erlbaum, pp. 1–27.

Hughes, M., Desforges, C., Mitchell, C. with Carré, C. (2000) *Numeracy and Beyond: Applying Mathematics in the Primary School*. Buckingham: Open University Press.

Liebeck, P. (1990) *How Children Learn Mathematics*. Harmondsworth: Penguin Books.

Mason, J. (2005) *Developing Thinking in Algebra*. London: PCP.

Mooney, C., Briggs, M., Fletcher, M. and McCullouch, J. (2012) *Primary Mathematics: Teaching Theory and Practice*, 6th edn. London: Learning Matters.

NNS (2002) *Learning from Mistakes and Misconceptions in Mathematics*. London: DfES.

Skemp, R. (1979) *The Psychology of Mathematics*. Harmondsworth: Penguin.

Skemp, R. (1991) *Mathematics in the Primary School*. London: Taylor & Francis.

Suggate, J., Davis, A. and Goulding, M. (2010) *Mathematical Knowledge for Primary School Teachers*, 4th edn. Abingdon: David Fulton.

Thompson, I. (2003) *Enhancing Primary Mathematics*. Buckingham: Open University Press.

Thompson, I. (2008) *Teaching and Learning Early Number*. Buckingham: Open University Press.

Turner, S. and McCullouch, J. (2004) *Making Connections in Primary Mathematics*. London: David Fulton.

Waters, M. (2007) *Big Picture*. London: QCDA. Available online at: http://www.teachfind.com/national-strategies/seal-secondary-schools (accessed June 2011).

West-Burnham, J. and Coates, M. (2005) *Personalizing Learning*. Stafford: Network Educational Press.

CHAPTER 4

WHAT SHOULD TEACHERS KNOW AND WHY?

Aims

By the end of this chapter you should:

- understand the *background* subject knowledge a teacher should possess in order to teach mathematics effectively;
- understand what *pedagogical* subject knowledge a teacher should possess in order to teach mathematics effectively;
- understand what *curricular* subject knowledge a teacher should possess in order to teach mathematics effectively;
- understand how the interrelationship between background, pedagogical and curricular subject knowledge empowers teachers and teaching.

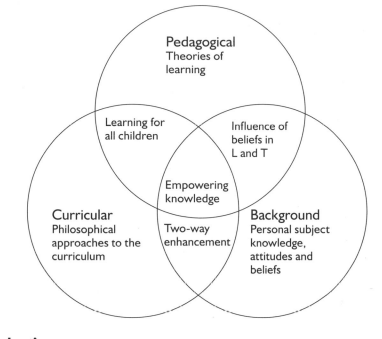

Introduction

At a time when the government is indicating more autonomy will be given to schools and teachers, it is important that teachers feel sufficiently confident to make and take decisions, particularly if they work in academies and free schools where they will be able 'to depart from aspects of the National Curriculum where they consider it appropriate . . .' (DfE, 2011). All primary teachers are expected to have the subject knowledge to teach the full curriculum. However, from the Plowden Report (DES, 1967) to the Williams Report (2008), teacher subject knowledge has been cited as an issue that needs to be addressed in order to improve teaching. Researchers here and in the USA have tried to categorise subject knowledge to examine what it is that teachers need to know to be effective. Shulman (1986) devised the term Pedagogical Content Knowledge (PCK) to describe the interrelationship between content and pedagogy. He carried out a longitudinal study of secondary teachers in their training and beginning of their teaching career. He believed there to be a symbiotic relationship between what he called 'subject matter knowledge' and 'PCK', i.e. the process of developing PCK led to stronger forms of the subject matter knowledge.

Major categories of teacher knowledge

- General pedagogical knowledge, with special reference to those broad principles and strategies of classroom management and organization that appear to transcend subject matter
- Knowledge of learners and their characteristics
- Knowledge of educational contexts, ranging from workings of the group or classroom, the governance and financing of school districts, to the character of communities and cultures
- Knowledge of educational ends, purposes, and values, and their philosophical and historical grounds
- Content knowledge
- Curriculum knowledge, with particular grasp of the materials and programs that serve as 'tools of the trade' for teachers
- Pedagogical content knowledge, that special amalgam of content and pedagogy that is uniquely the province of teachers, their own special form of professional understanding

(Shulman, 1987: 8)

Such findings have significant implications on how teachers can be taught to teach mathematics in terms of enhancing their personal mathematical understanding. More recently, Rowland et al. (2009) considered the ideas of Shulman in devising their 'Knowledge Quartet' based upon observation of the subject knowledge of mathematics content knowledge exhibited while on teaching practice.

Knowledge Quartet

Foundation refers to subject knowledge and beliefs about mathematics and mathematical pedagogy.

Transformation refers to how trainees are able to transform what they know to make it accessible to children.

Connection refers to decisions made about progression, sequencing in learning and conceptual connectivity within the lesson, including the relationship to previous lessons and pupils' knowledge.

Contingency refers to the ability to respond to the unexpected such as children's responses and questions.

(Rowland et al., 2009)

What is clear from both forms of categorisation is that the subject knowledge required for teaching requires more than a candidate with strong academic qualifications ready to learn a repertoire of teaching strategies. This chapter will discuss subject knowledge in detail and how it is developed on teaching programmes and in the classroom. Chapter 1 introduced subject knowledge in general terms and three broad categories were offered: background, pedagogical and curricular.

Background subject knowledge

Teachers require mathematical skills and understanding as well as their underpinning values and philosophy. Student teachers bring this prior knowledge to their teaching programmes where it gradually evolves through taught and school-based studies. It will continue to evolve when in post through experience and CPD activities.

Mathematical skills and understanding

The government's White Paper *The Importance of Teaching* (DfE, 2010) confirmed the commitment to developing a mathematics specialism in primary schools. This builds on the recommendation in the Williams Report (2008) which stated: 'There should be at least one Mathematics Specialist in each primary school, in post within 10 years, with deep mathematical subject and pedagogical knowledge.'

The Mathematics Specialist Teacher (MaST) Project

The aims of the programme acknowledge previous findings in that teachers do not necessarily have to have a mathematics background to undertake MaST, but they need *enthusiasm* for the subject. The programme covers *subject knowledge* of the mathematics contained in the Early Years Foundation Stage and primary curriculum, going into Key Stage 3, understanding of a range of approaches to teaching and learning and analysis of a range of coaching and mentoring skills in order to support others in strengthening their teaching and learning. The longer-term vision is that this group of skilled teachers promotes mathematics by making it more attractive to children, colleagues and parents and that local centres of influence lead to improvements nationally in attitudes, expectations and standards. (DfES, 2010)

The focus of the MaST programme clearly highlights research into the importance of enthusiasm, engendering positive attitudes in children, colleagues and the wider population as well as curriculum content and teaching and learning strategies. Knowledge, as is demonstrated in GCSE mathematics, is not sufficient for effective teaching. Berenson et al. (1997) used the terms procedure-centred and concept-centred to classify the extremes of knowledge in their study of trainee perceptions of teaching. It is the conceptual understanding that is fundamental to making connections within mathematics. Some teachers do not have such concept-centred knowledge as they have learnt and remembered mathematics in a compartmentalised way. Curriculum guidance documents can do no more than offer content and teaching strategies but these implicitly relate to a static curriculum and method of teaching. However, teaching in a classroom is ideally a dynamic process which requires numerous instant decisions to be made in order to adjust teaching to class responses and the varying evolving needs of individual children. Static curricula and teaching methods tend to lend themselves to instructional input and general dissemination of information and have a place in lectures, documentaries and such school practices as assemblies. This is not to say that adults and children do not learn from such practices, but they are not the core of teaching that takes place in school. It is the unique, dynamic relationship that a teacher has with class members that gives school teaching possibilities of such potency, particularly in the primary years when teachers and children have extended time together. As such, becoming a primary teacher requires knowledge acquired both from course work and experience of school.

One of the dilemmas that can take place is when teachers are unsure about what they are teaching, are unable to connect what is taught to previous learning experiences or are concerned about giving children opportunities to ask questions to which they may not know the answer. At this point teachers can adopt an instructional way of teaching which manifests itself in an emphasis on teaching standard methods and applying them to problems when alternative strategies may be more appropriate (Askew et al., 1997).

Although Askew et al. (1997) found that being highly effective did not necessarily relate to levels of mathematical qualifications, his research was with practising teachers only who develop their knowledge through the teaching of the curriculum. Initially, beliefs will be strongly influenced by personal competence and confidence. Personal beliefs should be recognised by providers of Initial Teacher Education (ITE) as their role is to enable student teachers to become sufficiently competent and confident in order to be enthusiastic teachers of mathematics.

Look at the following four categories and note examples of your mathematical knowledge under the relevant category. You may need to look at online resources to prompt you. A reliable source is the BBC Bitesize webpages that have information at Key Stages 1–3 and GCSE. Although you will have a GCSE in Mathematics or its equivalent you may find it helpful to start looking at Key Stages 1, 2 and 3 to remind you of the scope of the mathematics curriculum.

- Knowledge you had, understood, could apply and have used since school.
- Knowledge you had, understood, could apply but have rarely used since school. For example, you may have understood what a congruent triangle was at one time but forgotten as the word is not in day-to-day usage.
- Knowledge you had but did not fully understand.
- Knowledge you did not understand at all.

Identifying knowledge in categories will help you make sense of any areas that may need more time to develop and those that just need to be revised in order to prompt your memory. You may find that if you identify mathematics in the latter two categories it could be that you did not have conceptual understanding but just learnt procedures. This is particularly common with topics such as fractions and is a good example of how pedagogical and curriculum insights through planning a series of work can support and enrich your knowledge as you are must identify progression. This relationship will be explored later in the chapter when considering the two-way enhancement of curricular and background subject knowledge.

Underpinning values and philosophy

Although beliefs about mathematics teaching and learning will be significantly affected by personal competence, they will also be affected by your philosophical views of education. All teaching students and teachers have a philosophy of education but do not necessarily articulate it to others or even themselves. It can be helpful to read about the philosophies of others to prompt you when considering your own beliefs. Rudolf Steiner

(1861–1925) and Maria Montessori (1870–1952) had very specific beliefs about education which is evident in schools operating today under their philosophy. Information can be found on the Steiner Waldorf Schools Fellowship website http://www.steinerwaldorf.org and the Montessori website http://www.montessori.org.uk.

Broadly, the philosophy of education is dependent on the relationship between the individual and society whereas the psychology of education depends on the relationship between the innate and external factors that affect learning. As such, philosophy and psychology in terms of education are interwoven. Psychological perspectives are evolving as more is discovered about the brain through neuroscience which, in turn, challenges philosophical perspectives of education. The philosophical stance on mathematics education – indeed education as a whole – depends on a range of factors. Learning mathematics, just as learning any body of knowledge, depends on how its purpose is perceived, what will be learnt and how it will be learned. It may seem that its purpose is obvious but it depends whether you veer towards believing mathematics to be a life skill that is also a prerequisite of employment or one that relates more to mathematics having intrinsic worth to which children should have access for personal development or in terms of how that individual acts within society. As already discussed, personal experience is a powerful influence on teacher opinion and will be formed by both *being* a pupil and *teaching* pupils. Similarly, views of success in learning mathematics will fall within a spectrum from one extreme being that ability is inherent in the individual to the other that ability develops in response to the teaching and experience received. The standpoint taken on the purpose of mathematics teaching and learning theory will influence both curricular content and classroom-based teaching and learning pedagogy.

Influence of beliefs on learning and teaching

Students accepted on to any ITE programme, whether providers are university or school-based, come with a wide range of mathematical knowledge gained through qualifications and experience. As such these levels of 'background' knowledge present challenges, not just in measurable factors such as grades of qualifications or experience in the classroom, but in the 'baggage' they bring with them in the form of attitudes, beliefs and their approach to learning to teach mathematics. This 'baggage' does not necessarily have to be negative. The best case scenario is the person who deems themselves 'good' at mathematics based upon qualifications and positive memories about the subject. Such a person is likely to approach the teaching of mathematics positively. However, the converse scenario is also possible. Factors such as confidence and enjoyment about specific subjects are not necessarily evident at the time of interview. One potential issue for providers of ITE, especially on short PGCE courses, is enabling student teachers to develop a sufficient depth of understanding of mathematics in order to become confident and enthusiastic teachers of mathematics.

Pedagogical subject knowledge

This form of knowledge can be defined as the art of teaching, i.e. *how* mathematics is taught or learned. It involves knowing about a range of learning theories and making choices to translate mathematical knowledge into a form that children can understand.

Theories of learning

Although teaching is essentially a practical activity, it is a manifestation of a range of theoretical perspectives. Understanding *why* you are doing what you are doing in any sphere helps promote competence and confidence. It can be seen as relating to Skemp's view of relational understanding discussed in Chapter 3. Think about examples such as learning how to ski or learning a new language. If you understand your current situation or level and you are given ideas on how to make improvements and why they are effective, you are more likely to achieve success and be more positive about the process. Having a part to play in devising a programme to achieve a goal can only enhance competence and confidence with a sense of ownership. In fact, this is one of the main elements behind the 'Assessment *for* Learning' strategy promoted by the government in the curriculum in relation to children's learning. At the same time, talking to someone who understands what the next steps could be will strengthen the likelihood of a successful outcome.

Learning, as defined from a psychological perspective, is a change in behaviour. However, learning is not always observable or the result of one clear process. In an educational sense, learning is seen as changes in the way a person understands the world around them and uses that experience. How to foster learning within the individual is of particular significance to teachers and is their main *raison d'être*. Teaching and learning are reciprocal processes that depend on and affect each other. Teachers offer approaches that aim to create learning experiences and the types of experience depend on how it is thought the learning process takes place. The overview of learning theories given in the table on

p. 69 provided very broad categories. At one end of the spectrum were behaviourists who defined learning as a change in behaviour caused as a result *external* factors, a view attributed to such psychologists as Skinner. Cognitive theories explain learning as an *internal* mental process. Piaget, a developmental psychologist, was significant in developing such theories. Piaget's work evolved extensively and led to constructivist ideas: learners taking an active part in 'constructing' learning through direct experiences of the world. These experiences may challenge their existing perception of the concept (called a schema), so it involves learning to accommodate these new experiences by modifying their schema to assimilate new information. Once this process of assimilation and accommodation has taken place a state of equilibrium is attained. Vygotsky and Bruner's work evolved from these ideas and led to a consideration of the impact of social experience in learning.

Recently, emphasis in teaching has been given to 'humanistic' theories of learning relating to the needs of the whole person. Such ideas were first put forward by Maslow (1954) in his hierarchy of needs. These ideas are used today in trying to prepare positive conditions for learning in the classroom. For example, if a person's basic physiological needs are not met it is unlikely they will learn effectively. Also, a 'social' perspective of learning, attributed to Bandura, has become prominent, particularly in the Early Years. It considers how people learn from each other by observation, imitation and modelling and places emphasis on the importance of memory and motivation. As such this theory falls within the spectrum between behaviourist and cognitive learning theories.

Other factors that have influenced practice are studies on learning styles through work originally by Honey and Mumford (1982) and Kolb (1984). Learning is seen as the end product of direct experience, reflection, adjustment to fit in with existing ideas and experimentation. Here, there are parallel ideas with constructivism. Other models, such as identifying types of learner as visual, auditory or kinaesthetic (VAK) or including reading/ writing (VARK), have led to teaching practices and learning opportunities that cater for individual style preferences.

As mentioned briefly at the beginning of this chapter, recent developments in neuroscience have also led to alternative perspectives on learning, identifying particularly receptive periods for learning in the first years of life. Previously, theories about the learning process have been based upon *external* methods of identifying the process during activity or behaviour through such methods as observation. It is now possible to use methods to view the activity that occurs internally in the brain while the activity or behaviour is occurring. Such research is still in its infancy but is likely to have significant implications for teaching in the future.

Literature to explore theoretical perspectives is given at the end of this chapter as this broad outline of theories is insufficient to fully understand them. However, this overview may clarify your understanding of initiatives you may have experienced in school either as a pupil or a teacher. For example, constructivism supports the importance of making connections to ideas within mathematics and areas of the curriculum. The Every Child Matters agenda, although initiated by the Laming Report (2003) which identified inadequacies in the then current child support system, relates clearly to Maslow's ideas of the hierarchy of needs in terms of its outcomes.

The issue emerges of whether generic theories of learning are relevant to all areas of learning. As previously stated, mathematics has unique characteristics in terms of language, structure, notation and hierarchy. Developing teaching and learning strategies based upon understanding of theoretical perspectives is challenging enough in itself but modifying them to fit specific subject areas can be particularly challenging to the novice teacher.

Teaching and learning strategies

This area of pedagogical knowledge requires teachers' understanding of cognitive and developmental theories that illustrate how knowledge can be acquired or constructed. These are generic skills that all teachers learn by practical experience in the classroom supported by theoretical underpinning. They are the 'nuts and bolts' of teaching and could be seen as technical knowledge. However, this view implies a set way of teaching with the teacher in as much control of the teaching as possible, almost in the form of a trainer. Teachers will be given theoretical ideas on classroom management, teaching and learning models, observe other models in school, attempt to copy them and eventually develop their own style in the context in which they work. One of the issues with primary teaching is that teachers must have differing knowledge across a range of subject areas in terms of content *and* teaching and learning strategies. The generalist role of a primary teacher can obscure subject-specific pedagogical knowledge. In mathematics there is theory related to how mathematics is learnt and how to present mathematics to children in terms of the language, images, connections, resources and examples used. Teachers have been given strong recommendations through National Strategy guidance in the types of strategies they should use to teach mathematics and may not have had the opportunities to make active choices in how they teach mathematics.

Look at the grid of generic teaching skills (opposite) to assess your confidence rating in relation to subject areas. You may want to look at your lesson or weekly plans to guide you. For example, you may believe you have very good skills and are confident in using ICT such as a whiteboard and associated programs but is your opinion based across all subject areas or just some? Use the grid to support identifying mathematics-specific knowledge you would like to develop and particularly note your confidence score in relation to your teaching and learning style.

Engaging with this review of teaching skills should support you in identifying any areas of mathematical pedagogical knowledge you believe need addressing. For instance, you may feel confident differentiating work in English but feel uncertain how to either meet the learning needs of individuals in mathematics or know what makes an activity sufficiently challenging across the whole curriculum. Take the example of a lesson in which the outcome was the same for all children, e.g. to know the number bonds to one hundred. Differentiation for children who might find this difficult could include resources such as structural counting equipment or arrow cards (which show place value). However, if the outcome was to understand a method such as addition on a number line then differentiation may relate not to resources but to the choice of numbers, with the most challenging being using numbers that crossed the tens boundary, e.g. 57 + 28, and the least challenging being numbers that were both of less value, e.g. below 30, and did not cross the tens boundary, e.g. 17 + 11.

Learning for all children

Current Professional Standards for teachers (TDA, 2007) and the National Curriculum (DfEE, 1999) provide a framework for inclusive practice and clear entitlement for all learners. As such they present a vision that all children learn a broad range of knowledge, skills and understanding in mathematics. Children may be affected by social, emotional and language issues that

Generic teaching skills

Score on confidence rating 1–10 with 1 having minimum confidence and 10 being very confident.

	Foundation Stage		Key Stages 1 and 2											
	PSRN	CLL	Mathematics	English	Science	ICT	PE	History	Geography	RE	Art	Design and Technology	Modern Foreign Language	
Teaching style (Look at the overview of learning theories on p. 69 in Chapter 3 to guide you and make notes briefly under each heading)														
Planning • Lesson • Weekly • Longer term														
Organisational grouping														
Structuring activities														
Choosing resources including information technology														
Explaining concepts and subject specific terminology														
Questioning														
Differentiation														
Formatively assessing														
Target setting														
Knowing and planning for common misconceptions														

can potentially impair their opportunities for success. Additionally there are those children who are particularly gifted in mathematics and equally require additional intervention to provide suitably challenging experiences. However, there are also children whose are affected by specific problems with mathematics. Such problems broadly fall into three areas.

- Dyslexia – a learning disability that impairs fluency or comprehension in reading and spelling.

- Dyscalculia – a specific learning disability involving difficulty in learning or understanding mathematics.

- Children who have neurological, genetic or developmental problems.

Support should be available for class teachers in school through the 1996 Education Act and the Special Educational Needs Code of Practice 2001. Additionally schools can buy in specialist services. However, supporting all children in a class is potentially challenging for class teachers. They must develop knowledge to identify *and* support such children, not just in a generic way across the curriculum but specifically in mathematics. Further reading is given at the end of this chapter.

Curricular subject knowledge

This area of knowledge is the mathematical content to be taught and learnt by children. Depending on the type of school in which you teach, your level of ownership of the curriculum will vary. Currently, content is set out in the National Curriculum but in recent years the content has largely been driven by government guidance as found in such non-statutory documents as the National Numeracy Strategy (1999) and the Primary National Strategy (2006). The result has been that independence in teaching content has lessened. This is not necessarily detrimental as it can make for a more coherent experience for children. However, a curriculum that is well founded on research and which is open to debate by interested parties whether they be teachers, parents, employers or representatives from local and national government is likely to emerge more robust as it is based on shared beliefs. One of the challenges of increased school autonomy is ensuring sufficient cohesion of school-based curricula as children pass through their school lives and will require strong transition arrangements to be in place.

Two-way enhancement

Earlier in this chapter, two-way enhancement of the background mathematical skills and understanding with pedagogical and curricular knowledge identified was highlighted in relation to the work of Shulman (1986). Teaching programmes cover pedagogical and curricular knowledge but in the process have the power to support the development of a teacher's personal mathematical skills and understanding. Equally, school-based elements of programmes supplement such understanding and continue to do so once a teacher is in post. Below are examples of how mathematics knowledge skills and understanding has been developed by four teachers. The teachers were asked to consider the mathematics curriculum for the age range they were qualified to teach and any connections they could make. Additionally, they were asked to identify their confidence levels. Students A and B have just completed university teaching programmes and X and Y have been in post for three and four years respectively.

- Student A has completed a teaching programme for the 3–7 age range. Her experience has mainly been with the 4–6 age range.

- Student B has completed a training programme for the 5–11 age range and she has had experience across the full range.

- Student C has completed a training programme for the 5–11 age range taking the majority of her experience in Key Stage 2. She teaches in a two-form entry junior school and has taken Year 5 for two years and Year 3 for one year.

- Student D has completed a training programme for the 5–11 age range. She teaches in a two-form entry infant school.

Student examples clearly indicate that teachers significantly develop pedagogical and curricular subject knowledge through being in school whether as a student or qualified teacher.

Student A

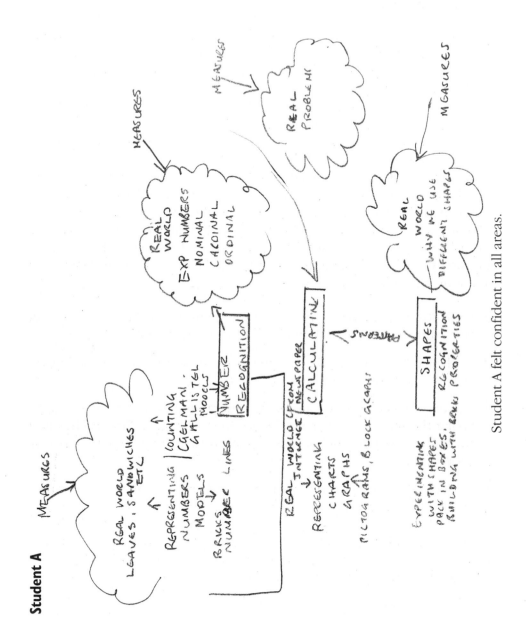

Student A felt confident in all areas.

Student B

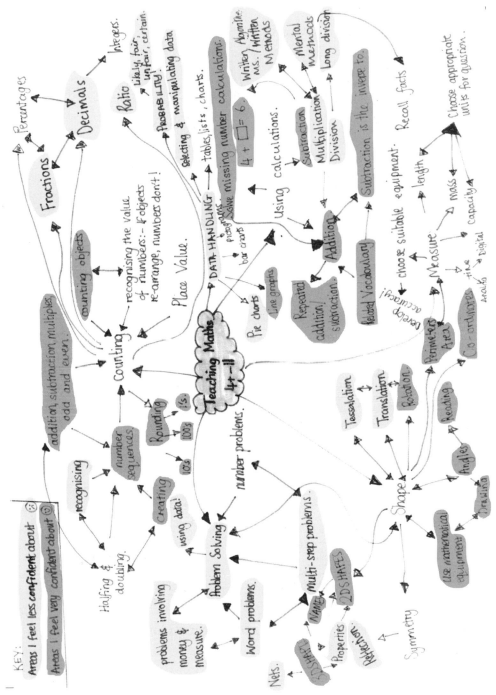

Student C

Counting
Calculating
Graphs
Algebra
Shape — area
perimeter
Sharing –
Grouping
Measures
concepts
from
real life
experience

Student C felt confident in all aspects of the curriculum.

Student D

Giving change — Role play.
↗ finding totals
Money
Coin recognition ↙

Word problems.

Comparing weights ↗

Measures → Capacity
Water ↘
Measuring length tray !
in non standard & standard units

Sorting Shape
e.g. number of sides,
faces, etc.

Number recognition
Reading ↘ Writing
number number

Pattern
(Shape)

Counting

Mathematical language

Sequencing

* 1:1 Correspondence, touch Counting
* Grouping to count a number of objects

Number Sentences
+, −, ×, ÷.

Handling Data
- tally charts
- pictogram
- bar graphs

Student D

Teaching Year 6

I would feel totally daunted and not at all confident in teaching year 6 because I feel I don't have adequate subject knowledge. I found maths very hard as a child & always had to have a practical approach towards it. I transfer this practical approach to numeracy into my teaching & feel it is easier to do so at foundation/key stage 1 level as there are always opportunities for role play, drama, real life experiences etc. I think numeracy can be taught much more creatively at KS1, as it can be linked in to a topic based curriculum. I enjoy teaching counting, using out door environment etc to do so.

Devise your own version of the mathematics curriculum you are training or qualified to teach. Similarly, identify connections and annotate the curriculum to identify your confidence level. You may want to do this activity with colleagues as part of whole school CPD or you may prefer to complete it individually to self-assess and identify your strengths and possible areas for development.

Summary

This chapter has considered the range of teacher knowledge that is required to teach mathematics under three broad headings – background, pedagogical, curricular – and their interfaces. It has highlighted the scope of the subject knowledge that teachers require to teach effectively.

Conclusion

The Council for the Accreditation of Teacher Education (CATE) engaged in imposing a model of curriculum design for undergraduate programmes that required a focus on subject specialism for two out of the three or four years of the degree (Select Committee, Education and Science, 1986). This change *potentially* marginalised the other areas of the curriculum such as child development which is of particular importance for those on primary education programmes (Young, 1985). Over the years issues have changed but the active intervention of the government has not. The current curriculum may look less prescriptive than its predecessors, but if ITE inspection by Ofsted continues in its current form, it means that the government still has a significant role in dictating the content of initial teaching programmes compared to other non-vocational undergraduate programmes. This causes the dilemma raised in the introduction – are teachers being educated or trained to teach? If teachers are to be given more autonomy over how to teach they will need to understand a wide range of teaching and learning approaches in order to justify a chosen approach or approaches. This is particularly a challenge in routes into teaching that are school-based where there is more likelihood of learning about a narrow range of teaching approaches.

The significance of having a narrow version of programmes is that it can disempower teachers in that they may not understand sufficiently what they are doing. Skemp's view of instrumental understanding – knowing what to do by the application of rules – could be related to elements of some current teacher training programmes. To develop practice you need to know what to do, not by the application of the rules given by others but by developing your own ideas with other experienced professionals in education on how to move forward. This activity demands knowing the purpose of what you are doing and considering the beliefs that support this purpose – in other words developing a philosophical stance.

Of course the individual teacher rarely has the option to put their own views into practice but it will affect their response to government initiatives, regional guidance, staff-room discussion and how they would plan and teach a mathematics curriculum given more autonomy. Additionally, with moves towards different types of school being a reality such as teaching in an academy or free school, the views of individual teachers may have more direct influence on the curriculum that emerges.

Review questions

Your response to this chapter will depend on the stage you are at in your teaching programme or career. You may believe you need to first explore a philosophical approach to teaching as well as consider a range theories on learning before you can engage in curricular issues. Alternatively, you may consider that you need to immerse yourself in the classroom before you can begin to understand how children learn, what they should learn and why they should learn it. The further reading below provides a range of literature to support you in each area.

References

Askew, M., Brown, M., Rhodes, V., Wiliam, D. and Johnson, D. (1997) *Effective Teachers of Numeracy: Report of a Study Carried Out for the Teacher Training Agency.* London: King's College, University of London.

Bandura, A. (1977) *Social Learning Theory.* New York: General Learning Press.

Berensen, S., Van der Valk, T., Oldham, E., Runesson, U., Moreira, C. and Brockman, H. (1997) 'An international study to investigate prospective teachers' content knowledge of the area concept', *European Journal of Teacher Education*, 20 (2): 137–50.

DCSF (2010) *The Mathematics Specialist Teacher Programme: Information and guidance to Participating Local Authorities.* London: DCSF.

DES (1967) *Children and Their Primary Schools* (Plowden Report). London: HMSO.

DfE (2010) *The Importance of Teaching: The Schools White Paper.* London: DCSF. Available online at: http://www.education.gov.uk (accessed 10 July 2011).

DfEE (1999) *The National Curriculum.* London: HMSO.

Honey, P. and Mumford, A. (1992) *The Manual of Learning Styles*, 3rd edn. Maidenhead: Peter Honey.

Kolb, D. A. (1984) *Experiential Learning Experience as a Source of Learning and Development.* Englewood Cliffs, NJ: Prentice Hall.

Laming, W. (2003) *Report of an Inquiry.* London: HMSO.

Maslow, A. (1954) *Motivation and Personality.* New York: Harper & Row.

Ofsted (2008) *Mathematics: Understanding the Score.* London: Ofsted.

Rowland, T., Turner, F., Thwaites, A. and Huckstep, P. (2009) *Developing Primary Mathematics Teaching: Reflecting on Practice with the Knowledge Quartet.* London: Sage.

Select Committee, Education Science and Arts (1986) *From UPTEC to NaPTEC: From Exasperation to Enhancement.* Available online at: http://www.naptec. org.uk/docs/story.pdf (accessed February 2012).

Shulman, L. S. (1986) 'Those who understand, knowledge growth in teaching', *Educational Researcher*, 15 (2): 4–14.

TDA (2007) *Professional Standards for Teachers.* London: TDA.

Williams, Sir P. (2008) *Independent Review of Mathematics Teaching in Early Years Settings and Primary Schools.* London: DCSF.

Young, R. (1985) 'Child development under threat: its place in initial teacher education for the years of primary schooling', *Journal of Further and Higher Education*, 9 (3).

Websites

BBC Bitesize: http://www.bbc.co.uk/schools/bitesize/
                  http://www.bbc.co.uk/ks2bitesize/
                  http://www.bbc.co.uk/schools/ks3bitesize/
                  http://www.bbc.co.uk/gcsebitesize
                  http://www.bbc.co.uk/schools/bitesizeprimary
                  (accessed 25 November 2011)

Further reading

Apple, M. W. and Beane, J. A. (eds) (1999) *Democratic Schools: Lessons from the Chalk Face.* Buckingham: Open University Press. See the section called 'A Democratic Curriculum' on pp. 14–21 identifying reasons why some sections of the community appear able to gain from education while others appear not to.

Barnes, J. (2011) *Cross-Curricular Learning 3–14*, 2nd edn. London: Sage.

Challen, A., Machin, S. and McNally, S. (2008) *Schools in England: Structures, Teachers and Evaluation*, FGA Working Paper No. 1. London: London School of Economics.

Dewey, J. (1916) *Democracy and Education*. Toronto: Macmillan, pp. 231–49.

Ernest, P. (2009) *What Is First Philosophy in Mathematics Education?* Keynote speech, Annual Conference of International Group for the Psychology of Mathematics Education (PME 33), Thessaloniki, Greece, July.

Ernest, P. (1991) *The Philosophy of Mathematics Education*. Abingdon: RoutledgeFalmer.

Gewirtz, S., Ball, S. J. and Bowe, R. (eds) (1995) *Markets: Choice and Equity in Education*. Buckingham: Open University Press.

Kelly, A. V. (2009) *The Curriculum: Theory and Practice*, 6th edn. London: Sage. See the chapter entitled 'The Curriculum and the Study of the Curriculum', pp. 5–31.

Lewis, G., Gewirtz, S. and Clarke, J. (eds) (2000) *Rethinking Social Policy*. Milton Keynes: Open University in association with Sage.

Quicke, J. (1999) *A Curriculum for Life*. Buckingham: Open University Press.

Ross, A. (2000) *Curriculum: Construction and Critique*. London: Falmer.

Teaching and Learning Research Programme (TLRP) (2011) *Neuroscience and Education: Issues and Opportunities*. Available online at: http://www.tlrp. org/pub/documents/Neuroscience%20Commentary%20FINAL.pdf (accessed 2 December 2011).

Tubbs, N. and Grimes, J. (2001) 'What is education studies?', *Educational Studies*, 27 (1): 3–15.

Dyscalculia

Attwood, T. (2002) *Dyscalculia in Schools: What Is It and What Can We Do?* Corby: First and Best in Education.

Attwood, T. (2002) *Methods of Teaching Maths to Children with Dyscalculia*. Corby: First and Best in Education.

Attwood, T. (2002) *Tests for Dyscalculia*. Corby: First and Best in Education.

Butterworth, B. (1999) *The Mathematical Brain*. London: Macmillan.

Butterworth, B. (2002) 'Dyscalculia', *Interplay*, Summer, pp. 44–7.

DfES (2001) *Guidance to Support Pupils with Dyslexia and Dyscalculia*, Circular 0512/2001. London: DfES.

Kay, J. and Yeo, D. (2003) *Dyslexia and Maths*. London: David Fulton.

QCA (2001) *Planning, Teaching and Assessing the Curriculum for Pupils with Learning Difficulties: Mathematics*. London: QCA.

Staves, L. (2001) *Mathematics for Children with Severe and Profound Learning Difficulties*. London: David Fulton.

CHAPTER 5

TEACHING APPROACHES

Aims

By the end of this chapter you should be able to:

- understand the mathematical, societal and local influences on learning and teaching;
- promote positive experiences in making sense of mathematics for all children;
- identify the importance of ongoing professional development;
- provide examples of approaches to teaching primary mathematics.

Introduction

Chapters 1 and 2 considered mathematics and how its nature can bring about both negative and positive perceptions of it as a subject. Chapters 3 and 4 have considered the primary curriculum and the knowledge this requires of teachers. This chapter will draw on the preceding chapters and consider the factors that influence the creation of positive learning experiences for children and suggest some teaching approaches to mathematics to engender a positive attitude.

National agenda influences

As teaching approaches in recent years have been strongly affected by government curriculum documentation (DfEE, 1999: DfES, 2006), they have the potential to limit the approaches teachers use. As discussed in Chapter 2, the Foundation Stage curriculum is based upon constructivist principles and the role of the adult in facilitating rather than directing *learning* whereas in Key Stages 1 and 2 approaches have been characterised by direct *teaching* through demonstrating, questioning and explaining to children in a structured three-part lesson. There have been adjustments advocated in guidance documents such as *Excellence and Enjoyment* (DfES, 2003) which called for a more creative learning experience in supporting children's development of literacy and numeracy skills. It included assessment strategies that took account of the child's role in the learning process with emphasis on assessment *for* learning rather than *of* learning.

1.14 We want schools to feel freer to take control, and to use that freedom to:

Take a fresh look at their curriculum, their timetable and the organisation of the school day and week, and think actively about how they would like to develop and enrich the experience they offer their children. (DfES, 2003)

However, these changes had the potential to cause uncertainty in schools. While being encouraged to take ownership of the curriculum with the guidance of best practice identified by Ofsted, schools still had to focus on raising standards in Literacy and Numeracy using an interactive, structured lesson approach. According to Brehony (2005), Froebel Professor of Early Childhood Studies at Roehampton University, freedom appears to be offered but only when a structure is established that severely restricts it.

Empowering teachers to be able to take more ownership of the curriculum and how it is taught are key foci of the new government's education policy (DfE, 2011). However, in order to be successful, all teachers have to develop the confidence to make changes. Such confidence comes from an understanding of what and how children should learn rather than just being able to implement an imposed pedagogy.

There has been significant research into learning over many years but, with a few exceptions such as the work on Effective Teachers of Mathematics (Askew et al., 1997) and Black and Wiliam (1998) on Assessment for Learning, it has not been clearly related to government initiatives. Although there were many positive features of the NNS in terms of the professional development it provided in mathematics, it failed, as have subsequent initiatives, to acknowledge, in any detail, the theoretical underpinning to the changes being introduced. This can have the effect that many teachers have no clear rationale for their teaching of mathematics using such government guidelines.

Government legislation in non-statutory provision for children from 0 to 5 (DCFS, 2008) is underpinned by a markedly different philosophy to statutory education in terms of learning and development. The Consultation on a Revised Early Years Foundation Stage (EYFS) (2011) following the Tickell Review (2011) has largely retained the play-based philosophy of the current EYFS. However, the Review does emphasise 'school readiness' and a summative assessment is required of children between 26 and 36 months. The challenge will be retaining Early Years education that has value in its own right, that is developmentally appropriate and that avoids 'labelling' children from an early age, in a climate of changing school provision. Academies and free schools have increased the range of statutory school provision. It is to be expected that such schools will have varying expectations of children entering the statutory phase of education in terms of the philosophy of the curriculum as well as the teaching and learning that the school adopts. Teachers working in Early Years settings will need to be able to articulate their philosophy of teaching and learning and support it with research-based evidence.

The introduction of the NNS was an endeavour to limit variables by prescribing a pedagogical approach to teaching. Following the introduction of the NNS in 1998 there was a target that 75 per cent of Year 6 children would achieve Level 4 as a minimum by May 2002. However, this was not achieved. Any national drive is flawed in terms of the individual, although it can be beneficial for the majority of the members within a society in terms of results (Williams, 2003). In many ways it was naive to assume that any national strategy will meet the needs of all as it does not take into account the inevitable variables related to the individual and the context. Teaching approaches that are firmly based upon knowledge of mathematics, research and assessment of children's needs are more likely to provide positive experiences and support children progress in mathematics. Research used on ITE programmes support students engaging in evidence-informed practice and some programmes have opportunities for students to engage in primary research. For practising teachers, use of research to identify best practice can be a very effective tool, significantly improving mathematics teaching (Askew et al., 1997; Jackson, 2008; Swann and Swain, 2010). A challenge can be accessing information from independent sources of evidence that are not influenced by politically driven agenda. There are sources such as 'The Best Evidence Encyclopaedia UK' (BEE UK) which is a free website maintained by the Institute for Effective Education (IEE). Based at the University of York, the IEE develops, evaluates and disseminates effective education programmes and promotes evidence-based policies. It is based on a version in the United States for Data-Driven Reform in Education. What is so useful is that it considers information from both the UK and an international perspective in order to develop best practice. The information is summarised but the full review is available. Another resource is the Nuffield Foundation (http://www.nuffieldfoundation.org) which provides a wealth of information. It is based on the belief in the importance of independent research evidence and its power to bring about change. It aims to improve social well-being by funding research and innovation in education and social policy.

The influence of generic teaching and learning theories and ideas on mathematics

One of the challenges for primary teachers as generalists is relating teaching approaches to specific subjects. Interactive, whole-class teaching that has characterised many primary schools in Key Stages 1 and 2 was intended for English and mathematics but, in some cases, the approaches used have permeated the whole primary curriculum. However, just as the nature of mathematics is different to that of English, so it is to other subjects. The application of generic theories should be considered in terms of how they take account of *mathematical* research and how theory supports the misunderstandings that can arise from mathematical representation and hierarchy.

Mathematical influences

Representation and theoretical perspectives

Chapter 2 explored how mathematics is characterised by its language, structure, notation, hierarchy and associated laws and rules. Understanding of one form of representation is supported by another. Representation will be discussed in detail in Chapter 7 but when considering teaching approaches it is important to remember that representation is central to the learning and use of mathematics. It demonstrates both the recording of the *result* of mathematical activity and the *process* of mathematical activity.

Understanding of mathematical relationships is expanded by using different forms of representations to organise, record and communicate ideas as well as to interpret and solve problems. Teachers should consider what representations will support learning. For example, if working on the concept of place value the following could be used.

- structural base-10 blocks;
- computer versions of base-10 blocks;
- a column diagram to identify places, i.e. tens and units/ones;
- a hundred square to show the relationship between numbers.

Not all representations will work for all children but teachers may offer representations and encourage children to devise their own representations. In this way representations support children in clarifying ideas as well as giving teachers an insight into their understanding, so supporting assessment and next steps in learning.

Bruner (1966), the social constructivist, saw representation in three stages. He suggested three modes of representation: enactive (direct experience), iconic (recording experience in images) and symbolic (language and mathematical notation).

Rather than neatly delineated stages he believed these modes of representation were integrated and only loosely sequential. Symbolic representation is the most adaptable form of representation as enactive and iconic representations have a fixed relationship to that which they represent. However, symbols can be manipulated and classified without the limitations of the action or image.

Bruner believed that all new ideas should be introduced in these three stages regardless of the age of the learner. Unlike Piaget who believed children went through sequential stages, he believed that new ideas can be understood, however young the learner, as long as the teaching is well structured. Bruner saw the curriculum as a spiral with at each successive level the learning developing at greater depth. The teacher's role was to foster this process by focusing attention and supporting articulation of ideas.

However, such views have been challenged. For example, Gates cites research of Kath Hart and colleagues carried out for the Economic and Social Research Council (ESRC) (Gates, 2001: 141) who concluded that often children failed to see the connection between concrete experience and the more formal symbolic stage. These findings may relate to the difference between *recording results* and *representing the process of doing* mathematics. When children are able to represent their mental methods on paper they can build on what they already know and understand. Recording what has already been found out through manipulating objects or pictures is different and may not be easy to translate into symbols. Carruthers and Worthington (2011 online) have carried out extensive work concerning young children's representations between 0 and 8 years. They used the term graphics to describe the range of children's own mathematical marks and representations. They believe that the graphics children use, including drawings, writing and maps, demonstrate children's mathematical thinking so enabling them to communicate mathematics and solve problems. The implications are that teachers should consider the interim stages between moving from concrete models taken from direct experience to their symbolic representation by enabling children to have the opportunity to devise their own representations and so develop their understanding.

Memory

Making ever increasing connections between mathematical ideas requires children to retain the ideas. Memory is fundamental to all learning as it allows a record of the information from a learning experience to be stored and retrieved. It is of particular importance in coming to understand mathematics due to its hierarchical nature. Making connections between previously learnt knowledge and transferring such knowledge to other situations is essential to understanding mathematics.

Mentally held conceptual frameworks or schemas support the organisation of one form of long-term memory, declarative memory. Declarative memory helps make sense of learning as the schema evokes memory to support recall of facts and events. When we learn something new that relates to previous learning, it constructs meaning and this is key to understanding and remembering information. Brain imaging has shown that an area of the left hemisphere is vital in the construction of meaning (TLRP, 2011 online). The other form of long-term memory, procedural memory, relates to acquired skills that, once mastered, come to be carried out almost automatically, e.g. times tables.

Additionally, in order to solve a calculation, it is important to 'hold' information for a short period of time. In the example 37 subtract 9, 27 has to be 'held' and then increased by 1: $(37 - 9 = (37 - 10) + 1$. Some teaching strategies actively foster short term or working memory by supplementing verbal information with visual cues supplied either by the teacher or by encouraging children to make their own jotting or representation. Observation of brain activity has identified that external jottings can be particularly helpful to learners as they can help offload demands on working memory (TLRP, 2011 online).

Brain-imaging evidence collected by Dehaene and his team (1999) has shown that approximate calculations take place in the brain's large-scale network and involve visual, spatial and analogical mental transformations. Exact calculations take place in an area usually reserved for verbal tasks. This part of the brain is activated when subjects have to remember verbal material although it is not a primary language area of the brain. Spelke and Tsivkin (2001) have found also that a rudimentary ability to approximate develops very early in humans with very young infants able to distinguish an array containing many objects from one containing fewer objects. Such research has implications for how number is represented to children and the opportunities children have for comparing sets of objects. A concise and clear overview of neuroscience and education is available from the Teaching and Learning Research Programme (TLRP) website (details at the end of the chapter).

Influence of perceptions of mathematics

As can be seen from Chapter 1, mathematics evokes strong reactions in people. Williams (2008) advocated the CPD programme for teachers (now known as MaST) with one goal being that such teachers would be mathematics champions 'to generate enthusiasm for learning the subject among children, parents and staff' (Williams, 2008: para. 76). Teachers should acknowledge the part played by children's families in forming attitudes as well as aiming to ensure that children are motivated to engage in mathematical activity. Additionally, teachers must acknowledge that their beliefs will be reflected in how they teach.

Local influences – teachers, children and their families

Teachers have personal approaches to teaching as they are individuals with different experiences, including their individual favoured ways of learning. Such approaches to teaching are a factor that has the power to engage all children in their learning but can be detrimental if they do not sufficiently engage the majority of children in the learning process. Although government guidance documents have sought to standardise approaches to teaching in order to develop best practice, research in 2003, five years after the NNS had been in place, suggests that the practice of teachers related to what they *believed* they should do rather than the guidance in the NNS. In relation to this finding, skilled teachers working in supportive schools still taught creatively despite increased guidance (Jeffrey and Woods, 2003; Ofsted, 2003). What did seem to evoke change was professional development. Strategies to improve the teaching of mathematics such as those given via web-based sources like the National Audit Office and Ofsted have value but have limitations. According to Alexander (2004), it is no good just using the 'what works' principle. Teachers need to be reflective and be willing to try out new ideas. The aim of the MaST programme is to recruit such teachers. Unfortunately, the new standards for teaching (DfE, 2011), while still retaining 'professional development' as part of Standard 8, point 4, make no reference to professional development in terms of reflection and innovation as outlined in the previous standards. It is to be hoped that professional development will view reflection and innovation as implicit and acknowledge their importance for practising teachers and students on ITE programmes.

Positive experiences engender positive attitudes and generally lead to a desire to repeat the experience. As adults, if we encounter negative experiences, we usually have the choice to either take avoidance strategies or actively engage in dealing with the cause of negative emotions. Children rarely have such choice. If children feel confused or discouraged by their mathematical experiences they may exhibit negative behaviour overtly or become withdrawn or disengaged from the activity and motivation can diminish. Teachers therefore must aim to be sensitive to children's responses and match the level of expectation to the individual's learning needs.

Consideration of your own reactions to negative experiences should help you identify children's reactions to events and how their responses can be turned into more positive experiences.

Think of a negative experience with which you have been involved recently, e.g. failing a driving test, being let down by someone, receiving a letter with potentially bad news such as the result of an interview. How did you react? Did you take avoidance strategies such as not opening the letter or not allowing yourself to think about the consequences? Alternatively, did you acknowledge what had happened and start to find a way of taking action? Do you think you react differently or similarly depending on the context? Record your thoughts in your learning journal.

Whatever approaches are taken to teaching mathematics one goal remains the same – making learning accessible. Teachers need to be aware of the factors that motivate or demotivate children in their engagement in and alienation from mathematics. In recent years motivation has been linked to assessment for learning (AfL) strategies yet motivation is more than that relation to assessment. Knowing what motivates children to learn is important in understanding the teaching and learning process.

Consider a mathematics lesson you have taught. What motivated the children, e.g. the task, the resources, the outcome, the way they worked together, how it related to other classroom activities? Were the children extrinsically or intrinsically motivated and did the type of motivation vary between class members?

Engagement can come from intrinsically motivating factors such as:

- interest
- enjoyment
- sense of purpose
- sufficient challenge

or from extrinsically motivating factors such as:

- rewards
- praise
- threat of disapproval or punishment.

Alienation can arise from:

- boredom
- lack of understanding
- confusion
- emotional factors.

If you are intrinsically motivated to learn you will feel more in control of the process in terms of the effort you make and understanding you develop. However, extrinsic motivation also has its place in engaging children. As adults we may give ourselves extrinsic rewards such as food or drink for completing a task we would rather not do or to initiate involvement in a task that, once started, is intrinsically motivating, e.g. having a cup of coffee before working in the garden. Extrinsic motivation in school can be generated through praise or rewards like stickers or merit points. Extrinsic motivation such as the threat of disapproval or punishment, may be effective in task engagement but is unlikely to enhance the learning experience of mathematics, or indeed of any subject.

Factors relating to intrinsic or extrinsic motivation are not fixed driving forces. What may interest or incentivise a child one day may not the next. Maintaining motivation is a key element of effective teaching and depends on knowledge of the child as well as the subject content. Equally, no one approach can do this for all children so teachers must tailor their approaches to meeting the needs of the majority of children while providing differing experiences for others by:

- explaining a particular idea in an alternative way;
- adjusting the language used to the level of development and mathematical understanding;

- offering a different representation;
- questioning and further discussion; or
- devising a similar but alternative task.

Such devices are commonly called differentiation. Differentiated teaching is not an approach but is based on the ideas of how children learn discussed in Chapters 3 and 4. The child is not seen as a receiver of teacher input from which output is expected; rather the child is seen as an active participant in the learning process, engaging with teacher input by finding ways to understand what the teacher offers whether it be facts or experiences.

Influence of meeting both national and local agendas

Government education policy is being influenced by international data. For example, the Schools White Paper on policy (DfE, 2010) stated that by 'drawing heavily on evidence from the world's best education systems' there was to be a radical reform. Improvement was to be led by schools rather than by centralised government policies yet rigorous assessment was to be retained. Although the wish to have school-led improvement is not necessarily at odds with rigorous assessment, the challenge to schools and government will be in enabling schools to have the confidence to make radical reforms if they are apprehensive of a centralised Ofsted inspection regime. Equally, decontextualising practice from one country to another and from a widening range of local authority, academy and free schools has the potential to limit pedagogical approaches to what has been tried and met with inspection approval. Supporting teachers in gaining confidence from a strong subject knowledge base would seem of particular importance if the government strategy is to be successful in changing both the culture surrounding mathematics and children taking the first steps towards becoming successful mathematicians.

Influences – key points

- Teachers must develop the confidence to initiate change through research-based evidence in order to provide positive learning experiences for children *and* justify approaches taken in relation to national requirements and guidance.
- Teachers must have subject-specific confidence to address the specific learning issues that mathematics can present to children.

• Teachers must work at a local level to promote a positive mathematics culture both within and outside the classroom.

Teaching approaches

Here are some ideas for approaches to teaching mathematics. They are not intended to be seen as *ways* of teaching mathematics but as types of strategy that could be included in any lesson.

You may find it useful to consider the following ideas by relating them to the diagram opposite which indicates the broad spectrum of the teacher's role and the curriculum. Additionally, consider if each quadrant indicates a particular philosophy of education. For example, when statutory education was introduced in 1870 the purpose was to have workers with sufficient knowledge to work in the factories. As such, it had a set curriculum that was teacher-led and aimed to support society in terms of maintaining the class system. This could be identified on the paradigm at the extreme point of the top left-hand quadrant.

Real-life

Chapter 1 identified the disconnection that people found between real-life and 'school' mathematics. Making these connections can support children's motivation by seeing the relevance of what they are doing. Consolidation activities support memory. Boaler (2009) is a strong advocate of 'real' mathematics and concerned that much mathematics teaching is based upon problems that do not happen in real life. She believes mathematics retains its mystique if problems are contextualised in unrealistic situations which leads to children ignoring the context and working with just the numbers. This, in turn, can lead to nonsensical answers (Boaler, 2009: 45–7).

Taking mathematics outside the classroom

Children encounter real mathematics all the time outside the classroom. Literally taking mathematics outside can help ensure mathematics is

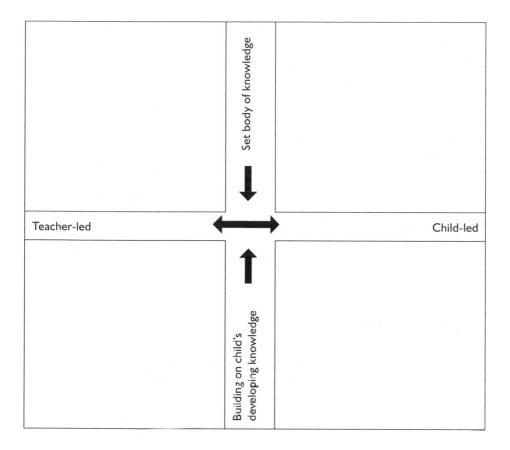

real. However, even though mathematics in the environment is evident, it needs to be focused upon if children are going to gain mathematically rather than just improve their observational skills. Many organisations in historic and natural sites put on 'Mathematics Trails' to support learning but they can easily be carried out around a local environment. The focus should provide opportunities for children to explore and develop strategies for solving a variety of problems. The change of environment can help increase motivation as the learning takes place in a different setting and can enhance memory and perhaps encourage children to be more willing to offer suggestions. It is important to give purpose to activities rather than move activities outside that could be carried out just as well in a classroom. For example, the outcome of a local trail could be planning a route to a local church, green space or other local place of interest for another year group. The mathematical focus would be related problem-solving, communicating and measurement.

Cross-curricular approaches – relating mathematics to the whole curriculum

Leading on from teaching mathematics outside the classroom is viewing mathematics within the whole curriculum. Cross-curricular approaches can be, but are not necessarily based-around child-centred discovery approaches to learning: it depends on the role taken by the teacher in managing the learning. For example, in the topic 'Water' mathematical components could relate to measurement in terms of volume, time and associated calculation but the learning could span every curriculum area. Again children can become well motivated as they can relate mathematics learning to other learning they are encountering so giving it purpose. Thematic approaches that try to relate the whole mathematics curriculum to other subjects can present problems in terms of children progressing in a structured way. Chapter 2 identified a number of ways that mathematics can be incorporated into the curriculum.

Games and puzzles

Not all mathematics is context-based. Mathematics has intrinsic value and engagement in mathematics in games and puzzles can lead on to developing skills that can apply to context-based problems. Games tend to involve two or more players, have a competitive element to them with winners and losers, and involve either chance or strategy. Puzzles can be participated in collaboratively or individually. They have a wealth of benefits in terms of motivation, encouraging collaboration and providing the opportunity to apply skills in meaningful situations. As such, they support differentiation by enabling participation without the constraints of attainment and language barriers. Usually, games contain some form of symbolic representation which allows children to discover and explain relationships. Games and puzzles also allow children to practise skills and support their memory. They can be either teacher- or child-devised and adjusted by resource in terms of numbers used or by rules.

One example is a 'snap' game using domino cards to identify equivalence. For example, versions could be made to relate to various aspects of mathematics:

- equivalent multiplication and division facts, e.g. $3 \times 4 = 2 \times 6$, $\frac{2}{3} = \frac{4}{16}$;
- properties of 2D or 3D shapes, e.g. different types of four-sided shapes, all of which could be classed as quadrilaterals.

Such snap games could be developed further. For example, a player places a card and has to give the connection to the previous card, e.g.

- 4 connects with 8 as they are multiples of 4;
- 7 connects to 2 by adding 5.

The NRICH website has a wealth of ideas to support teachers in finding games and puzzles.

Homework and consolidation activities

The use of games and puzzles can foster home–school links. Homework ideas like a game bag to take home to play with family members encourages family participation and can increase motivation. Other forms of homework can be a way of relating to real life as well as increasing children's understanding. Homework provides opportunities to practise and apply new learning to a real context as well as sharing school experiences. It should not be approached as an afterthought to the school day, but as a focused strategy for increasing understanding. Of course, there are always issues as there are limitations based upon how children are supported at home. These can be kept to a minimum by making sure that homework is shared by the teacher with parents by means of a display outside the classroom, in a newsletter on a school website or by e-mail and by ensuring that, if necessary, the amount of parental intervention required is minimised.

Analogy and classification

Analogy is very much part of the teacher's resource toolkit. In general terms it refers to the process of transferring a principle from one context to another. Analogy has two key purposes. Firstly, it relates to a child's prior learning and helps take the mystique out of a new process by comparing it with a familiar situation. Secondly, it supports children in making connections between ideas within and across subject areas. Analogy is strongly related to classification which requires learning to distinguish differences and similarities in order to identify features of a set of numbers, group of shapes or set of data. For example, 'as a banana is part of a set of fruit so 2 is part of the set of even numbers'. This strategy could lead children to thinking about what other sets 2 could belong to. The original analogy could support this development by trying to get children to think of what other sets a banana could belong to, e.g. set of yellow food. This type of approach to teaching fosters the identification of relationships and connections.

Analogies relate classroom mathematics to real life so giving purpose to what is being taught and learnt, and they actively engage children in making connections to experiences they understand and can then apply not only to mathematics being taught within the classroom but also to previous mathematical learning. For example, if the topic is finding half of a quantity, reference could be made to everyday experiences such as dividing fish fingers or playing cards between two children. However, relationships can also be made due to the fact that finding a half is the same as dividing by two. In this way the relationship between areas of mathematics is made explicit. However, if teachers are to make use of analogic relationships, they need to be secure in their subject knowledge. They have to understand overarching mathematical concepts such as classification and be able to apply them to everyday situations.

Challenging thinking – cognitive conflict and concept cartoons

Children can be aware that they do not understand but unsure of *why* they do not understand. It would seem that at the point of confusion, what the child expected to happen did not happen. This can manifest itself in a child not knowing what to do when given a task or making a mistake in the task. Mistakes can be an ideal teaching and learning opportunity just as they are in everyday life. If you consider the cognitive learning theories discussed briefly in Chapter 4, you will see that this confusion relates to accommodation and assimilation. Actively engaging children with statements or examples that do not initially seem to make sense is sometimes called 'cognitive conflict'. Such examples can be in the form of statements, e.g., 'multiplying can make a quantity smaller' or 'is it true that as the area of a shape gets bigger the perimeter gets bigger?' Also, children can be presented with worked examples such as a calculation that is incorrect and asked why it is incorrect. Cognitive conflict can arise unknowingly by teachers if their choice of examples has not been fully considered.

The use of concept cartoons is another way of challenging thinking. They offer scenarios that can generate cognitive conflict. For example, cartoon characters can give different solutions to problems and the child is asked for their opinion. They encourage active engagement by children and can enable collaborative learning to take place. Additionally they help teachers assess children's understanding. Keogh et al. (2008) are authors of the book *Concept Cartoons in Mathematics Education* which includes interactive material to adjust the level of demand as well as providing further guidance online.

Summary

The purpose of this chapter was not to advocate any one set of teaching approaches or learning theories to support them but rather to give a rationale for considering teaching approaches in terms of how they affect the experience of learning mathematics. Teachers must consider their choices based upon how such experience is influenced by the children and their families in their class, the school and community and statutory requirements.

Conclusion

Considering a variety of teaching approaches is not new to teaching. However, centralised policies have had the tendency to limit the approaches that teachers believe they can use which could be summarised as those associated with interactive teaching such as teacher questioning and those encouraging the active participation of learners. These approaches are not new but other approaches identified also have value in developing children's understanding. Awareness of a wide range of teaching approaches can only be a valuable asset to the teacher in supporting the learning process.

Review questions

1. Is it time to review aspects of your pedagogical, curricular or background knowledge?
2. What references in the Further reading at the end of this chapter would it be useful to follow up?
3. Record your ideas in your learning journal.

References

Askew, M., Brown, M., Rhodes, V. and Wiliam, D. (1997) *Effective Teachers of Numeracy: Report*. London: TTA.

Black, P. and Wiliam, D. (1998) 'Assessment and classroom learning', *Assessment in Education*, 5 (1): 7–74.

Brehony, K. (2005) 'Primary schooling under New Labour: the irresolvable contradiction of excellence and enjoyment', *Oxford Review of Education*, 312 (1): 29–46.

Boaler, J. (2009) *The Elephant in the Classroom. Helping Children Learn and Love Maths.* London: Souvenir Press.

Bruner, J. (1966) *Towards a Theory of Instruction.* Cambridge, MA: Harvard University Press.

Carruthers, E. and Worthington, M. (2011) *Children's Mathematics.* Available online at: http://www.childrens-mathematics.net (accessed 2 November 2011).

DCSF (2008) *Practice Guidance for the Early Years Foundation Stage.* Nottingham: DCSF.

Dehaene, S., Spelke, E., Pinel, P., Stanescu, R. and Tsivkin, S. (1999) 'Sources of mathematical thinking: behavioral and brain-imaging evidence', *Science*, 284: 970–4.

DfE (2010) *The Importance of Teaching: The Schools White Paper.* London: DfE. Available online at: http://www.education.gov.uk/publications/standard/ publicationDetail/Page1/CM%207980#downloadableparts (accessed 14 March 2012).

DfE (2011) *Michael Gove Speaks to the Royal Society on Maths and Science* (online) London: DfE. Available online at: http://www.education.gov.uk/inthenews/ speeches/a00191729/michael-gove-speaks-to-the-royal-society-on-maths-and-science (accessed 1 March 2012).

DfEE (1999) *The National Numeracy Strategy: Framework for Teaching Mathematics.* London: DfEE.

DfES (2003) *Excellence and Enjoyment.* London: DfES.

DfES (2006) *Primary National Strategy: Primary Framework for Literacy and Mathematics.* London: DfES.

Gates, P. (ed.) (2001) *Issues in Mathematics Teaching.* London: Routledge.

Jackson, E. (2008) 'Mathematics anxiety in student teachers', *Practitioner Research in Higher Education*, 2 (1): 36–42.

Jeffrey, B. and Woods, P. (2003) *The Creative School: A Framework for Success, Quality and Effectiveness.* Abingdon: RoutledgeFalmer.

Keogh, B., Dabell, J. and Naylor, S. (2008) *Concept Cartoons in Mathematics Education.* Sandbach: Millgate House.

NNS (1999) *Mathematical Vocabulary.* London: DfEE.

Ofsted (2003) *Expecting the Unexpected: Developing Creativity in Primary and Secondary Schools*, HMI 1612. Available online at http://www.ofsted.gov.uk.

Spelke, E. S. and Tsivkin, S. (2001) 'Initial knowledge and conceptual change: space and number', in M. Bowerman and S. Levinson (eds), *Language Acquisition and Conceptual Development.* Cambridge: Cambridge University Press.

Swan, M. and Swain, J. (2010) 'The impact of a professional development programme on the practices and beliefs of numeracy teachers', *Journal of Further and Higher Education*, 34 (2): 165–77.

Teaching and Learning Research Programme (TLRP) (2011) *Neuroscience and Education: Issues and Opportunities.* Available online at: http://www.tlrp. org/pub/documents/Neuroscience%20Commentary%20FINAL.pdf (accessed 2 November 2011).

Tickell, C. (2010) *The Tickell Review of the Early Years Foundation Stage.* London: HM Government.

Williams, J. (ed.) (2003) *Proceedings of the British Society for Research into Learning Mathematics*, 23 (2). Available online at: http://www.bsrlm.org.uk/IPs/ip23-3/BSRLM-IP-23-3-4.pdf (accessed 1 March 2012).

Williams, Sir P. (2008) *Independent Review of Mathematics Teaching in Early Years Setting and Primary Schools*. London: DCFS. Available online at: https://www.education.gov.uk/publications/eOrderingDownload/Williams%20Mathematics.pdf (accessed 1 March 2012).

Websites

Nuffield Foundation: http://www.nuffieldfoundation.org.
Teaching and Learning Research Programme (TLRP): http://www.tlrp.org/.

Further reading

Askew, M. and Brown, M. (2001) *Teaching and Learning Primary Numeracy: Policy, Practice and Effectiveness*. Southwell: BERA.

Barnes, J. (2011) *Cross-Curricular Learning 3–14*, 2nd edn. London: Sage.

Butterworth, B. (1999) *The Mathematical Brain*. London: Macmillan.

Carruthers, E. and Worthington, M. (2010) *Children's Mathematical Graphics: Understanding the Key Concept*, NRICH, University of Cambridge. Available online at: http://nrich.maths.org/6894.

Clarke, S. (2005) *Unlocking Formative Assessment*. London: Hodder & Stoughton.

Cotton, T. (2010) *Understanding and Teaching Primary Mathematics*. Harlow: Pearson Educational.

DCSF (2009) 'Children thinking mathematically: PSRN essential knowledge for Early Years practitioners', *The National Strategies*. London: HMSO.

Dehaene, S. (1997) *The Number Sense*. Oxford: Oxford University Press.

Dehaene, S. (1997) *The Number Sense: How the Mind Creates Mathematics*. Oxford: Oxford University Press.

DfEE (1999) *National Numeracy Strategy*. London: DfEE.

DfEE/QCA (1999) *The National Curriculum: Handbook for Primary Teachers in England*. London: HMSO.

DfEE/QCA (2000) *Curriculum Guidance for the Foundation Stage*. London: DfEE.

Gellman, R. and Gallistel, R. (1978) *The Child's Understanding of Number*. Cambridge, MA and London: Harvard University Press.

Haylock, D. (2010) *Mathematics Explained for Primary Teachers*, 4th edn. London: Sage.

Haylock, D. and Cockburn, A. (2008) *Understanding Mathematics in the Lower Primary Years*, 3rd edn. London: Sage.

Haylock, D. and Thangata, F. (2007) *Key Concepts in Teaching Primary Mathematics*. London: Sage.

Hughes, M., Desforges, C. and Mitchell, C. with Carré, C. (2000) *Numeracy and Beyond: Applying Mathematics in the Primary School*. Buckingham: Open University Press.

Liebeck, P. (1990) *How Children Learn Mathematics*. Harmondsworth: Penguin Books.

Mooney, C., Briggs, M., Fletcher, M. and McCullouch, J. (2001) *Primary Mathematics: Teaching Theory and Practice*. Exeter: Learning Matters.

Sousa, D. (2008) *How the Brain Learns Mathematics*. London: Sage.

Sousa, D., Ansari, D. and Christodoulou, J. A. (eds) (2010) *Mind, Brain, & Education: Neuroscience Implications for the Classroom*. Bloomington, IN: Solution Tree Press.

Spelke, E. S. (1999) 'Infant cognition', in R.A. Wilson and F. Keil (eds), *The MIT Encyclopedia of the Cognitive Sciences*. Cambridge, MA: MIT Press.

Spelke, E. S. and Tsivkin, S. (2001) 'Language and number: a bilingual training study', *Cognition*, 78: 45–88.

Suggate, J., Davis, A. and Goulding, M. (2010) *Mathematical Knowledge for Primary School Teachers*, 4th edn. Abingdon: David Fulton.

TDA (2009) *Guidance to Accompany the Professional Standards for QTS and Requirements for ITT*. London: TDA.

Thompson, I. (2003) *Enhancing Primary Mathematics*. Buckingham: Open University Press.

Thompson, I. (2008) *Teaching and Learning Early Number*. Buckingham: Open University Press.

CHAPTER 6

ASSESSMENT AND PLANNING IN MATHEMATICS

Aims:

By the end of this chapter you should be able to:

- explain how the current view of assessment in mathematics has evolved;
- identify the role of the teacher in assessment and planning mathematics;
- identify the role of the child in assessment and planning mathematics;
- identify the expectations of society in assessment.

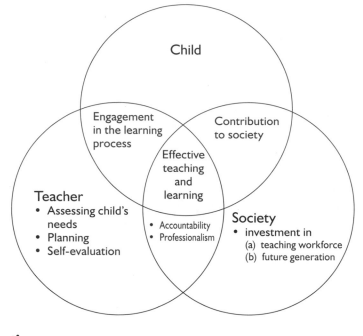

Introduction

Assessment and planning are fundamental parts of a teacher's role. However, assessment is often cited as an issue of concern for both student teachers and practising teachers. The current government stated in the Progress Report on KS2 testing, assessment and accountability *'assessment continues to be an area in which schools need to improve'* (DfE, 2011).

There is a tendency to view assessment and planning as separate entities when, in fact, they are part of the same process. If you accept that you are

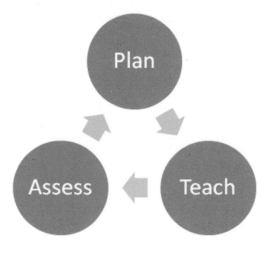

clear about *what* you want to teach and *what* you want the children to learn such a cycle appears simple but, as can be seen from the diagram above, the term assessment has come to be used generically to cover not just assessing children but as means of evaluating teaching achievement and accountability. It is not surprising that assessment raises issues for teachers, particularly those at the beginning of their career. This chapter will consider the cycle of assessment and planning in terms of:

- society – in providing an accountability framework to develop the teaching workforce and future generations;
- the teacher – in supporting the process of teaching mathematics;
- the child – in engagement in the process of learning mathematics and developing into an active member of society.

Society: professionalism and the evolution of assessment practice

In order to consider the current situation it is useful to identify how it has arisen. In the 1970s teaching had been seen as an 'easy' job. The teaching profession has never had the same status as other professions in the UK such as careers associated with medicine and law. Long school holidays and a short school day of no more than seven hours are factors that could be cited and may have been valid. Increased professionalism was developed when teaching became a graduate profession in the 1980s but the most significant change has been the accountability of teachers that is now associated with the role. In the 1990s the Conservative government became concerned about variable local inspection regimes with the result that the government inspection system was restructured and was named the Office for Standards in Education (Ofsted) under the Education (Schools) Act 1992. Following the advent of Ofsted inspection, a national scheme of inspections was set up to inspect every state-funded school in the country with reports being published for the Secretary of State. Although there have been some changes to the process in the intervening years, the system has remained broadly the same, the aim being to 'promote improvement and value for money in the services we inspect and regulate, so that children and young people, parents and carers, adult learners and employers benefit' (Ofsted, 2011).

Although public attitudes to teachers' workload have still persisted to some degree, in January 2003, a National Agreement was signed by school workforce unions, local government employers and the government. As part of this agreement 'planning, preparation and assessment' (PPA) time was introduced in 2005 in response to concerns about workload pressures on teachers. As a result, from 2005, teachers have been entitled to a minimum of 10 per cent of their timetabled teaching time as PPA time. This decision was a significant move as it acknowledged that planning, preparation and assessment were fundamental to the teaching process and not activities that could be fitted in around a school day.

Society and the teacher: accountability

The explicit, active role of the teacher in assessment is a relative new aspect of the role of the teacher that has evolved over the last twenty years. Before the National Curriculum (1988) informal summative assessments such as mental mathematics and tables tests were made. Such summative assessments would form the basis of grades on school reports but these grades were not collected outside the school on either a regional or national basis. At the end of the primary phase, summative assessment in the form of the 11+ examination was administered to all children in their last year of primary education on a national basis. The results were used to allocate places for admission to the various types of state secondary schools available at that time: grammar school, secondary modern school and technical school.

The 11+ examination is now only used in a few counties and local authorities in England that retain grammar schools alongside comprehensive schools. It is interesting to note that this 'tripartite' system as it was called was based on the idea that different skills required different schooling. The philosophical stance behind the Butler Education Act 1944 recognised the importance of education from a societal and individual perspective. Education of the individual was perceived as being the basis of the education of the society in the sense that the community's and individual's needs are not just academic.

This linear diagram illustrates such a model of assessment and planning. The teacher plans work for the child which is assessed summatively and society responds by allocating a label to each child in terms of what is deemed to be the most suitable further education for the child. In such a model the child has no active involvement in the process. Such a model *can* exist whatever approach to teaching and learning is taken but generally it is associated with a didactic model where the onus for learning rests with the child not the teacher as the teacher makes limited adjustment to the needs of the child.

The advent of the National Curriculum marked a significant change in the way assessment was viewed. Schools were held accountable for children's achievement as gauged by Standard Assessment Tests (SATs). Such tests were introduced in phases starting in 1991. The first version at Key Stage 1 did not use the term 'test' but 'task'. The tasks were generally practical but a combination of the teacher time it took to administer them and the fact that tasks could not be taken simultaneous by schools due to their nature, led to a test-based assessment. By 1998, there were tests for 7, 11 and 14 year olds. They were designed to assess whether a pupil had reached the average level for their age but the average then became the expected level. Factors such as concerns about consistency in marking procedures, increased stress caused to children and the narrowing of the curriculum have led to them being phased out in England in 2008 for 14 year olds. From 2005 Key Stage 1 testing has been based upon teacher assessment. If the teacher assessment and test results differ, the teacher assessment results are reported. At the time of writing (Autumn 2011) England is the only country in the UK to retain SATs at KS2, although their status is being reviewed. Key Stage 1 tests are available but were not a legal requirement from 2011. In Wales, Northern Ireland and Scotland they have been replaced by teacher assessments.

This diagram illustrates such a cyclical model of assessment and planning

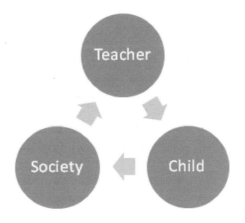

whereby assessment takes on a role beyond assessing the child but instead as a form of assessing the teacher, i.e. accountability, but then relates back to how the teacher plans.

The teacher: subject knowledge and the role of assessment and planning in the teaching process

The diagram above illustrates the model which is prevalent today whereby the child is seen as having more active involvement in the process of assessment so has an influence on how work is planned by the teacher. What assessment means in terms of teaching is more than acknowledging the requirement for teachers to be accountable but to understand how assessment is an integral part of teaching and learning as indicated in previous chapters. Assessment is an everyday process with which we all engage in some form every day.

Consider the following scenarios. What sort of judgements do you think happen to the designated expert and learner during or at the end of the event?

- Job interview
- Driving lesson
- Teaching your granny to send a text

Write down your response in your learning journal.

Using these analogies, you may think that the lessons or interview went well or not. Whatever form of assessment they take, they can affect your future responses, particularly when things have not gone as well as you hoped. You may want to take avoidance action and not repeat the event or you may look at ways to improve. If you gain the opinion of someone other than yourself it may increase the strength of your opinion or make you challenge it. However, rarely do we wait to form an opinion until after an event has taken place. Ongoing assessment takes place instead. An interview is an example of an assessment that is summative as a final judgement is made whereas the driving lesson is a form of ongoing formative assessment with the instructor adjusting the teaching to directly meet the needs of the learner driver. Teaching your granny a skill will require using your comparative expert knowledge with personal knowledge of her to ascertain what she does know and what she does not understand in order to work out the best teaching approach to help her learn the skill of texting. This approach will include considering the misconceptions that could arise as well as the anxieties that may form. Although a type of formative assessment, such assessment is diagnostic in nature.

However, in practice, assessment is not so clear cut. For example, in the case of the interview, although the final assessment is the one that matters, both interviewer and interviewee are constantly revising their assessment depending on the responses each is receiving. Skills on the part of the interviewer may elicit the information that is required from the candidate whereas some candidates may be able to interpret signals from the interviewer instinctively and so be more adept at influencing the outcome during the process. In this way, an oral summative assessment can be influenced in a formative way. Assessment in teaching is not dissimilar and broadly comes under one of the following three types.

- *Summative* assessment makes a judgement after the event such as an interview or a test.
- *Formative* assessment is an integral component of teaching and supports the success during the event such as a driving lesson.
- *Diagnostic* assessment supports active identification of understanding and confusion during the event such as teaching your granny to text.

A summative assessment is usually given to children after a specific point in teaching to assess their understanding. Examples of summative assessments are national examinations, end-of-year tests or even weekly tests. Many textbooks include questions for teachers to use for a summative assessment. Formative assessment is usually embedded within the teaching process as it takes place *during* the process. It can be used to determine what needs or focus should be addressed next for the class, group and/or individual child. Teachers use formative assessment to find the gaps between what children understand and where they are uncertain. Formative assessment evolves from noting children's responses to activities and developing interactive discussion. It includes engaging children in identifying what they need to do to succeed and giving them opportunities to assess themselves as well as receive feedback from the teacher identifying where children did well and offering specific suggestions for improvement to help them reach the next level of learning.

Diagnostic assessment is a more in-depth practice of formative assessment.

It is assessment that usually takes place before teaching. It could be in the form of a test but generally it is in the form of an activity or discussion that is aimed at eliciting information about each child's prior knowledge in order to help in developing lesson plans and to meet children's needs. Meeting the particular needs of children is made by a variety of adjustments to the planning of teaching called differentiation. As such, it requires a secure level of mathematical subject knowledge as well as knowledge of the personal and learning needs of children. Primary teachers have particular opportunities to develop strong knowledge of children's personal and learning needs as they are with children for the majority of the school day.

Summative assessments have their place but do not give sufficient information to support teachers planning teaching on a daily basis. Formative assessment is required to enable children to make progress. However, this process has to be in more depth than is possible during a busy lesson so there needs to be opportunities for diagnostic assessment to take place such as at the beginning of a new school year, at the start of a new topic of work or when children seem to be struggling with the work provided. What can be confusing is that the mode of assessment does not necessarily indicate its purpose. For example, an oral mental mathematics test could have a formative rather than summative purpose to see if children had quick recall of number facts. The purpose could be to ascertain the methods the children were using rather than their ability to give the correct answer.

Assessment and teacher subject knowledge

Although the various types of assessment can be confusing and their uses considered controversial, it is important to remember that they should be used as a structure to inform the teaching process. Ultimately, the knowledge gathered from assessment should be used to support individual children in their learning. It is interesting to note that three of the eight Standards for QTS in Part 1: Teaching, relate to assessment.

The 2011 Standards for Initial Teacher Training, effective from 1 September 2012 (DfE, 2011) state teachers must

Make accurate and productive use of assessment [in the following four areas]
- know and understand how to assess the relevant subject and curriculum areas, including statutory assessment requirements
- make use of formative and summative assessment to secure pupils' progress

- use relevant data to monitor progress, set targets and plan subsequent lessons
- give pupils regular feedback, both orally and through accurate marking, and encourage pupils to respond to the feedback.

Promote good progress and outcomes by pupils
- be accountable for pupils' attainment, progress and outcomes
- plan teaching to build on pupils' capabilities and prior knowledge
- guide pupils to reflect on the progress they have made and their
- emerging needs
- demonstrate knowledge and understanding of how pupils learn and
- how this impacts on teaching
- encourage pupils to take a responsible and conscientious attitude to their own work and study.

Adapt teaching to respond to the strengths and needs of all pupils
- know when and how to differentiate appropriately, using approaches which enable pupils to be taught effectively
- have a secure understanding of how a range of factors can inhibit pupils' ability to learn, and how best to overcome these
- demonstrate an awareness of the physical, social and intellectual development of children, and know how to adapt teaching to support pupils' education at different stages of development
- have a clear understanding of the needs of all pupils, including those with special educational needs; those of high ability; those with English as an additional language; those with disabilities; and be able to use and evaluate distinctive teaching approaches to engage and support them.

Assessment and planning are the tools by which evidence is provided to identify adaptations to teaching necessary to promote good progress. It involves background knowledge of competence in *mathematics*, pedagogical knowledge in terms theories and experience of learning and teaching *mathematics* and curricular knowledge of the *mathematics* and whole curriculum with other statutory requirements. Relating generic assessment knowledge to mathematical knowledge is key to successful teaching and learning.

Assessment and planning can take place without learner engagement. The participation of learner and teacher in assessment is similar to that of teaching styles identified in the diagram on p. 69 in Chapter 3, and is dependent on ideas about learning and teaching.

Overview of how learning theories can relate to teaching styles

Learning theory		
⇐ Behaviourist	Cognitivist	Constructivist ⇒

Teaching style		
⇐		⇒
Didactic		Child-centred
Characteristics: – learning by transmitting knowledge, telling information, giving instructions to the learner – teacher controlled	Use of a range of styles that stimulate more senses and forms of communication than hearing, i.e. speaking, using visual aids, demonstrating, etc. Children assess their own performance against criteria	Characteristics: – investigative approach to learning, reflecting on actions to make generalisations – teacher acting as facilitator – teacher- and child-controlled guided discovery

Assessment type		
⇐	Summative Formative	⇒

However, child engagement in the learning process is now firmly embedded in the Standards, denoting a teaching style that fosters active learning by the child. Teaching is not done *to* the child but *with* the child. However, this does not mean that teaching style is child-centred. The teacher is more than a facilitator, but an active leader in the learning process.

Teacher/child engagement in assessment and planning

Motivation usually relates to children understanding the purpose of what they have been asked to do and having a sense of what they are aiming to achieve. Such ideas originate from the work of David Ausubel, an American psychologist working in the 1960s and 1970s (Ausubel et al., 1978). Ausubel took a constructivist view that the key influence on learning was what the learner already knows. He believed that teachers should provide organisational strategies to support new learning by explaining next steps and highlighting new information so that the learner can process and understand it. More recently, these ideas were developed in the UK and brought to prominence by Professors Paul Black and Dylan Wiliam in their seminal article 'Inside the Black Box: Raising Standards through Classroom Assessment'. Strategies suggested include active involvement of pupils in their own learning, setting explicit objectives and giving effective feedback to children. These strategies are evident in the Assessment for Learning initiative that is evident in most schools today. Organisational ideas can be based upon acronyms such as WALT (We Are Learning To), WILF (What I'm Looking For) and TIB (That Is Because) or 'traffic lights' and 'thumbs up/thumbs down' to allow children to show their level of understanding to the teacher. Such strategies *can* support motivation and memory but understanding the theory behind the strategies is important if they are going to be addressed effectively by teachers and explained appropriately to children. Ofsted (2003) stated that:

Formative assessment or 'assessment for learning' is most effective when it:

- is embedded in the teaching and learning process
- shares learning goals with pupils
- helps pupils to know and to recognise the standards to aim for
- provides feedback for pupils to identify what they should do to improve
- has a commitment that every pupil can improve
- involves teachers and pupils reviewing pupils' performance and progress
- involves pupils in self-assessment.

Assessment for learning (AfL) been a key element of all ITE programmes as it has been explicitly referred to in the QTS Standards (TDA, 2007). Although the revised Standards (DfE, 2011) do not make reference to the term 'assessment for learning' its strategies are evident. AfL makes sense when seen in practice but can be challenging for the student teacher who is just beginning to develop skills in teaching. Black himself raises these concerns, stating that:

'doing assessment for learning' may fail to implement those key features whereby pupils are helped to become more confident and effective learners . . . changes involved make heavy demands on teachers and schools in that they are required to rethink their roles . . . the essential requirement is that teachers should be supported by a commitment sustained within the whole school over several years . . . (Black, 2007)

Teachers starting out in the profession must understand the basics of assessment in the cycle of teaching before they can begin to understand such formative strategies. The core elements of assessment are:

- What children know and what they should learn next.
- What teachers need to maintain/adjust/change in their teaching.

Plan – using knowledge of misconceptions, etc. progression in mathematical learning to support progression including engagement of the child in the process of assessment

Teach – to ensure the individual learning needs of children are met including mathematical progression

Assess – have mathematical subject knowledge to be able to make assessments including those required to meet statutory requirements

Concept cartoons, discussed in Chapter 5, would be an example that *does* support putting the principles of AfL into practice. They enable children to demonstrate their level of understanding or confusion in such a way that it can be taken account of by the teacher as a lesson progresses, leading to in-depth questioning that can support the child becoming aware of the source of a misconception.

It can be seen that assessment is at the heart of teaching and learning. It relates to how well children are learning and how well the teacher is teaching. One of the challenges when teaching mathematics – or indeed any subject – is the specific mathematics knowledge required to make formative assessments. Such knowledge includes awareness of misconceptions, strategies to expose or clarify such misconceptions, connections that can be made to other branches of mathematics and so on. In fact it is the knowledge that evolves from background mathematical competence and knowledge of the nature of mathematics in terms of language, structure, notation and hierarchy discussed in Chapter 2.

As an example of the role of assessment and planning in the teaching process and the importance of subject knowledge, think of the misconceptions associated with recognising and representing numbers symbolically in the form of a numeral, i.e. 3.

Make a record of your thoughts in your reflective journal.

Such activities are basic to understanding the place value system. Even at this preliminary level, basic place value is complex:

- Numerals are abstract concepts.
- Numerals bear no relation to the concrete objects with which children are familiar when they learn to count.
- The language used to denote number is:
  (a)   not consistent, e.g. the word for 17 – 'seventeen' – starts with a unit value and then ten whereas the word for 31 – 'thirty-one' – starts with the value of the tens and then the units; and
  (b)   the numeral is not written as a recording of language, e.g. sixty-seven is 67 not 607.
  This leads on to:
- The place of the numeral denotes its value: 6 in the tens column and 7 in the units column represents 6 tens and 7 units or 67.
- The use of zero '0' acts as a place holder, e.g. 102 is 1 hundred and 2 units so must be written as 102 not 12.

If the focus for a Year 2 class was:

Read and write two-digit and three-digit numbers in figures and words. (PNS, 2011)

The teacher would have to assess their knowledge, skills and understanding through an awareness of the potential misconceptions identified above and an understanding of an assessment activity which would elicit such information. Children could play 'bingo'-type games to assess their reading of numerals. The numbers would have to be carefully chosen to include those that could potentially cause confusion, e.g. 16. Another version of a 'bingo' game would assess their writing of numbers by having a 'caller' who gives numbers for children to record. The children are then asked to match their numbers to a bingo card. Such activities could be completed in small groups so assessment could be detailed. Other than the mathematical concepts involved, such activities may indicate those children who are inhibited by their fine motor skills in holding a pencil or following instructions. These activities would not be teaching as such but assessment, the means by which planning for effective teaching could take place.

Planning

The purpose of a plan is to ensure you have considered such elements. The detail of the plan depends on numerous factors – experience, subject knowledge of what is being taught, the children. Purpose is a key driver. If the plan is to support the teacher and children then the plan must make sense to the teacher. However, if the plan has a dual purpose to support the teacher *and* be used as evidence of meeting QTS standards, Ofsted criteria or school appraisal, then it becomes a shared document and must be in a form that is easily understood. It can be the same document but its fitness for purpose can be obscured. As a student teacher you may feel that assessment and planning take up considerable time. This is probably because the documents produced have shared purposes. Unfortunately what is often lost is the idea that the plan is a supportive element of learning to teach and developing teaching skills. It has another positive purpose in that it acts as a means of explaining to colleagues shared thinking when planning as part of a team. As a student teacher, it is usually the case that you plan each lesson or activity in detail but as experience develops certain elements of planning such as organisational factors are internalised.

Look at the annotated example of a plan by an undergraduate student in her final year of training, working at the beginning of the academic year with a Year 2 class. Its purpose was two-fold: to support teaching *and* to give evidence for an external examiner of aspects of the Standards that could be readily or fully observed such as the ability to plan and have secure subject knowledge.

As a student teacher you must be guided by school policies but you must also indicate understanding and show awareness of a range of teaching approaches and the areas of contention. Reading and writing numbers may seem a straightforward activity but there is debate about how children should be taught and what representations should be used, as discussed in Chapter 5. Place value is an example of notation that represents numbers in symbolic numerals according to their place, an issue cited in Chapter 2 that has the potential to confuse children. Here are some of the aspects you will need to consider in order to assess children:

- the types of misconceptions children may make (see plan);
- the types of questions and discussions at the beginning, during and the end of the lesson to ascertain understanding/decide whether any mistakes are misconceptions or errors;

Lesson Plan

Lesson plan format	Example	Purpose
Age of children, time of day, duration of activity/ lesson:	**Year 2** September 28th for 1 hour between 11 a.m. and midday.	Useful information for personal review and later stage/enables tracking of series of activities/ lessons.
Focus of activity/lesson/ lesson objectives: We Are Learning Today . . .	Today we are going to see how we can read and write numbers so we can play a game.	May seem obvious but supports you in explaining the focus to the children in language they can understand and gives purpose to what the children are expected to do.
Student/teacher focus:	Make sure that if the most able children have exhausted the designated game possibilities they have sufficient resources to adapt the game by making their own rules.	This element relates to the teacher's self-reflection and observation by tutors/colleagues, e.g. challenging the most able children.
Links to children's previous experience:	Work relates to pre-topic assessment to identify understanding of reading and writing numbers and the quantity they represent.	Identifying and relating work to previous/future lesson/activity/other area of curriculum helps support both teacher and children in making connections.
Learning objectives/ intentions:	Read and record numbers from 0 to 100 and recognise that the position of a digit gives it its value • **All** children – know how to read and record numbers 0–30. • **Some** children – know how to read and record numbers 1–100. • **Most** children – understand that the first digit shows the number of tens and the second digit the number of units/ones. • **All** children – use their knowledge and understanding to play a variety of games suited to group/individual needs. • **All** children – develop cooperative work in a small-group activity.	Learning objectives/intentions: Useful to think in terms of: • KNOW (knowledge) • UNDERSTAND (concept) • DO (skill). These may be introduced to children using WALT (We Are Learning To . . .) As well as PSE/PSMSC focus.
Success criteria/target setting: **What I'm Looking For (WILF)**	**All children** Remembering 11 and 12 as special numbers to know the place value quantity. Thinking about the 'tricky' numerals 13–19. Reading numerals (as related to group) correctly. Using my knowledge of reading numbers to play a game. **Some children** Using my knowledge of numerals to write numbers.	Should relate to the identified Learning Objectives/intentions and provide children with a clear indication of the specific steps to meeting lesson objectives.

Planned assessment	Each group will be supported by an adult – class teacher, student (me), TA and parent support. Each adult will have a proforma to note whether children achieve objective and write additional comments.	*The assessment should identify how assessment is to take place.*
Possible errors and misconceptions:	(1) Children cannot remember the strategies taught to remember 11 and 12 + tricky numbers, e.g. arrays of 12 in egg boxes and 1 and 1 make 11 fun. 1 and a 2 tell 12 what to do. 1 and a 3 send 13 up a tree. 1 and a 4 tell 14 shut the door. 1 and a 5 keep 15 alive. 1 and a 6 make 16 pick up sticks. 1 and a 7 send 17 to heaven. 1 and an 8 make 18 great. 1 and 9 make 19 shine. (2) Children may not be able to relate their knowledge of reading numbers to a game as it is not fully consolidated. (3) Some children who are to play record a running total in the exchange game may be confused in the recording process even though they can read the numbers.	*This should demonstrate subject knowledge in terms of concepts and strategies to support understanding. They may include teaching approaches to be used as identified in Chapter 5.*
Resources/roles of other adults/other forms of differentiation:	**IWB** Range of numbers displayed including 'tricky' numbers displayed and specific children asked. Individual white boards – numbers called children record (group 1 to work with TA) in corner of room) Each group supported by an adult to • Assess activity • Keep children on task • Negotiate/support turn taking in game **Games** Prepared bingo boards for group 1 and 2 – group 1 numbers 1–30 and group 2 numbers 1–100. Groups 3 and 4 (group 3 one die and group 4 two die). Large group dice. Individual white boards and pens for recording. Some children may require structural material to exchange units for tens.	*Resources including role of adults need to be clear.* *Differentiation needs to be clear, i.e. how the task will be adapted to meet children's needs.*

| Lesson/activity structure: | • 'Child speak' learning objective.
• Whole-class activity using IWB (on carpet with group 1 seated to left so they can move away without disrupting whole group). (Make sure whole class time limited to maximum 10 minutes due to wide ability range.)
• Remind of 'tricky' numbers rhyme and say together.
• Group 1 leave to play bingo game which will include 'tricky' numbers.
• Call numbers including 'tricky' numbers but extending to 100 – children record on boards and show.
• Group 2 leave main group to play bingo game – 1–100.
• Model exchange game using numbers 0–30 with big die –how long will it take us to get to 30 – set timer. First child rolls die and teacher records number. Second child roles die and adds to number (support by recording on whiteboard, i.e. 5 + 4) – total kept on board – continue until 30 reached – could develop so exact total reached, i.e. got to 28 so must role 2).
• Groups 3 and 4 disperse – note engagement of group. Group 3 play game of keeping running total – first child to get to target number of 30 wins. Group 4 use two dice and carry out similar activity. Adjust target number depending on response to who e-group activity.
• Adaptation – groups 1 and 2 reduce range of numbers as indicated.
• Extension – groups 1 and 2 – identified child becomes caller.
• Adaptation – groups 3 and 4 – provision of structural apparatus and/or 100 squares to support keeping running total.
• Extension – extend target number/change game rules. | *Format of lesson should be clear with 'stage directions' introduction.*
Ground rules, i.e. behaviour.
Sequence of events.
Timings for each part of the lesson.
Extensions for early finishers and plans for those who have need for further support.

After planning it may be helpful to write key points on card. |
| **Plenary** | IWB – images of numbers from environment – quick-fire questions to targeted children to assess their reading of number.
Children write down their numbers, e.g. number of people in their family, number of pets etc.
(Record any issues on class list.)
Return to learning WALT and demonstrate examples of WILT. | *Relate back to beginning of lesson and identify what will happen in next lesson in general terms – use assessment information to:*
(a) inform lesson objectives for next lesson
(b) identify the success of your planning |

- the questions you will ask other adults who have been supporting groups.

Once the information is gathered it should help you plan effectively for the next lesson.

The child and society: provision for the teaching workforce

Children are taught by teachers with varying degrees of expertise. All can bring different strengths, from new ideas to a wealth of knowledge drawn from experience with children. Student and novice teachers need to be aware of the debates about teaching and learning and have the opportunities to share the knowledge of more experienced colleagues.

If schools are to become more autonomous as indicated in the White Paper (DfE, 2011) with some gaining 'teaching school' status, providing opportunities for all teachers, whether they are students, novices or experienced, is essential if true professional communities are to form.

The following diagram illustrates such a model of assessment and planning. It may also be useful to consider the model from a bird's eye view with each process spiralling forward so deepening the child's understanding, through ongoing review.

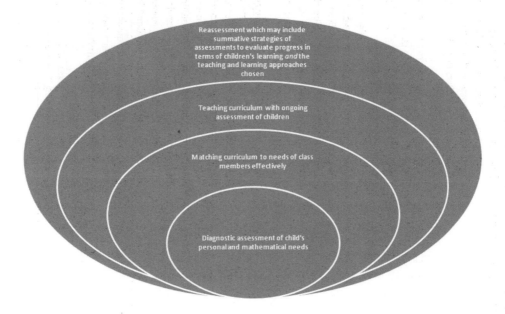

Reassessment which may include summative strategies of assessments to evaluate progress in terms of children's learning *and* the teaching and learning approaches chosen

Teaching curriculum with ongoing assessment of children

Matching curriculum to needs of class members effectively

Diagnostic assessment of child's personal and mathematical needs

Teacher engagement with this process will vary according to experience.

Look at the following diagram and identify what forms of support would develop your understanding or what support you could offer to colleagues.

Level of process	Support
1. Initial assessment (diagnostic)	• Records of children's previous work • Discussion with colleagues of previous teaching of the topic – planning diagnostic activity • School planning documents • Statutory planning documents • Related literature • Internet sources of information
2. Planning	• Discussion with colleagues about interpreting the results to devise appropriate teaching and learning • Revisit school planning documents, statutory planning documents related literature and Internet sources of information
3. Teaching	• Colleague observation • Self-evaluation
4. Reassessment	• Further discussion with colleagues re teaching approach taken and learning responses of children
Repeat 2, 3 and 4 for allocated/ agreed period of time	• Summarise outcomes for children and further action • Summarise teaching approaches in terms of successes and what could be improved

All teachers can gain from having opportunities to discuss their teaching openly and honestly to win support just as less experienced teachers need opportunities to share their research. The ultimate aim is to provide a positive and effective learning experience for all children.

Meeting national and local agenda

One of the challenges of devolving more power to schools is finding ways to meet evolving conflicting agendas. A potential example is the role of assessment and planning in the EYFS and National Curriculum. The EYFS takes a different stance to assessment and planning. Formative assessment takes place in the form of such data as observations, photographs, drawings and parental information, and is currently based upon six areas of learning that emphasise the provision of enabling environments that support children learning at different rates and in different ways. Although the review of the EYFS (Tickell, 2011) recommends rationalisation of the current format of the profile by which each child's progress is checked, it still would be summary of all the formative assessment towards the early learning goals. The aim is for it to be used to guide planning in KS1. As a result, planning in the Foundation Stage is aimed at meeting the needs of the individual rather than meeting the needs of the individual within a set statutory curriculum with annual expectations of progress.

The role of the teacher or practitioner in the Foundation Stage is to provide an environment where individual learning needs can be met. Although each area of learning cannot be planned in isolation, if we take the example of reading and recognising numbers, children will need to be provided with opportunities to see number symbols. One element of planning is providing such opportunities.

The other element of planning is to assess children's current progress according to the levels indicated in the EYFS and provide a balance of child-initiated and adult-led play activities with an aim of encouraging a particular aspect of learning. Although as a result of the Tickell Review (2011), it is likely that more detailed assessment of children in the Foundation Stage will concentrate on the areas of personal, social and emotional development, and communication and physical development, mathematics will remain as an area of learning. A 'number-rich' environment would include clocks, telephones, machines such as microwaves, money and signs. It is important that children can read numbers but it is also important that they have experience of different uses of numbers. An example of the nominal use of numbers would be telephone numbers whereas numbers on money and machine displays would indicate a value and support children in developing the cardinal principle of number. Numbers on clocks or on the pages of a book denote the ordinal aspect of numbers and support children developing the stable-order principle of counting. As children's fine motor skills develop they will need opportunities to represent numbers. Such representations *may* include numeral symbols but could also be representations more related to the objects they represent. It can be seen that the expectations for mathematics at this stage may appear straightforward but the teacher or practitioner must have secure mathematical subject knowledge to make plan to and assess children.

Summary

This chapter has raised three key issues relating to assessment and planning:

- the meaning of assessment in terms of teachers' accountability *and* progression in children's learning;
- the difference in types of assessment and how they relate to teaching and learning;
- the importance of having secure mathematical subject knowledge to make assessments and plans.

Conclusion

Chapter 7 will consider how resources relate to the teaching process in terms of choice of approach and the influence of assessment and planning within this process. The fundamental nature of representation to understanding mathematics will be discussed in terms of the roles of teacher and learner.

Review questions

This chapter may have raised issues with which you are not yet familiar. A good starting point would be to read work by Paul Black and Dylan Wiliam. You may also want to consider the cycle of assessment, planning and teaching and how it relates to the mathematics lesson plans you have written.

1. How did you know what to teach?
2. How did the plans support meeting the needs of the children?
3. How effective was your assessment in future planning?

References

Ausubel, D. P., Novak, J. D. and Hanesian, H. (1978) *Educational Psychology: A Cognitive View*, 2nd edn. New York: Holt, Rinehart & Winston.

Black, P. J. (2003) *Testing Times: Role of Assessment for Learning*, Curriculum Briefing 2:1. London: GL Assessment.

Black, P. J. and Wiliam, D. (1998) *Inside the Black Box*. Southwell: BERA.

DfE (2011) *Review of Key Stage 2 Testing, Assessment and Accountability: Progress Report*. DfE. Available online at: https://www.education.gov.uk/publications/ standard/publicationDetail/Page1/DFE-00035-2011 (accessed 19 September 2011).

Ofsted (2003) *Good Assessment Practice in Mathematics*, HMI 1477. London: Ofsted.

Ofsted (2011) *About Us*. Available online at: http://www.ofsted.gov.uk/about-us (accessed 11 November).

TDA (2007) *Professional Standards for Teachers*. London: TDA.

Tickell, C. (2011) *The Early Years: Foundations for Life, Health and Learning. An Independent Report on the Early Years Foundation Stage to Her Majesty's Government*. London: HMSO.

Further reading

Askew, M., Brown, M., Rhodes, V. and Wiliam, D. (1997) *Effective Teachers of Numeracy: Report*. London: TTA.

Aubrey, C. (1997) *Mathematics Teaching in the Early Years: An Investigation of Teachers' Subject Knowledge*. London: Falmer Press.

Black, P. J. (2007) 'Full marks for feedback', *Making the Grade (Journal of the Institute of Educational Assessors)*, Spring 2007, pp. 18-21.

Black, P. J. and Wiliam, D. (1998) 'Assessment and classroom learning', *Assessment in Education*, March, pp. 7–74.

Clarke, S. (2001) *Unlocking Formative Assessment*. London: Hodder & Stoughton.

Clarke, S. (2003) *Enriching Feedback in the Primary Classroom*. London: Hodder & Stoughton.

Clarke, S. (2005) *Formative Assessment in Action*. London: Hodder Murray.

Cockburn, A. and Littler, G. (2008) *Mathematical Misconceptions*. London: Sage.

Cotton, T. (2010) *Understanding and Teaching Primary Mathematics*. Harlow: Pearson Educational.

Ginsburg, H. (1977) 'Learning to count. Computing with written numbers', in H. Ginsburg, *Children's Arithmetic: How They Learn It and How You Teach It*. Austin, TX: Pro-ed, pp. 1–29, 79–129.

Haylock, D. (2010) *Mathematics Explained for Primary Teachers*, 4th edn. London: Sage.

Mason, J. (2005) *Developing Thinking in Algebra*. London: PCP.

Mooney, C., Briggs, M., Fletcher, M. and McCullouch, J. (2012) *Primary Mathematics: Teaching Theory and Practice*, 6th edn. London: Learning Matters.

NNS (2002) *Learning from Mistakes and Misconceptions in Mathematics*. London: DfES.

CHAPTER 7

RESOURCES FOR MATHEMATICS

Aims

By the end of this chapter you should be able to:

- identify resources for specifically *teaching* mathematics;
- identify the role of resources for specifically *learning* mathematics;
- understand issues relating to how resources represent mathematics;
- identify questions about resources that you need to consider further.

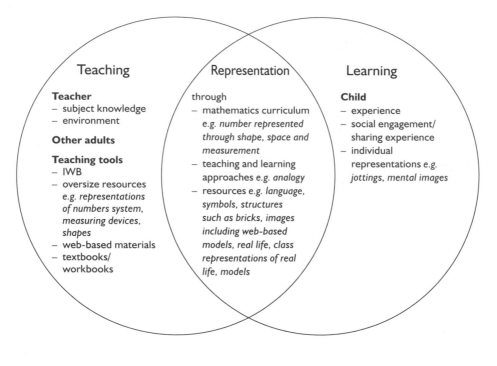

Introduction

The term 'resource' has a wide range of meanings depending on its context. It can either be seen as synonymous with the term 'equipment', conjuring up an image of a collection of plastic or wooden items stored in corner of the classroom, or with web-based resources available from government or commercial websites. However, a resource, in its broadest sense, is a means of support whether it is tangible such as counting cubes or help from an adult or intangible such as analogy to support an explanation. This chapter will focus on such a broad definition of resources in relation to the primary school by considering those that:

• support teaching
• represent mathematics
• support learning.

Teaching resources

The choice of teaching resources is generally guided by:

• the perspective taken on teaching and learning;

- what is being taught;
- the individual needs of children being taught.

The teacher

It is easy to overlook the key resource in the modern classroom with its plethora of equipment – the teacher. In a Victorian classroom a blackboard, a globe and possibly an abacus would be the only resources other than the teacher. The teacher was the source of knowledge. The aim of teaching was to transmit this knowledge to the child. Although such a model of teaching and learning is neither evident nor thought desirable today, there are teachers that are able to transmit the knowledge they possess in a form that inspires.

> The NRICH website gives information on what it was like to be taught mathematics in a Victorian classroom.

Examples of inspiring teachers can be found easily through television. There are those that make what may seem complex accessible to the viewer. For example, Professor Brian Cox albeit with a huge range of resources at his disposal, enables the viewer to make sense of particle physics, not a subject usually accessible to the layman. Identifying what he or others do that make knowledge accessible to you is a useful step in developing your own teaching skills. Additionally, much can be gained by either considering the qualities of teachers that inspired you during your school days or observing colleagues who you believe inspire children. Focused observation can give you ideas of how you could inspire others to learn. It may be their secure command of subject knowledge, their use of analogy, the humour they include or even just their enthusiasm.

>
>
> Teaching at some level is a performance. It needs to engage the learner as well as offer knowledge and support in learning, understanding and the development of skills. A worthy aspiration for any primary teacher would be to be the most effective classroom resource for teaching mathematics!

Government initiatives

It can be seen that investment in teachers by society is fundamental to effective teaching and learning. One of the unfortunate results of the National Strategies was that at the same time as supporting teachers, they had the potential to limit creativity that could emanate from the teacher. This led to some generic government initiatives such as Creative Partnerships (Creativity, Culture and Education, 2002, online) in response to the Robinson Report (NACCCE et al., 1999), *Excellence and Enjoyment* (DfES,2003) and *Learning Outside the Classroom* (DfES, 2006) emphasising aspects of teaching that are so relevant to mathematics. The National Strategies have resulted in micro-management of the curriculum in some schools over the last few years so that opportunities for some teachers to use their own initiative in teaching has been marginalised. *Excellence and Enjoyment* is a case in point. It was introduced as a result of an Ofsted Report (2002) that observed that the best practice was found in schools which had a rich and varied curriculum and that this was not evident in the majority of primary schools. Emphasis moved from *what* was being *taught* to *how* it was *learnt*. The relative inflexibility of the former curriculum had provided assurance for some schools that they were covering what was expected of them. This difference in response to seemingly prescriptive strategies highlights the importance of staff being able to justify their chosen practice in a climate of greater autonomy being given to schools.

The physical environment

Although there has recently been emphasis on the outside environment, teachers are responsible for provision of the whole physical environment. The role of the environment in learning can be exemplified again through considering a Victorian classroom. The environment was not meant to have a positive effect on learning. If anything it was meant to cause the least distraction possible. Windows were often beyond child height so children would not be distracted from their work by looking outside. The environment is seen quite differently today in learning: it not only is conducive to learning in terms of being organised and attractive but as a resource for learning. The role of the physical environment in the Reggio Emilia approach to Early Years education is such that it is seen as a third teacher in terms of its relationship with educational philosophy and practice (Thornton and Brunton, 2010: 63). Such a philosophy is evident in Early Years settings in England through the principle of enabling environments in the EYFS.

A rich and varied environment supports children's learning and development. It gives them the confidence to explore and learn in secure and safe, yet challenging, indoor and outdoor spaces. (EYFS, 2006: 3.3)

Consider the physical environment where you currently teach or one where you taught recently. In what way did it support mathematical learning?

Creating a mathematically 'rich' environment requires knowledge of the connection between different branches of mathematics and the rest of the curriculum. It could include provision of representations of mathematics from the real world from role-play areas to displays of patterns in nature, mathematics games such as snap or even hand-held games consoles as well as an environment that allows children to play with mathematics in a less structured way, creating patterns and other constructions. Playing with toy bricks even holds attraction for adults, to the extent that there is a website devoted to adult fans of Lego (http://www.brickish.org/)! There would seem no reason to limit such activities to younger primary children. Finding enjoyment in mathematics from an early age is important if positive attitudes to it are to be formed. There can be no richer place than the world outside the classroom in terms of mathematics. It is where mathematics originates. Such spaces around the classroom can be enhanced with structures such as seating and planting. Alone, these features give scope for studying number, pattern, shape and measurement. Exploring beyond the vicinity of the school increases possibilities to support the whole curriculum as well as mathematics. Visiting museums, parks and other centres of interest adds further opportunities.

However, going outside in itself does not support mathematics. It needs just as much thought as any other learning experience offered in terms of how it will enable children to gain from the encounter and how it will connect to other learning experiences. The types of questions that need to be asked to promote its effective use are:

- Does it provide a genuine purpose for the activity? Purpose was cited in Chapters 2 and 5 in relation to intrinsic motivation and its importance in engaging with mathematics.

- Does it promote a wider range of experiences than within the classroom? For example, if the focus of the activity was naming shapes considering exclusive and inclusive definitions then an outdoor environment would provide a wider range of examples than the classroom. It would challenge children's thinking so their experiences were wider than the prototypes of shapes commonly available in a classroom and lead them into justifying the names they give to shapes.

The emotional environment

Chapter 1 referred to the role of emotion in learning mathematics and the fear of mathematics which had been engendered in classrooms. Creating an environment where children feel safe, intellectually stimulated and it is acceptable to make mistakes are all part of a positive school and classroom ethos. It is teachers who set the tone for such an ethos in their engagement with each other and with children, so modelling behaviour to foster positive engagement among children.

Teachers have a concurrent role in as much as they are learners too. Not only do they develop their pedagogic subject knowledge through the experience of teaching; they act as a resource to model learning. Children can be supported by such strategies as teachers explicitly verbalising mental thought processes and using language accurately to form logical arguments.

Other adults

'Other adults' is a generic term used to denote adults in a class beyond the class teacher. They can be employed or working in a voluntary capacity having a range of titles such as teaching assistant, learning support assistant, classroom assistant, student or may be a parent helper. Other adults work in a negotiated partnership with teachers, depending on their experience and the policies within a school.

The introduction of the National Strategies in Numeracy and Literacy at the end of the 1990s led to schools employing increasing numbers of assistants to support raising children's performance, many of whom have completed relevant qualifications through, for example, programmes leading to NVQ qualifications and Foundation degrees. As a consequence other adults in the classroom have become an increasingly skilled workforce that can complement the teacher. Ofsted's Review of Primary Education 1994–98 (1999) stated: 'Well-trained teaching assistants are a key resource and are used effectively in many primary schools.' More recently the issues of qualifications was again cited by Ofsted (2010) when it was identified that relevant qualifications of support staff had an impact on whether schools were effective or not. This highlights the importance of schools considering all adults who support children in their learning when devising CPD, not just teachers.

Information and communication technology

Today ICT has become an implicit part of nearly all teaching and learning experiences. Already certain teaching resources such as chalkboards have become obsolete, being replaced by interactive whiteboards (IWB). As a multi-faceted resource for teaching alone, technology has enabled teachers to share planning more effectively using IWBs and to use a high level of sophistication in the quality of the virtual images they can offer to children. However, just as time in planning can potentially be reduced, so can it be increased by the overwhelming range of resources from which to choose. Teachers have to be discerning about what resources they make. Technology alone will not enhance teaching and the appropriate use of technological resources must be based on secure mathematical knowledge, not take the place of more appropriate non-technological means such as questioning and using tangible resources that exemplify the mathematics being taught. For example, in a problem-solving activity, if the aim was to consider different perimeter dimensions to a vegetable plot to allow a certain number of seeds to be planted, looking at the potential plot may yield ideas which could then be transferred in sketches to paper. However, it may be helpful to:

- take a digital photograph to explore ideas and act as a reminder of the nature of the plot in terms of limiting factors such as a wall to one side;
- use a spreadsheet to extend the activity by considering maximum/ minimum areas.

If the mathematics related to developing an understanding of equivalent fractions then application to a situation that had meaning such as money would enable children to use their prior knowledge to make sense of the mathematics. For example,

$\frac{1}{2} = 50\text{p}$
$5/10 = 5 \times 10\text{p} = 50\text{p}$

Such resources may better support understanding than specific models which are either in hard copy or electronic form such as a number wall. Effective use of ICT comes with experience. As a guide the following questions may support you in the decision-making process. Additionally, children should learn to engage in these decisions when considering their choice of resources.

Does the use of ICT support:

- more *effective* teaching by engaging children and supporting their understanding?
- more *efficient* teaching in terms of time and quality of resources?
- more *effective* and active learning that meets the child's needs?
- more *efficient* learning in terms of enabling solutions to be explored within reasonable time limits and using the resources available?
- collaborative opportunities for independent practice of application to concepts?

A Google search under 'mathematics resources for teachers' will identify almost over 60 million sources. Although Internet sites provide a wealth of ideas caution needs to be taken as to their provenance as well as awareness of the fact that resources being found on a site legitimises neither their quality nor their value in terms of appropriateness for the children being taught. Making appropriate choices can be challenging so it is valuable if such decisions involve school management teams. Criteria that you would apply to any resource in terms of fitness of purpose should also be applied to online sources but it is important also to consider their provenance in terms of the credentials of the author or organisation.

Here are some sites that have a clear provenance.

Primary Resources: http:// www.primaryresources.co.uk/

Primary Resources was launched in 1998 by Gareth Pitchford who shared worksheets he had created. It expanded to include materials sent in by teachers. It is currently hosted by RM Education. It has extended to include some commercial sources and resources of photographs and images. The site enables teachers to share resources across a potentially worldwide community.

The National Centre for Excellence in the Teaching of Mathematics (NCETM): http://www.ncetm.org.uk/

NCETM was launched in 2006 as part of the government's Science, Technology, Engineering and Mathematics (STEM) programme and aims to improve mathematics teaching by supporting a wide range of professional facilities.

BEAM (Be A Mathematician): http://www.beam.co.uk/

BEAM is a commercial site and part of Nelson Thornes, the educational publisher. BEAM specialises in teaching and learning materials for 3–14 year old children and includes consultancy and CPD activity.

The NRICH Project: http://nrich.maths.org/public/

NRICH started in 1996 and is based in both the University of Cambridge's Faculty of Education and the Centre for Mathematical Sciences. It encompasses free mathematics enrichment resources for children of all ages, discussion forums and face-to-face CPD, a range of publications and a mathematics thesaurus. The team of NRICH is made up of qualified teachers.

BBC Learning: http://www.bbc.co.uk/learning/ – a range of resources to support teachers as well as parents and children.

Local authorities often have resources on their websites to support teachers. They are usually password protected but valuable as they have gone through a level of scrutiny in terms of quality before reaching teachers.

Textbooks and workbooks

Textbooks and workbooks were used commonly in primary schools for many years. A significant number were published in the 1980s which led to a wide diversity of practice in the primary school mathematics curriculum (Gray, 1991). When the National Curriculum was first published in 1988, a structure was in place which led to more homogenous practice in terms of content in primary schools. Gray noted that such resources could be 'a prop' for a teacher's lack of knowledge and Harries and Spooner (2000) noted the influence they had on teachers' thinking. As such they can be seen as both a teaching and a learning tool and Ofsted (2005: para. 63), albeit specifically in regard to worksheets, identified that less effective teaching was associated with their use. However, although textbooks and workbooks cannot be sufficiently fine-tuned to meet the needs of individual learners and the contexts in which learning takes place, they yield the same benefits as resources that can be found online, i.e. by giving teachers ideas. More recently, it could be assumed that increases in ICT sources and the cost of investment in commercial schemes will lead to them not having a place in primary mathematics. However, research carried out for the Nuffield Foundation by Mike Askew and Jeremy Hodgen

(Askew et al., 2010), albeit with secondary school children, found that *good* textbooks are more important for high attainment in mathematics than factors such as ICT. They found that in countries that perform well in mathematics, carefully constructed textbooks were the primary means of teaching. By comparison, use of mathematics textbooks in English schools is relatively low, and English textbooks use routine examples and are less mathematically logical than those in other countries. Additionally, children in high-performing countries were more likely to use textbooks at home and their use was supported by parents. Textbooks and workbooks in schools can be useful resources but decisions about their use must relate to teaching and learning policy within the school and the criteria that would be used for any resource in terms of fitness for purpose.

Representation

Chapter 2 discussed how the range of representations in mathematics can set up barriers to learning mathematics for some people. Chapter 5 introduced the idea of two elements of representation: the recording of the *result* of mathematical activity and the recording of the *process* of mathematical activity. Representation is fundamental to mathematics understanding as it used to organise, record and communicate mathematical ideas as well as to translate these ideas to solve problems and interpret mathematics. Mathematics is represented through language, images and symbols which, at primary level, are based upon real experiences through solving problems. ICT software enhance how such representations can be seen dynamically rather than as static representations so showing another fundamental element of mathematics – change. Furthermore, the very nature of the topics in the mathematics curriculum can be seen as a form of representation, for example number represented through shape, space, data and measurement. Go back to the schema devised by teachers on pp. 90–94 in Chapter 4. You will be able to identify that much of what is included originates from number and most other areas of mathematics are forms of representation of number such as data-handling and measuring.

Making connections between different forms of representation is fundamental to the teaching and learning process. Just as the content of the curriculum and the approach to learning mathematics depends on the teaching and learning perspective taken, so does the use of resources. Teachers need to make choices that support understanding of the concept being taught. Resources can be divided into broad areas:

- structural and visual resources;
- real-life resources;
- modelling formats;
- multisensory resources.

All resources have strengths and weaknesses, are open to debate and are dependent on the teaching and learning perspective being taken. A useful and still valid summary of these debates is *Teaching and Learning Primary Numeracy: Policy, Practice and Effectiveness*, edited by Mike Askew and Margaret Brown (2001). It can be found on the British Educational Research Association (BERA) website and relates to a national seminar in 2000 in conjunction with the British Society for Research into the Teaching of Mathematics. The papers discuss the change in emphasis on ordinal rather than cardinal number in the Early Years and the timing of the introduction of place value and quantity value. Other relevant topics were concerned with the limited effect of ICT on standards in the long-term and the influence of teacher's beliefs on the practice used.

Structural and visual resources

The National Numeracy Strategy (DfEE, 1999) signalled a shift in how mathematics was taught in the primary school. Mental strategies became a dominant part of the numeracy agenda and there was a move away from the use of structural apparatus to visual images such as digit cards, number lines and 100 squares which supported children in developing visual images of the number system to aid mental calculation. This came at a time when an increasing number of visual resources became available on the Internet. Formerly, physical teaching aids had dominated the teaching of calculation. Their use was based upon the constructivist approach to representation attributed to Bruner (1966) as discussed in Chapter 5. There was the sense that children need initially to manipulate physical resources in order to understand notation and calculation processes. These physical resources involved physical representations of objects such as toy cars as well as teaching aids such as interlocking cubes. However, there has been increasing evidence that although children need to manipulate *ideas* to make connections between different representations, it is the way that teachers refer to such physical resources that encourages children to form mental images. Aubrey (cited in Thompson, 1997) found that 5-year-old children were able to find their own way of representing numbers. Thompson (1997) believes the issue is that children in this country are meant to record their calculations as a form of evidence of learning whereas calculations happen in the mind. Ginsberg, in his seminal work, believed that assimilating formal concepts into children's informal knowledge may often cause a problem for children because of the symbolic nature of calculation. According to Ginsberg (1977) there are three stages in understanding place value:

1. Writing the number correctly but being unable to explain why.
2. Recognising when a number has been written down incorrectly.
3. Understanding what each digit represents, a level not easily achieved during the primary years.

(abridged from Dickson et al.,1984)

This view is in sharp contrast to government guidance over the last 10–15 years, originating in the National Numeracy Project (1996) (Straker, 1999), whereby children are expected to understand what each digit represents from Year 1. There is another debate surrounding how notation should be represented in the teaching and learning process. Apparatus has been in use for many years. For centuries, throughout the world, calculations were made using an abacus, a frame with beads or balls on sticks. Although the abacus is still in use in parts of Asia today, the Hindu Arabic notation has replaced it largely as a result of commercial use. However, the abacus is a form of representation of numbers and the version based upon base 10 was still used to teach children about place value until the 1960s. Electronic versions are even available today. Other apparatus includes individual bricks or joined bricks to represent units, tens, hundreds and thousands. However, research by Cobb in the 1980s suggested that, as a form of representation, such apparatus does not support children's understanding of place value as a concept and only makes sense to those who have already grasped the concept (Cobb and Merkel, 1989). Place value by its very definition *is* a form of representation and a concept that needs to be understood. The question would seem to be whether you develop the concept of place value by considering other forms of representation or whether it is an 'imposed' concept to aid in calculation so should be learnt as a representation using the notation of the number system.

The aim of using mental imagery of the number system was that children would be able to calculate without always using an algorithm or set method based upon 3D teaching aids that represented the number system such as Dienes' equipment. Look at the example below.

$$\begin{array}{r} 99 \\ +38 \\ \hline 137 \\ \hline {}_1 \end{array}$$

Structural equipment *could* lead children to adding the units first and carrying a ten to add together with the other tens whereas 38 can easily be added to 100 to make 138 and adjusted by 1 as 99 is 1 less than 100.

The strength of physical representations lies in the opportunity they allow children to form appropriate images to support their understanding of a concept. Barmby et al. (2009) believe that if mathematics is to be in the mind it must be in some form, i.e. an image, symbol or language. How we represent an idea in mathematics is a key part of the process by which we develop an understanding of and give meaning to that idea (Barmby et al., 2). Teachers must consider what resource would best explain the concept that is being taught and learnt. Look back at the use of resources in the lesson plan on p. 129 in Chapter 6. If the concept was place value then a physical resource either in 3D or 2D form such as Dienes' material would be best as the aim is to make explicit the value of a numeral in a particular place. However, if the aim was to consider the value of a number then arrow cards would be a more appropriate resource. Another issue for consideration is how teaching aids represent real life. Barmby et al. (2009) advise that if Dienes' apparatus is used, then it should be explained as representing real objects that come in tens and hundreds to bridge the gap between the abstract and the real such as sections of chocolate, particularly with young children.

Arrow cards are rectangular cards which are narrowed at the right to form an arrow shape. Each rectangle is divided into a square to denote a base 10 place. Thus 534 would be made from placing first a 500 card on top of which would be placed a 40 card and finally the top card denoting 4.

Dienes' apparatus is a form of structural apparatus which was available in bases 2–10. Base 10 apparatus includes unit cubes, 10 rods, 100 flats and 1,000 blocks. Such apparatus illustrates the relationship between each 'place'.

The difference between supporting children in developing their own images and those offered in teaching will be influenced partly by the prior knowledge each child brings to the interpretation of teaching but also by the level of flexibility in the use of a resource. Some resources are designed to be used flexibly, e.g. an empty number line. Others can give a false notion of an image by limiting images to prototypes. In measurement, use of resources such as real clocks and real money can enhance children's ability to transfer their knowledge to solve everyday problems.

Real-life resources

Bridging the gap between the real world and the classroom does not just mean going outside. Everyday representation of numerals, arrays, patterns and shapes through photographs can support children in relating mathematics to the outside world, particularly if it relates to 'their' world in terms of the school grounds or the local environment which could again connect with other curricular areas.

Gather examples of 'real' mathematical representations that could be used with children. For example, you could take photographs of different examples of the numerals 0–9, arrays of cakes in a baker's shop – the list is endless. As a development of the activity you could take a group of children with you to take their own photographs if possible.

Solving the mathematics that such an activity generates encourages children to think mathematically. The teacher's skill lies in enabling children rather than finding the solution for them. For example, if the children made a large cake as a group activity and decided on a way of distributing it that led to them finding half of a quarter, the solution would not come from working out $\frac{1}{2} \times \frac{1}{4}$ but practically – finding a quarter first and then halving it. Such experiences can support children in gaining a sense of calculating with fractions which they can then apply in other situations. Suppose children were told that 72 bottles of soft drinks had been donated to a sale in equal amounts of orange, lemon and lime flavours, half the lemon bottles had special stickers to denote they were to get an extra prize, and the children had to find how many prizes they would need. The task could be carried out by sharing out the bottles into groups although such a method would not be that practical. Different solutions could be found. The skill of the teacher would be to enable but not to lead. Teachers can provide support by questioning, building on the input of the children's suggestions or if necessary taking more direct involvement by suggesting what children would do if they had a much smaller number of bottles such as 12. Children may be able to 'see' the solution and then apply it to the larger numbers.

Simultaneous equations are normally part of the Key Stage 3 curriculum but arise quite naturally in mathematics. For example, on a visit to a museum a child may have £1.50 to spend. He wants to buy a pencil and a drink but is not sure if he has enough. One friend has bought three pencils and a drink which came to £1.80 and another has bought one pencil and two drinks and have cost £2.45.

What type of representations could you devise to support possible solutions without resorting to a standard simultaneous equation?

Just as real mathematics does not necessarily come in what could be considered age-appropriate levels nor do the numbers involved. Calculators support children finding solutions that could be too complex for them to work out. What is important is that knowing how to work out a solution, not necessarily always finding an exact solution. Such understanding relates to how memory is stored by the brain as discussed in Chapter 5.

Modelling formats

Models to structure children's thinking can support them to find solutions to problems. There are a wide range of such models available but they all basically relate to the model developed by Polya (1971) for classroom practice which has four basic steps.

1. Understand the nature of the problem.
2. Draw up a plan to solve the problem.
3. Try out the plan.
4. Monitor the outcome of the plan.

Forming generalisations is important in the development of problem-solving and hence in mathematical understanding. It is a process in which children apply the knowledge they have gained from specific problems by organising that information into a format to look for patterns. Such forms of representation can be in 3D such as cubes to represent numbers that give a visual pattern, or hand-drawn representations using grids or tables, or interactive resources that enable children to record their own patterns. For example, a child in Year 3 may be recording the results of adding on 9 on a hundred square starting from 0. This could lead the child to look for patterns in the digits of each highlighted number table to form a generalisation about any number that was a multiple of 9. Offering appropriate forms of representation is part of the teacher's role in supporting children to find effective forms of representation.

Multisensory resources

It is very easy to discount senses which relate to more than the written and spoken word but we frequently say *I see* what you mean, that I get *a feel* of something or that *I hear* what you are saying. Such a multisensory approach replicates the way mathematics is used on an everyday basis such as in buying goods, following a recipe, decorating a home or appreciating art. Learning through the senses helps form mental images which support understanding and memory, particularly with young children. As well as seeing mathematics in representations, feeling familiar objects to match with a memory of the object and clapping numbers and rhythm can support children's developing mental imagery of number.

Learning

Just as it is easy to dismiss the teacher in discussing resources so the learner can be overlooked. As we develop ideas about the world in which we live, so we develop personal meanings. Our understanding is based upon experiences. The greater the representations of an idea the more scope there is to develop understanding. Of course this may lead to initial confusion as new representations do not fit into our prior experience. Not only are children a resource in the sense of their experience, neurological research suggests we are all born with a cardinal sense of number (Butterworth, 1999).Such ideas echo the thinking of Loris Malaguzzi, instigator of the Reggio Emilia system of early education. Children are seen as possessing many resources at birth, including the means to build up their own thought processes. Such an approach resonates with ideas of child-centred education and building on a child's prior experience.

Another aspect of children as resources is their role in teaching. A Victorian classroom relied heavily upon children for teaching purposes. The teacher taught the more able children who then taught groups of children. Today there are versions of this practice in the form of peer tutoring and mixed-ability grouping. Such initiatives support practices advocated by Boaler (2009) that were discussed in Chapter 1 in terms of resisting labelling children by attainment and engaging them actively in learning. Opportunities for collaborative learning in the constructivist tradition have been opened up by ICT which enables children to interact with the technology and with each other. Inevitably technology will change the relationship between and hence role of the teacher and learner, allowing children to exert more choice over how they approach learning. Technology has the power to adapt knowledge to make it accessible to learners whether it be simply to increase the size of a font or to find interactive resources that are sufficiently flexible that they can be tailored to the specific learning need of a child.

Summary

This chapter has considered resources of teaching and learning and their role in representation, an implicit element in the nature of mathematics. The role of the teacher as a fundamental resource has been emphasised including their unique position in providing a resource-rich environment for learning to take place. The resources learners bring with them in both a teaching and a learning capacity have been explored.

Conclusion

Resources are an integral element of teaching and learning mathematics. The influence of international data on changes to education in England has been discussed in previous chapters. The following chapter will consider international perspectives in teaching and learning mathematics in more detail by considering the range of sources of evidence and the importance of viewing the evidence in the context from which it has arisen.

Review questions

This chapter has raised a number of issues concerning decisions you need to make in your choice of resources:

1. What strategies do you need to employ to become an inspiring mathematics teacher?
2. How can you create a mathematically resource-rich environment?
3. How will you support other adults in the classroom?

4. What factors can support you in identifying the appropriateness of a resource?
5. How will you select ICT to support (a) your teaching and (b) children's learning?
6. How will you make use of the experiences that children bring to learning mathematics?

References

Anghileri J, (2000) *Teaching Number Sense*. London: Continuum.

Askew, M. and Brown, M. (2001) *Teaching and Learning Primary Numeracy: Policy, Practice and Effectiveness*. Southwell: BERA.

Askew, M., Hodgen, J., Hossain, S. and Bretscher, N. (2010) 'Are Poor Quality Maths Textbooks Letting English Pupils Down?' Available online at: http://www.kcl.ac.uk/ (accessed 8 October 2011).

Barmby, P., Harries, T., Higgins, S. and Suggate, J. (2009) 'The array representation and primary children's understanding and reasoning in multiplication', *Educational Studies in Mathematics*, 70 (3): 217–41.

Boaler, J. (2009) *The Elephant in the Classroom. Helping Children Learn and Love Maths*. London: Souvenir Press.

Bruner, J. (1966) *Toward a Theory of Instruction*. Cambridge, MA: Harvard University Press.

Butterworth, B. (1999) *The Mathematical Brain*. London: Macmillan. Available online at: http://www.mathematicalbrain.com/ (accessed 8 October 2011).

Catling, S. (2006) 'Planning for learning outside the classroom', in J. Arthur, T. Grainger and D. Wray (eds), *Learning to Teach in the Primary School*. Abingdon: Routledge, pp. 159–78.

Cobb, P. and Merkel, G. (1989) 'Thinking strategies as an example of teaching arithmetic through problem solving', in P. Trafton (ed.), *New Directions for Elementary School Mathematics*. Reston, VA: National Council of Teachers of Mathematics.

Creativity, Culture and Education (2002) *Creative Partnerships*. Available online at: http://www.creative-partnerships.com/ (accessed 1 March 2012).

DCSF (2008) *Practice Guidance for the Early Years Foundation Stage*. Nottingham: DCSF.

DfEE (1999) *National Numeracy Strategy: Framework for Teaching Mathematics from Reception to Year 6*. London: DfEE.

DfES (2003) *Excellence and Enjoyment: A National Strategy for Primary Schools*. London: DfES.

DfES (2006) *Learning Outside the Classroom Manifesto*. London: DfES.

Dickson, L., Brown, M. and Gibson, O. (1984) *Children Learning Mathematics*. Eastbourne: Holt.

Ginsberg, H. P. (1977a) 'The psychology of arithmetic thinking', *Journal of Children's Mathematical Behavior*, 1 (4): 1–90.

Ginsberg, H. P. (1977b) *Children's Arithmetic: The Learning Process*. New York: Van Nostrand.

Gray, E. (1991) 'The primary mathematics textbook, intermediary in the cycle of change', in D. Pimm and E. Love (eds), *Teaching and Learning School Mathematics*. London: Hodder & Stoughton, pp. 122–36.

Harries, T. and Spooner, M. (2000) *Mental Mathematics for the Numeracy Hour*. London: David Fulton.

National Advisory Committee on Creative and Cultural Education, Department for Education and Employment and Department for Culture, Media and Sport (1999) *All Our Futures: Creativity, Culture and Education* (Robinson Report). London: DfEE.

OECD (2009) *Annual Report*. Online: http://www.oecd.org (accessed 8 October 2011).

Ofsted (1999) *Primary Education: A Review of Primary Education*. London: HMSO.

Ofsted (2002) *The Curriculum in Successful Primary Schools*, HMI 553. London: Ofsted.

Ofsted (2005) *The National Literacy and Numeracy Strategies and the Primary Curriculum*, HMI 2395. London: Ofsted.

Ofsted (2009) *Mathematics: Understanding the Score – Improving Practice in Mathematics*. Available online at: http://www.ofstcd.gov.uk (accessed 8 October 2011).

Ofsted (2010) *Workforce Reform in Schools: Has It Made a Difference?* Available online at: http://www.ofsted.gov.uk/publications/ (accessed 8 October 2011).

Polya, G. (1971) *How to Solve It. A New Aspect of Mathematical Method*, 2nd edn. Princeton, NJ: Princeton University Press.

Straker, A. (1999) 'The National Numeracy Project: 1996–99', in I. Thompson (ed.), *Issues in Teaching Numeracy in Primary Schools*. Buckingham: Open University Press, pp. 39–48.

Thompson, I. (1997) *Teaching and Learning Early Number*. Maidenhead: Open University Press.

Thornton, L. and Brunton, P. (2010) *Bringing the Reggio Approach to Your Early Years Practice*. Abingdon: Routledge.

Topping, K. J. and Bamford, J. (1998a) *The Paired Maths Handbook: Parental Involvement and Peer Tutoring in Mathematics*. London: David Fulton.

Websites

BBC Learning: http://www.bbc.co.uk/learning/teachers (accessed 8 October 2011).

Be A Mathematician (BEAM): http://www.beam.co.uk/ (accessed 8 October 2011).

The Brickish Association (Lego): http://www.brickish.org/ (accessed 8 October 2011).

National Centre for Excellence in Teaching Mathematics (NCETM): http://www.
ncetm.org.uk/ (accessed 8 October 2011).
NRICH: http://nrich.maths.org/ (accessed 8 October 2011).
Primary Resources: http://www.primaryresources.co.uk/ (accessed 8 October
2011).

Further reading

Cunningham, K. (2007) 'The environment and the outdoor classroom as a
mathematical resource', in D. Drews and A. Hansen (eds), *Using Resources to
Support Mathematical Thinking*. Exeter: Learning Matters.

Drews, D. and Hansen, A. (eds) (2007) *Using Resources to Support Mathematical
Thinking*. Exeter: Learning Matters.

Fabian, H. (2005) 'Outdoor learning environments – easing the transition from the
Foundation Stage to Key Stage 1', *Education 3–13: The Professional Journal for
Primary Education*, 33 (2): 4–8.

Fox, B., Montague-Smith, A. and Wilkes, S. (2001) *Using ICT in Primary
Mathematics – Practice and Possibilities*. London: David Fulton.

Hansen, A. (2005) *Children's Errors in Mathematics: Understanding Common
Misconceptions in Primary Schools*. Exeter: Learning Matters.

Headington, R. (1997) *Supporting Numeracy*. London: David Fulton.

Maynard, T. and Walters, J. (2007) 'Learning in the outdoor environment: a missed
opportunity?', *Early Years*, 27 (3): 255–64.

O'Brien, E. and Murray, R. (2005) *A Marvellous Opportunity for Children to Learn:
A Participatory Evaluation of Forest Schools in England and Wales*. Surrey:
Forest Research.

Pound, L. and Lee, T. (2011) *Teaching Mathematics Creatively*. Abingdon:
Routledge.

Skemp, R. (1991) *Mathematics in the Primary School*. London: Taylor & Francis.

Thompson, I. (2008) *Teaching and Learning Early Number*. Buckingham: Open
University Press.

Thornton, L. and Brunton, P. (2010) *Bringing the Reggio Approach to Your Early
Years Practice*. Abingdon: Routledge.

Waite, S. (2007) 'Memories are made of this: some reflections on outdoor learning
and recall', *Education 3–13*, 35 (4): 333–47.

CHAPTER 8

WHAT CAN WE LEARN FROM OTHER COUNTRIES?

Aims

By the end of this chapter you should:

- have an awareness of sources of comparative information that support the development of effective teaching and learning in mathematics;
- be aware of international measures of mathematics education and the effect on government policy;
- understand the relationship between global perspectives and teaching and learning mathematics within the school context;
- have knowledge of how international data on mathematics education can inform debate on educational change.

Introduction

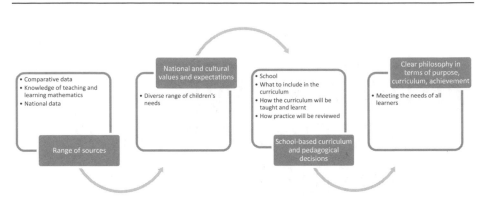

Comparative education is the study of educational theory, systems and practice in different countries and the historical, cultural, social, political and economic dimensions in which it has evolved and is being shaped. Apart from being a field of study in its own right, at one time comparative education was an element of teacher education programmes. Today, it is more likely to be studied at postgraduate level. In recent years there has been more focus on using comparative data from assessments of children to identify best practice in terms of learning outcomes. Different systems and practices are examined to identify their strengths and weaknesses with the purpose of supporting the improvement of education on a worldwide basis. Instigating change in one country based on practice in another is implicitly problematic as systems and practice do not operate in a vacuum. However, comparative study can help broaden perspectives by identifying alternatives to current practice.

This chapter will consider a range of sources of comparative information and the efficacy of its use in informing education policy to improve teaching and learning in mathematics. It will explore the decisions required in planning a framework and consider the juxtaposition of global data with individual, national and cultural perspectives.

International evidence of practice

There are many evidence-based sources of information. One that has already been cited is the Best Evidence Encyclopaedia UK (BEE UK) maintained by the Institute for Effective Education (IEE). It is based at the University of York with the aim of evaluating and disseminating evidence-based education programmes (see: http://www.bestevidence.org.uk).

Look at the Best Evidence web page (http://www.bestevidence.org.uk) and follow the links for primary mathematics (http://www.bestevidence. org.uk/reviews/primary_maths/index.html) and then follow the link for key findings (http://www.bestevidence.org.uk/reviews/primary_maths/ findings.html) under 'What works in teaching maths?'.

How do the findings reflect your experience? Record your response in your learning journal.

The National Foundation for Educational Research (NFER) (http://www. nfer.ac.uk) was founded in 1946 as a centre for educational research and development in England and Wales. The work of NFER includes educational research, the evaluation of education and training programmes, and the development of assessments and specialist information services, for example it is a repository for international assessments and analysis such as the Programme for International Student Assessment (PISA) and Trends in International Mathematics and Science Study (TIMSS). NFER is also involved with:

- EURYDICE at NFER (http://www.nfer.ac.uk/eurydice) is the website for the unit for England, Wales and Northern Ireland in the European Commission information network on education. It provides comparative information on education systems and policies in Europe.
- The International Review of Curriculum and Assessment (INCA) website (http://www.inca.org.uk/) provides descriptions of government policy on education in a range of countries. It focuses on curriculum, assessment and initial teacher education.

Select a country, subject and age phase on the INCA website (http://www.inca.org.uk). Other than for general interest, how could you use this information effectively in your professional role? Here are some ideas to act as prompts:

- To support any research you are undertaking
- To find out more about reports on educational practice in the media

National governments in English-speaking countries (as well as those in which you may be fluent in the language) can be a source to prompt discussion of current practice. For example, the webpage http://www. deewr.gov.au for the Department of Education, Employment and Workplace Relations in Australia enables access to policies and guidance on Early Childhood and Schooling such as the Early Years Learning Framework, an equivalent to the EYFS.

Further information on publications and literature is given at the end of this chapter.

Significance of comparative data

One of the main reasons given for national changes in the teaching curriculum in the last 15 years has been concerns that England compares unfavourably in international league tables (DfEE, 1999; DfES, 2006; DfE, 2010). Analysis by both the NFER (2010) and Askew et al. (2010) suggests this is not an accurate assessment but the fact that such claims are being made means comparative data cannot be ignored. The study that is cited frequently in current government debate is the PISA run by the Organisation for Economic and Cooperative Development (OECD). Recent events in the global market have shown that the economies of nations have become inextricably linked and that individual national policies can influence those of other nations.

The relevance of global markets may seem far removed from the teaching and learning of mathematics within a school, yet this global dimension is becoming increasingly apparent in national policy-making, as is evident in the document *A World-Class Mathematics Education for All Our Young People* (Vorderman et al., 2011) from the task force commissioned in 2009 by David Cameron and Michael Gove and published in summer 2011. It concluded that urgent action should be taken as financial numeracy is important both for individuals and for the economy. One way to relate global markets to practice in school is to consider the influences on a child's environment.

Bronfenbrenner (1989) developed the ecological systems theory identifying four levels of influence upon the individual as illustrated in this simple model based on his work:

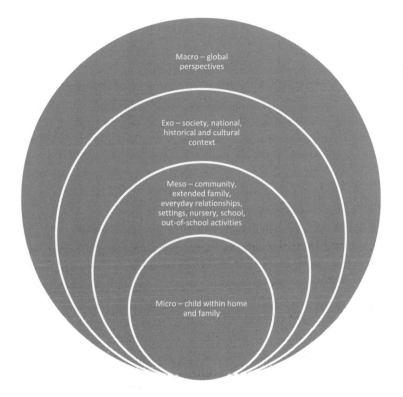

Using the ideas of Bronfenbrenner, the diagram illustrates how government recommendations based on international data could be interpreted as having a direct impact upon the child in school.

The Organisation for Economic Cooperation and Development (OECD) is an international economic research and discussion organisation based in Paris with the purpose of using 'its wealth of information on a broad range of topics to help governments foster prosperity and fight poverty through economic growth and financial stability' with a goal to 'build a stronger, cleaner, fairer world' (OECD, 2011). The OECD has evolved from the Organisation for European Economic Cooperation which was established after the Second World War to coordinate aid under the Marshall Plan intended to help European economic reconstruction. There are 34 member countries which include both developed and emerging economies. The OECD also works closely with strong emerging and developing economies and membership is increasing.

The PISA and TIMSS studies are available online and are published in England on the National Foundation for Educational Research (NFER) website (http://www.nfer.ac.uk) under International Studies. Information is given on PISA 2012 and reports for each country in the United Kingdom are available via the search engine. A report on the United Kingdom entitled *Viewing the United Kingdom Through the Prism of PISA* is available on the OECD site (http://www.oecd.org). Information on TIMSS 2011 is available as well as the 2007 report for England.

As each country within the UK is treated individually ranking can be confusing as analysis relates to individual countries *and* to the UK as a whole.

*Notes at the end of the article explain why there are concerns about sampling in the UK in 2000 and 2003 which is why data from these years is not in the PISA analysis.

The PISA study

The OECD Programme for International Student Assessment (PISA) is an internationally standardised assessment that was jointly developed by participating economies and administered to 15-year-olds in schools (OECD, 2010a). Although organised through the OECD, the test design, implementation and data analysis is delegated to an international consortium of research and educational institutions led by the Australian Council for Educational Research (ACER). ACER runs the development and execution of sampling procedures and helps with checking sampling outcomes. Countries and partnership economies outside the OECD are also included in the study.

The study has taken place since 2000 and tests reading, mathematics and science every three years on a rolling programme, with a focus on one area although the other two are tested as well. Four assessments have so far been carried out in 2000, 2003, 2006 and 2009. Every period of assessment focuses on one of the three areas: reading, mathematics or science. After nine years, a full cycle is completed. Reading was again the focus in 2009, the last available assessment.

In 2000 the UK was placed eighth in the PISA test when 43 countries participated. In 2006, when 57 countries participated, England was ranked 24th and in 2009, when 65 participated, England was ranked 28th. The highest performing region across all the tests is Shanghai–China, followed by Korea and then Finland. The results for England indicated that mathematics had fallen as well as reading and science. The difference *could* be attributed to the implementation of the National Strategies. For example, in 2000, when England came eighth internationally in the PISA, the students aged 15 would not have been affected by government initiatives. However, English cohorts of children who participated in the 2009 PISA and 2007 grade 8 TIMSS would have been approximately aged 4 and 5 respectively when the NNS was launched and so were likely to have been taught in the manner the strategy advocated. Does this mean that the NNS supported children more in content- rather than context-based questions and, if so, does this mean that a more problem-solving approach was more common prior to the introduction of the NNS which supported children in the PISA 2000?

Of course it is not possible to draw such direct conclusions as other factors come into play. The results have to be interpreted in the light of the facts that the PISA 2000 sample in England could have skewed the results favourably, that the number of participants increased in PISA 2009 and that high performers, Shanghai–China and Singapore took part for the first time. Additionally, although the ranking for mathematics was 22nd, this is an estimate and the ranking could fall between 17 and 25 (OECD, 2010b). The analysis by Ruddock et al. (2006) of PISA 2000 and 2003 and TIMSS 2003 found that English students were not favoured or disadvantaged by either PISA or TIMSS but one key difference was that the PISA mathematics assessment required significantly more reading.

However, the data from PISA reveals more than test scores and ranking. It gives a range of material that includes information for contextualising and so interpreting the results such as learning strategies deployed, the learning environment, school organisation, resources and arrangements for assessment and accountability.

Look at the summary in the National Reports on the NFER and OECD websites. What are the key points that you take from this analysis? Ideally work with colleagues and identify a focus and how it relates to your school or your experience in schools. For example, how do schools manage diversity? Does this resonate with your findings? Why do you believe this may be so? What type of action could offer solutions in your school?

The TIMSS

Another study similar to the PISA in terms of its international engagement is the Trends in International Mathematics and Science Study (TIMSS) study. Like the PISA study, the TIMSS study is worldwide. The TIMSS, as its name suggests, provides data about trends in mathematics and science achievement. It assesses the knowledge and skills of children aged 9–10 and 13–14. It also gives data on background information about the quantity, quality and content of teaching which can be used to make comparisons between participating countries. TIMSS 2007 involved approximately 425,000 pupils in 59 countries around the world. Two UK countries, England and Scotland, participated in TIMSS 2007. It takes place every four years; the most recent results are for 2007 but the 2011 results will be published shortly.

Look at the TIMSS 2007 assessment information on the NFER website in relation to mathematics. What differences and similarities do you find between the PISA and TIMSS studies? You may want to look at the differences between the information gathered such as how each test assesses mathematics or how each relates to the curriculum, or look at the similarities and differences in analysis that relate to a particular school focus such as gender differences in attainment or enjoyment levels. As the reports are long and detailed it is useful to choose a focus. Ideally, work with colleagues and share the information you gather.

TIMSS 2007 – overview – England

	TIMSS 2007	
	Year 5	**Year 9**
Ranking	5th after Chinese Taipei, Korea, Singapore, Hong Kong	6th after Chinese Taipei, Korea, Singapore, Hong Kong and Japan

PISA 2009 – overview – England

	Year 10	Notes
Ranking	20th* * England has maintained its position relative to the OECD average. Shanghai–China and Singapore did not participate in PISA 2006, and their high performance in 2009 has increased the number of countries with scores significantly higher than England's from 18 in 2006 to 20 in 2009.	England's performance in mathematics was not significantly different from the OECD average. Compared to results in 2006, proportion of low achievers changed little but that of high achievers decreased. Boys in both years score higher than girls and gap has increased. In 2009, as in 2006, boys scored significantly higher than girls. It appears that the gender gap in England has increased slightly between the two PISA cycles.

Test content

The tables show ranking for England and it can be seen that the results are significantly different between PISA and TIMSS assessments. A similar pattern is found in many countries other than those around the Pacific Rim which do well in both PISA and TIMSS. In general terms, PISA tries to find how children apply their knowledge while TIMSS tries to find what they know. As such, the PISA project is concerned with how children make use of knowledge they gain from school in everyday situations whereas TIMSS is concerned with how the curriculum is taught and learned. It would seem that both perspectives could be judged as valid but the fact that PISA and TIMSS aim to assess different features of learning means it is reasonable to expect different findings from each. However, the fact that results across the two studies has led to significantly different rankings has given rise to much debate. An electronic search leads to a significant amount of literature. Catherine Wu, a research fellow in the Graduate School of Education at the University of Melbourne, has worked at ACER since 1992 and has close involvement in the TIMSS and the PISA studies in terms of mathematics and problem-solving, writing, test development and analysis. She compared the mathematics results for PISA and TIMSS 2003, a year when the tests coincided, and found the following:

- Variations between Western and Asian countries in terms of differential performance in the tests could be directly attributed to the types of items in each test. For example, application questions dominate PISA whereas TIMSS contains more context-free questions involving formal mathematics.
- The fact that the source language is English means that the structure and vocabulary used were not easily translatable into other languages. This can lead to Asian students misunderstanding questions.
- Western students perform better on everyday real-life questions where they bring knowledge from outside the classroom whereas Asian students rely on mathematics gained in the classroom. Wu noted, however, that an almost exclusive emphasis on real life is likely to lower mathematics content and so not reflect all the content taught which may affect its future use by students.

(Wu, 2009)

Svein Sjoberg, a professor of science education at Oslo University, has raised some concerns about the cultural dimension to international testing. Test questions go through scrutiny with the aim of removing cultural bias but Sjoberg believes it may not be realistic to assess real-life mathematics skills by paper and pencil tests and, moreover, questions whether it is possible to depict real life in over sixty countries. He also notes the potential bias arising from the differences seen in the significance of the tests for children. In Taiwan, for example, success in the tests is seen as a source of national pride with the children being urged to do their best by teachers and parents alike. In countries where the tests have no significance in terms of the individual it is likely the motivation to do well will be limited (Sjoberg, 2007).

Significance of international assessments

Daniel McGrath is the PISA representative and Director of the International Activities Program at the National Center for Education in Washington. A document from the Center providing background information to interpret the TIMSS 2007 results with PISA and the National Assessment of Educational Progress (NAEP) concluded that the differences in the assessments made comparisons unhelpful but provided different 'lenses' by which to view and understand the US student performance (NAEP, 2004). However, the PISA project is not an academic exercise but one that is *meant* to produce results to influence policy-making. Although the PISA analysis takes an economic rather than an educational stance, economics are important in justifying the funding of education and so the PISA results are significant in devising policy. Additionally, the PISA results give plausible data to the media and public of the quality of education in terms of resources, teaching and outcomes (Sjoberg, 2007). It would appear that what is needed is to establish what the headlines mean.

It would seem that currently the PISA has supplanted the TIMSS as a source of evidence to support government policy. This may be because the last set of such results came from PISA and the TIMSS 2011 is yet to be published. The Coalition government is identifying the PISA rankings and results of 2009 as evidence for making change. The Schools White Paper, *The Importance of Teaching* (DfE, 2010) has set out an agenda to reform the school system. In December 2010, Michael Gove, Secretary of State for Education, stated:

> Today's PISA report underlines the urgent need to reform our school system. We need to learn from the best-performing countries. Other regions and nations have succeeded in closing the gap and in raising attainment for all students at the same time. They have made opportunity more equal, democratised access to knowledge and placed an uncompromising emphasis on higher standards at the same time. These regions and nations – from Alberta to Singapore, Finland to Hong Kong, Harlem to South Korea – should be our inspiration. (DfE, 2010)

This general statement leads into proposed policy that clearly takes its evidence base from the PISA 2009 report. The White Paper states:

> Drawing heavily on evidence from the world's best education systems, it [the White Paper] outlines how we will raise the prestige of the teaching profession, and how we will transform the quality of initial training and continuing professional development:

- Powers for teachers to improve discipline, and trialling a new approach to exclusions
- A vision for a transformed school curriculum supported by rigorous assessment and qualifications
- More academies and free schools and a strong strategic role for local authorities
- Changes to school performance tables, Ofsted inspections and governance
- A fairer funding system including a pupil premium to channel more money to the most deprived children
- School-led school improvement replacing top-down initiatives.

(DfE, 2010)

These changes also involve the training of teachers. The pamphlet entitled 'Teaching Schools' by the National College states:

> It is widely acknowledged that the quality of teaching and the quality of leadership are the most important factors in raising standards. Top performing systems around the world are focused on creating and supporting school improvement networks, spotting talent and growing teaching and leadership potential within and between schools, rather than through formal courses.

Examples of some initiatives such as school-led school improvement, channelling more money to deprived children and the introduction of 'teaching schools' can be seen as directly relating to the PISA analysis in the document *Viewing the United Kingdom School System Through the Prism of PISA* (OECD, 2010b: paras 25, 42 and 78). There are many other such examples that can be found by analysing the documents. However, evidence for the introduction of academies and free schools is somewhat tenuous once socio-economic background is accounted for, with public (i.e. state) schools outscoring privately managed schools by 20 points (para. 53).

Although it is not possible to always separate general government initiatives in order to view them in relation to primary education, let alone mathematics, one of the challenges in using data from the PISA is that it assesses only small, even insignificant, parts of curriculum coverage. As such it is questionable that it can give insight into what to include in a curriculum and guidance on teaching and learning across the whole curriculum.

The danger of using any evidence source to justify policy is that it can lead to selectivity. However, such selectivity must be seen in the context of other imperatives that must be juggled when deciding policy such as political will and funding.

There are other challenges in defining policy such as the dichotomy regarding assessment in schools. Is it possible to have 'a vision for a transformed school curriculum supported by rigorous assessment and qualifications' if the imposed assessment defines the school curriculum? As discussed in Chapter 6, assessment for learning is a strategy that has been widely used in recent years in the UK and USA and in England has been government-led in its implementation. Dylan Wiliam believes it has proven overall to be both effective in children's learning and cost-effective in comparison with increasing teachers' subject knowledge and reducing class size (Wiliam, cited in Boaler, 2009). However, Boaler, raises the issue that it is not possible to truly use such formative assessment when children are being prepared for SATs and such external accountability as they are in England (Boaler, 2009: 91). The challenge to schools, and particularly to those which gain more autonomy, will be devising a curriculum which supports both internally and externally devised strategies for assessment.

A way forward

Taking a fresh look at curriculum and teaching and learning approaches can be both invigorating and challenging for schools. Practice in other countries can enrich debate but, equally, too much information can be overwhelming. What is going to make any one school distinct from others nearby? It may be the role they wish to take in the school system or it may be influenced by the distinct approach to the curriculum and ways of teaching and learning.

School system

A review of comparative material usually encompasses sources relevant to a wide range of ages. At one level the age band is not relevant, as what happens in one age range affects another. However, it is useful to consider how countries organise their school system and whether each band has distinctive features. For example, most countries organise schooling with a pre-school phase of non-compulsory provision prior to a compulsory starting age between 4 and 7. Compulsory schooling is divided into two further phases equating to what would be called primary and secondary level in England, with post-compulsory education starting around 15–16. However, what makes each phase distinct is not clear. Does the role of each phase relate mainly to preparation for the next phase or has it specific characteristics related to a distinct purpose in terms of the curriculum and teaching and learning strategies. The EYFS is a distinct phase and has quite distinct guidance in teaching and learning but current curriculum documentation generally relates to National Curriculum areas of learning. Identifying whether to promote distinctive features in an age band is an important element in deciding the purpose of a curriculum. Comparative information can identify alternatives to be considered when planning how to organise the curriculum.

Using current comparative information in curriculum planning, teaching and learning

One of the challenges when instigating change is finding a range of material to support the full spectrum of debate, whether it be about textbooks, the gender gap or the use of ICT. In 2008 the Nuffield Foundation commissioned a team headed by Mike Askew from King's College to conduct a review of research literature on the features of mathematics education in those countries which perform well on international tests of mathematics attainment. They have produced a comprehensive review for the Nuffield Foundation of mathematics education in the high-performing countries of Finland and those from the Pacific Rim: China, Chinese Taipei (Taiwan), Hong Kong, Japan, Singapore and South Korea, with recommendations for England (Askew et al., 2010). The focus was evidence that gave insights into their high ranking. The results of this work led to a consideration of what constitutes and contributes towards high performance in mathematics learning. The report yields extensive information which is categorised into 14 broad themes relating to the interaction of children with mathematics in terms of their parents, teachers, lessons, textbooks and what is termed 'shadow education' – education taken as additional to school-based education.

The findings reveal some fascinating insights into what can contribute to high performance. Chapter 1 identifies a range of research that took place within the UK which considered the feelings of anxiety that mathematics can evoke and its negative effect upon performance (Buxton, 1981: Cockcroft, 1982; Williams, 2008; Jackson, 2008; Boaler, 2009; Haylock, 2010; Swan and Swain, 2010). This research could indicate that to become competent in mathematics it was important to develop confidence and enjoyment in the subject. However, the Nuffield research suggests that confidence and enjoyment were not necessarily prevalent emotions in those from high-performing countries. However, what was a key factor in higher performance was when curriculum content was closely matched to test expectations. This finding would suggest that caution needs to be taken when interpreting international results in different national contexts.

Two factors that have not received significant attention in this country are the use of textbooks and what is termed 'shadow' education, i.e. education such as private tutoring that supports education in school. It was found that textbook use was relatively low in England compared with other countries and that, when used, textbooks in England were not as well structured in terms of mathematical content as their counterparts in other countries and relied on routine examples. Although shadow education is evident in England, its use was much more prevalent in high-performing countries and was found to affect mathematics results positively, although it was also found to have adverse affects on social development. Textbook use and shadow education will be explored further in Chapter 9.

Recent research has identified the positive benefits of Early Years' education (Sylva, 2010) but the Nuffield findings suggest that such Early Years' education does not necessarily correlate to improved *mathematics* performance. Interestingly, it was also found that in countries with high performance in mathematics the gaps in attainment between different socio-economic backgrounds had not been reduced (Askew et al., 2010).

The implications of attitude, pre-school learning, textbooks, shadow education and managing diversity are clear areas for further investigation. One possibly surprising but fundamental finding was that high attainment may be '. . . more closely linked to cultural values than to specific mathematics teaching practices (Askew et al., 2010: 12). The fact that culture seems to have particular significance has led to the recommendation that further research is needed with culturally 'near neighbours' and schools that achieve high standards for all pupils (Askew et al., 2010: 47).

Askew et al. urge caution in embracing practices from higher-attaining countries in the hope they will lead to greater achievement here. They cite the example of raising teaching to a Masters profession, a goal that has been promoted by the government over the last five years based on the Finnish example. Teachers in Finland are indeed qualified at Masters level, but this is in the context of teaching in Finland being viewed as a high-status profession where there are strong levels of competition to enter teacher education. The fact that teachers are educated to Masters level and children reach high levels of attainment does not necessarily mean that if the same policy was adopted here, it would necessarily yield similar results as teaching does not have the same status in this country.

In conclusion Askew and the team felt that no country had the answer to successful mathematics teaching, and even those that had high-ranking in the PISA did not see their position as satisfactory. Korea was given as an example, being concerned that high ranking was based too much on test preparation leading to less emphasis on investigation. Values are seen as particularly important in mathematics education yet different cultures have different beliefs in what these values are within a culture.

Summary

This chapter has considered the role of comparative information in promoting good practice. It has considered sources of information, how these relate to the formation of government policy and the positive as well as the potentially problematic consequences of such action.

Conclusion

Comparative education has become an increasingly significant in a world of mass communication. Cultural and economic perspectives have become inevitably more globalised. They challenge national boundaries, economic relationships and personal identities as well as fostering greater interdependence. Study of comparative education enables you, as a teacher, to understand issues from a different perspective and a different cultural, political and social context. It allows you to examine, evaluate and analyse your own culture and educational assumptions. For example, is education a benevolent agent of change or a mirror of society with its inherent inequalities? Do our educational practices maintain the status quo or are they agents of change for both the individual and society? On a personal level, the study of comparative education can raise your awareness that you are part of a global community.

Review questions

Look at the activities you have carried out in this chapter and identify the following

1. What sources of information did you find particularly informative?
2. How does it support your understanding of teaching mathematics?
3. How could you use this information in your role as (a) a student teacher, (b) as a classroom teacher and/or (c) in a management role?

References

Askew, M., Hodgen, J., Hossain, S. and Bretscher, N. (2010) *Values and Variables: Mathematics Education in High-Performing Countries*, Nuffield Foundation Report. Available online at: http://www.nuffieldfoundation.org.

Black, P. (2005) 'Formative assessment: views through different lenses', *Instructional Science*, 16 (2): 134.

Boaler, J. (2009) *The Elephant in the Classroom: Helping Children Learn and Love Maths*. London: Souvenir Press.

Bradshaw, J., Sturman, L., Vappula, H., Ager, R. and Wheater, R. (2007) *Achievement of 15-year-olds in England: PISA 2006 National Report*, OECD Programme for International Student Assessment. Slough: NFER.

Bronfenbrenner, U. (1989) 'Ecological systems theory', in R. Vasta (ed.) *Annals of Child Development*, Vol. 6. p. 187-249.

Buxton, J. (1981) *Do You Panic About Maths? Coping with Maths Anxiety*. London: Heinemann Educational.

Cockcroft, W. H. (1982) *Mathematics Counts: Report of the Committee of Inquiry into the Teaching of Mathematics in Schools under the Chairmanship of Dr W. H. Cockcroft*. London: HMSO. Available online at: http://www.educationengland. org.uk/index.html.

DfE (2010) *The Importance of Teaching: The Schools White Paper*. London: DfE Available online at: http://www.education.gov.uk/publications/standard/ publicationDetail/Page1/CM%207980#downloadableparts (accessed 14 March 2012).

DfEE (1999b) *The National Numeracy Strategy*. Sudbury: DfEE Publications.

DfES (2004) *Primary National Strategy: Primary Framework for Literacy and Numeracy*. Nottingham: DfES Publications.

DfES (2006) *Primary National Strategy: Primary Framework for Literacy and Mathematics*. Nottingham: DfES Publications.

Haylock, D. (2010) *Mathematics Explained for Primary Teachers*, 4th edn. London: Sage.

Jackson, E. (2008) 'Mathematics anxiety in student teachers', *Practitioner Research in Higher Education*, 2 (1): 36–42.

National Centre for Education Statistics (2004) *Comparing TIMSS with NAEP and PISA*. Available online at: http://nces.ed.gov/timss/pdf (accessed 10 October 2011).

National College (n.d.) *National Teaching Schools*. Available online at: http://www. nationalcollege.org.uk/teachingschools (accessed 6 March 2012).

NFER (2010) *PISA 2009: Achievements of 15 year olds in England*. Available online at: http://www.nfer.ac.uk/publications (accessed 15 October 2011).

OECD (2010a) *PISA 2009 Results: What Students Know and Can Do – Student Performance in Reading, Mathematics and Science*. Available online at: http:// www.oecd.org/edu/pisa/2009 (accessed 6 March 2012)

OECD (2010b) *Viewing the United Kingdom School System Through the Prism of PISA*. Available online at: http://www.oecd.org/dataoecd/33/8/46624007.pdf (accessed 15 October 2011).

OECD (2011) Home Page. Available online at: http://www.oecd.org/ (accessed 15 October 2011).

Perie, M., Moran, R. and Lutkus, A.D., NAEP (2004) *Trends in Academic Progress: Three Decades of Student Achievement in Reading and Mathematics* (Washington, DC: US Department of Education, Institute of Education Services, National Center for Education Statistics, 2005. Available online at: http://nces-ed. gov/nationsreportcard/ltt/results2004/.

Ruddock, G., Clausen-May, T., Purple, C. and Ager, R. (2006) *Validation Study of the International PISA 2000, PISA 2003 and TIMSS 2003 Studies of Pupil Attainment*. London: NFER.

Sjoberg, S. (2007) *PISA and 'Real Life Challenges': Mission Impossible?* Available online at: http://folk.uio.no/sveinsj/Sjoberg-PISA-book-2007.pdf (accessed 6 March 2012).

Swan, M. and Swain J. (2010) 'The impact of a professional development programme on the practices and beliefs of numeracy teachers', *Journal of Further and Higher Education*, 34 (2): 165–77.

Sylva, K. (2010) *Early Childhood Matters: Evidence from the Effective Pre-school and Primary Education Project*. London: Routledge.

Vorderman, C., Budd, C., Dunne, R., Hart, M. and Porkess, R. (2011) *A World-Class Mathematics Education for All Our Young People*. DfE. Available online at: http://www.conservatives.com/News/News_stories/2011/08/~/media/Files/ Downloadable%20Files/Vorderman%20maths%20report.ashx (accessed 16 November 2011).

Williams, Sir P. (2008) *Mathematics Teaching in Early Years Setting and Primary Schools*. London: DCFS. Available online at: http://dera.ioe.ac.uk/8365/1/ Williams%20Mathematics.pdf (accessed 7 March 2012).

Wu, M. L. (2009) *A Critical Comparison of the Contents of PISA and TIMSS Mathematics Assessments*. Available online at: https://edsurveys.rti.org/PISA (accessed 15 October 2011).

Websites

Australian Council for Educational Research: http://www.acer.edu.au/ (accessed 10 October 2011).

Australian Government, Department of Education, Employment and Workplace Relations: http://www.deewr.gov.au/Pages/default.aspx (accessed 15 October 2011).

Best Evidence Encyclopaedia UK (BEE UK): http://www.bestevidence.org.uk.

Cambridge Primary Review: http://www.primaryreview.org.uk (accessed on 15 October 2011).

Information on Education Systems and Policies in Europe (EURYDICE): http:// eacea.ec.europa.eu/education/eurydice/index_en.php (accessed 15th October 2011).

International Review of Curriculum and Assessment: http://www.inca.org.uk (accessed 15 October 2011).

National Foundation for Educational Research: http://www.nfer.ac.uk (accessed 15 October 2011).

OECD: http://www.oecd.org.

Programme for International Student Assessment (PISA): http://www.pisa.oecd.org (accessed 20 October 2011).

Further reading

Black, P. J. and Wiliam, D. (1998a) 'Assessment and classroom learning', *Assessment in Education*, March, pp. 7–74.

Boaler, J. (2000) *Multiple Perspectives on Mathematics Teaching and Learning (International Perspectives on Mathematics Education)*. Westport, CT: Ablex.

Bray, M., Adamson, B. and Mason, M. (eds) (2007) *Comparative Education Research: Approaches and Methods*, CERC Studies in Comparative Education 19. New York: Springer. Available online at: http://jri.sagepub.com/content/8/2/228.

CHAPTER 9

RESEARCHING MATHEMATICS EDUCATION – A CASE STUDY

Aims

By the end of this chapter you should:

- be aware of how research can support the practice of teachers at any stage in their career;
- become aware of how to implement research;
- consider research to undertake to support your understanding of teaching and learning mathematics.

Map of Europe identifying Gambolò, Italy, Reggio Emilia, Italy, Malahide, Dublin and Jerez de la Frontera, Spain.

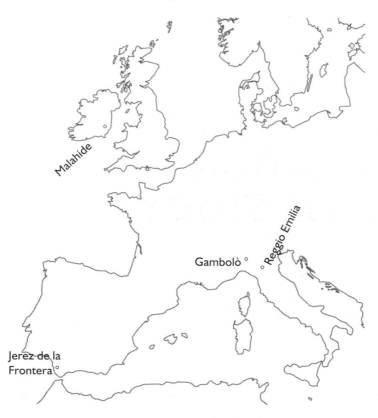

Introduction

The efficacy of reviewing comparative information to broaden national perspectives has been discussed Chapter 8. Apart from a national perspective, such a review can also be taken from a personal or school perspective. This chapter will consider a practical approach to gaining comparative information by reviewing the purpose of such research from the perspective of a teacher and identifying ways to start research. The discussion will be exemplified by research carried out by the author in Italy, the Republic of Ireland and Spain. It will be referred to as 'The European Research Study' (ERS). The structure for the model of research used is based on that given by Opie (2004).

Structure of Research Writing

Abstract
Introduction
Literature Review
Methodology and Procedures
Results
Analysis
Conclusion
Bibliography
Appendices

Adapted from Opie (2004: 49).

Educational research

Research is a systematic approach aimed at finding information by means of investigating sources and/or activities in order to collate original facts or establish new facts and draw conclusions. The purpose can be as straightforward as personal interest or as a means of identifying the best way to do something such as buying a car or a washing machine. Educational research has a more defined meaning. It generally implies finding information with the aim of improving practice or to act as an evidence base to inform a policy-making process. Research concerning the primary age phase will usually involve children who are 'vulnerable' in terms of not necessarily being able to make informed decisions about whether they wish to be observed or engaged in conversation. As a consequence, it will involve those who are 'gatekeepers' such as parents and teachers who control access to children. Making sure appropriate safeguards according to the values of honesty, confidentiality and respect are put in place is referred to as adhering to ethical guidelines. The British Educational Research Association (BERA) gives guidance in their document *Revised Ethical Guidelines for Educational Research* (BERA, 2011) about adhering to ethical guidelines and gaining ethical approval to carry out research. The process can support clarification of the purpose, specific aims and process of the proposed research.

Why do research?

Participating in research can enable the teacher to:

- *Become empowered*. The premise of this book is the possible disempowerment of teachers through increased intervention in what and how mathematics is taught at primary level. The process of engaging in research gives the opportunity to empower the individual teacher or group of teachers as it develops understanding and the confidence to engage in debate about practice (Brause and Mayher, 1991).
- *Take control of centralised intervention*. Research can enable teachers to take more control as well as adapt any centralised intervention at the school level (Hopkins, 1993).
- *Be professional*. As professionals, engaging in research enables teachers to strengthen their understanding of theory and practice and evaluate the research of others from a more knowledgeable point of view.
- *Justify classroom practice*. Research can provide the basis of a rationale to justify classroom practice to a variety of audiences, e.g. colleagues, tutors, parents.
- *Take on the role of a learner*. As discussed in Chapters 4 and 6, a good teacher is a good learner too and engaging in research can help in developing the ongoing process of learning. Taking the role of a learner helps the individual teacher to critically self-evaluate practice.

Beginning research

Purpose

In order to begin any research, a clear purpose is required. In the ERS the purpose was to explore alternative practices in terms of teacher training, curriculum design and pedagogy to illuminate practice in England with the overarching aim of finding alternative perspectives from which to review practice in England.

The basis of the literature review for the study came from the White Paper *The Importance of Teaching* (DfE, 2011) and the research by Askew et al. *Values and Variables: Mathematics Education in High-Performing Countries* (2010) but, as can be seen from the literature cited in previous chapters, there is a wide body of related evidence.

There could be a wide range of purposes for either a student teacher or a teacher employed in school but generally the purpose would be based upon:

- individual research – by reviewing practice to consider a specific teaching approach;
- identifying an objective in the school development plan or CPD work such as for the Mathematics Specialist Teacher programme and working individually or with colleagues, for example the development of counting across each age phase of the school. In an academy or free school the objective may be broader if the focus was a complete curriculum review.

Whatever the purpose, it should be justified by reference to school documentation, government and/or local authority documentation *and* a review of published literature.

Aims

Once the general purpose has been defined, clear aims should be identified in order that the research can be planned in terms of timescale, resourcing and logistical considerations.

In the case of the ERS the aims initially were to:

- identify a sample of European countries;
- identify key areas of research;
- identify contextual information for each chosen country in terms of key topics;
- explore the implementation of key areas of research.

Key areas of research

The areas of research have been based upon the content of previous chapters. When choosing such areas it is important to keep to those of concern yet be open to those that may explain what has been observed or stated. These areas can emerge in the data-gathering process.

Thus with the emphasis on mathematics the areas of concern were:

- international comparisons
- enjoyment of mathematics as a subject
- curriculum content
- teaching and learning strategies
- differentiation/SEN
- subject knowledge and teacher training
- assessment
- accountability
- resources.

Deciding the aims give rise to key actions that must be addressed – how the sample will be chosen and the relationship to limitations such as access, timing and resourcing. It could be at this point that the aims would need adjusting or refining to meet the inevitable limitations. In the case of the ERS there were limitations in terms of time and resources to spend in schools to develop contacts abroad.

It was decided that personal contacts would be used to facilitate access to schools. As teachers carrying out research, the use of personal contacts is a good means of gaining access to a setting that you believe will support the focus of your research. However, such use of contacts must be acknowledged as it may influence the outcomes of your research.

The decision to use personal contacts had two effects:

1. It identified the sample of countries and regions within those countries as Andalucía in Spain, County Dublin in the Republic of Ireland and Lombardy in Northern Italy. Such a sample is called convenience or opportunistic sampling. An illustration in a different context would be if it was decided to elicit the opinions of a group of people leaving a meeting by giving questionnaires only to those who left in the first ten minutes as this was the only time that the researcher had available. Of course, such a sampling technique cannot be said to be representative of all the people at the meeting, merely of those who left first, regardless of gender, age and other variables that may be relevant. Other types of sampling look at ways to represent the whole group from which the sample is taken.
2. Convenience sampling led to limiting the research to schools where access could be arranged within the given parameters of the required age phase. In this way 'case studies' emerged. Again this is a form of convenience sampling as it was at the convenience of or under the constraints imposed by those enabling access.

Research approach

Case study

Teachers may choose to carry out a case study or studies for different reasons. For example, the purpose may be to analyse a situation and identify interrelationships in that situation. The case or cases may be children and the focus could be to analyse the response to a specific teaching approach that was used. However, it would not be possible to generalise from such an approach: the data gathered is not reliable as it is unlikely that it could be reproduced, nor is it valid as it cannot be said to assess what it set out to do or how well it reflects what happened or was said.

Action research

Action research is a process that can be carried out by an individual or with colleagues, with the aim of improving practice in a familiar setting. The action could be related to the use of a resource or teaching approach in one classroom or across the school.

There are many other approaches to research but Opie (2004) suggests case studies and action research are the most 'doable' within the timescale associated with teaching programmes. Further research literature is given at the end of this chapter.

Research approach used for the ERS

The limitations imposed by the sample led to limitations in the research approach to be used. The sample had produced particular 'cases'. Case studies can be criticised as they cannot be used to establish reliability or generality of findings and can give rise to a biased interpretation of the issues. However, as the purpose of the research was an exploratory study of alternative practices to illuminate practice in England, a case study approach could be justified (Bassey, 1999). This situation may not always arise. The research approach could be identified first and then the sample decided.

Research procedures – gathering data

Once the sample and approach had been identified, contacts made and ethical protocols were in place, the process for gathering data was formulated. It may have been possible to collect all the data without arranging visits but two limitations prevented this course of action.

1. Although the key areas of interest had been identified, the value of case studies lies in the potential for illuminating practice beyond the bounds of the main focus. If the research was desk-based it would be less likely to elicit further explanatory information from participants. Additionally it would limit the methods for gathering data.
2. Language – the fact that research in two countries was dependent on the fluency of the participants and the support of translators meant that it would be unlikely that information could be elicited without supplementary questions 'in situ'.

It was concluded that contextual information on each country would be drawn from secondary electronic sources with a secure provenance and the primary research would come from semi-structured interviews and observation of classroom practice. Data can broadly be divided into two types: quantitative and qualitative. Quantitative data generally relates to large populations and is concerned with amounts and proportions as well as trends over an identified timescale. The INCA database, although extensive, is descriptive in content and could not be deemed to be quantitative. Qualitative data generally relates to small or medium-scale research with the purpose of searching for meanings and interpretations. As such, it was appropriate to the focus of the primary research.

As teachers are likely to be carrying out small-scale research, data will generally be qualitative in nature. However, the type of data does not dictate the data-gathering methods. For example, interviews could be used to gather both quantitative and qualitative data depending on the way in which they were designed and analysed. Teachers should evaluate a range of data-gathering methods before deciding the methods to be used.

As each country produced a different case, primary research varied in each setting. However, this was not considered an issue as the purpose was not to compare and contrast each case.

Gathering secondary data for the ERS

As discussed, contextual data for each country was gathered using secondary sources. The sources were the INCA and EURYDICE databases discussed in Chapter 8. As the provenance of the databases is transparent they can be deemed a reliable source of information. Such databases could be useful if research was to be carried out within the countries of the United Kingdom, such as Scotland.

It takes time to become familiar with such extensive information in electronic form and how it can be accessed. Look at the INCA and EURYDICE databases for Italy, the Republic of Ireland and Spain (see the websites at the end of the chapter). You will find that the organisation and detail of the information varies within and between each database for each country.

Write a short report on what you have found out.

Could you use it to compare and contrast the information with information on the English system of pre-primary education?

The databases can be seen to give the researcher useful background information which could be time-consuming to acquire in the individual country. It has the added advantage of being a stimulus to enable the researcher to formulate questions not previously considered, e.g. clarification of the process whereby textbooks are chosen by the Teachers' Assembly or what 'The freedom of teaching' principle means to teachers in Italy.

Obviously, there are limitations to such data. In the case of the ERS, the key focus is mathematics but very limited mathematics-specific data was found as the database related to the education system as a whole. Care needs to be taken over the accuracy of the information depending on the date given when information was made available.

Gathering primary data

Raw data is data that is collected directly from its source before it has been subjected to processing and interpretation. It has not been included in this chapter as the ERS is being used mainly to illustrate the value of research and, in this case, research of an exploratory nature. However, it is important to retain raw data as it can be used to corroborate findings and it can be used to illustrate discussion points.

Observations

Teachers usually understand two meanings of the word 'observation', the difference being whether the observation is 'of' or 'by' the teacher. If it is 'of' the teacher then it usually relates to some form of assessment and can evoke anxiety. However, if it is 'by' the teacher it is a learning experience, often associated with learning from the experience or expertise of a colleague. Even if the purpose of the observation is assessment of an experienced colleague, that colleague can gain personally from the process by examining and explaining their own practice in detail. When observation is used as part of a data-gathering exercise, then both interpretations of the word must be considered. If you are to observe either teachers or children it is a privilege and must be respected. In addition to the ethical protocols that should be in place, there should be empathy on the part of the researcher in terms of what it may feel like to be observed. This is particularly so of teachers. Equally, anything recorded from the observation should be shared by the observer with the observee; in fact such sharing of records can support later discussion of points noted. Prior to an observation taking place, thought needs to be given to how the observation is to be recorded. Filming classroom activity has the benefit of allowing the lesson to be viewed slowly so detail is not missed. This method of observation has become more viable in recent years with camcorder devices suitable for home use. It has the advantage of giving a continuous record of events. However, it has the disadvantage that ethical issues may restrict its use in terms of retaining the anonymity of those being filmed. Additionally it may heighten the effect of any observation in the way it can alter the behaviour of those being observed.

A simple method is to make a written record. It would be neither possible nor desirable to record everything that occurs in a lesson. Having a focus on a specific aspect of a teacher's practice enables the observer to maintain the purpose of the observation. There are many formats for recording written observations. Three common types are:

- *Narrative* – a continuous record of what occurs. The advantage is that it gives a full picture of what has occurred but the disadvantage is that it is time-consuming to record.
- *Prepared checklists/structured observation sheets* – these have the advantage of being quick to record but the disadvantage is that they give limited scope for recording the unexpected.
- *Time sampling* – involves making regular records of what occurs at specific intervals, for example every 5 minutes. It has the advantage of being quick to record but the disadvantage of not capturing what takes place between intervals.

A combination of written formats was used for the ERS. A checklist was devised identifying features such as resources used and child participation but space left for the inclusion of factors that emerged during the observation or required further information from the interviews and/or secondary research. Opposite is an example of an observation form.

Finally, in making observations, it is important to avoid making judgements, such as giving opinions about what is being seen and heard, as it can detract from observing accurately.

Semi-structured interviews

Semi-structured interviews have the advantage of enabling general views to be explored but by the same token care must be taken in making sure questions are not prescriptive or leading. Additionally, they allow for revision of the structure if ideas have arisen from other techniques for gathering data. An example is shown on page 191.

Example of an observation form

Date / time	Class / age / teacher
Tuesday, 5 April 2011, 8.30–9.30	*9–10 years*

Main curriculum subject focus	Key learning intentions for the lesson
Mathematics	*Calculating area of a regular rhombus*

Environment
Modern classroom with desks set out in twos in formal arrangement facing the teacher at the front

Focus of observation
Teaching and learning strategies

Children ready at the beginning with mathematics exercise books and textbooks and equipment. At the same time as the teacher gave brief instructions on how to complete the calculations, one child went around class with small pieces of paper containing 14 mental mathematics examples, the first one being solved to show what was required. The instruction at the top of the paper stated:

> Write the value of each digit as in the example. Pay attention to the zero
> $93.7m^2 \rightarrow 90m^2 + 3m^2 \rightarrow 70dm^2$
> $13.4 \, dm^2 \rightarrow$
> $0.9 \, dam^2 \rightarrow$

After approximately 10 minutes the children were told they should have finished. The examples were gone through by children volunteering the answer by raising a hand. There was a brief explanatory discussion when there were errors and then the children were told to write the date and stick the piece of paper in their exercise books. This activity was completed very quickly, children using personal glue sticks.

Children told to turn to lesson for the day in their textbooks. The textbook gave an introduction to finding the area of a shape. The teacher went through the 'lesson' with the aid of the textbook but she had her own lesson plan.

Despite appearing to be initially didactic, the lesson was very interactive. The teaching focus was eliciting information from the children by asking for ideas of how to find the area, proof, using previous knowledge, i.e. area of squares, perpendiculars, right angles, diagonals. At no time were the children told how to work out the area of the rhombus. If they gave an idea they had to say why. Although the learning outcome was the same for all children and it was hard to identify the level of differentiation – it appeared that some children who needed additional help were targeted with more detailed questions. Using the knowledge of the solution to the worked example, the same interactive technique was used to work out a formula using the diameters of the rhombus – D × d. The children were given a small 3 × 4 rhombus on squared paper to stick in their books. They drew in the diagonals and wrote their bisected lengths. They then made the 4 triangles into squares to show the method of proof and then wrote down the formula. The teacher then dictated the method of how to work out the area of a regular rhombus and they wrote it under their diagram. The lesson concluded with the children being directed back to the textbook and told to start the exercise of finding areas of rhombi which they were to complete for homework.

Reflection
The lesson was at quite a fast pace but when I went round the class all the children seemed to have completed the task. There was never silence but no one spoke over the teacher. Talk was more to do with borrowing rubbers or glue sticks. No issues of negative behaviour arose.

Further information needed on:
- the role of homework
- school equipment
- textbooks
- ICT
- class size
- teacher hours (teacher free to talk with me as her class were being taken by someone else).

Triangulation
It is useful to try to have more than one method for gathering data as it can strengthen its value if there is similarity in results from data gathered from different methods. This strategy is called triangulation.

Contextualisation
Contextualisation refers to the physical setting of the research. Although the studies are neither representative of a country or intended for comparison, it is useful to the reader to be able have some understanding of the context so as not to attribute issues raised by extraneous factors.

Discussion of ERS
The fact that the studies have been identified by convenience sampling means that the results can be biased so it is not appropriate to draw conclusions that can be said to represent any one country. The following discussion relates to data recorded in a variety of formats depending on the sources in each case study. However, as neither comparison nor generalisation is the purpose of the research, it is not seen as posing a problem.

Additionally, the fact that the researcher collected the data and interpreted the data can mean increased subjectivity even before the results are discussed. All the case studies are able to represent is an interpretation

Example of discussion with teachers

Table to show elicited themes from teaching observation and discussion		
Theme	**Description**	**Quotations**
GENERAL THEMES Curriculum and planning	The current curriculum was published in 2007. It places emphasis on the belief that educating cannot be reduced to knowledge and acquisition of skills with stress on the fact that the term educate comes from Latin *e-ducere*, get out: the child needs to be helped to discover the value of himself, and the reality of things. Education seen as: • delivering the cultural heritage; • preparing for the future; • helping to construct individual personality. There is particular emphasis on the family: 'no possibility that the school achieves its task of educating without sharing the family.' The family and society are seen as key assets in addition to economic resources. Mathematics emphasises problem-solving. The curriculum is broken into number, geometry, measurement and 'introduction to rational thought'. The document emphasises proof.	*Where does the curriculum come from?* *We have the little book which our planning is based on. We don't look at it that much but the textbooks are based on it so we know we cover it. We plan each subject for the year and then break it down in three-month cycles. Each week we meet to plan for two hours.* *Documents stress proof and discussion. How do you incorporate this into your teaching?* *Well maths is about proof – finding truth – you know the great mathematicians – that is what they did. Children must try to think like that.*
Teacher training	*Secondary data was supplemented by primary data through discussion and observation*	
School autonomy		
Use of data/external examinations		
Accountability		
Resources – school equipment/textbooks		
Teaching/learning theory		
EVOLVING THEMES	*These themes emerged through discussion or were identified during observation and later discussed.*	
The role of homework		
Differentiation/SEN		
Planning		
ICT		
Class size		
Teacher's role		

of regional and national policies. As such they act in an exploratory way to generate debate by giving an alternative perspective to that which is familiar.

Read through the synopsis of the ERS provided in Appendix 1 at the end of the book. It includes questions that may prompt consideration of practice in your school or schools where you have taught. How could such ideas support a school in developing policy?

Summary

This chapter has considered the practical aspects of engaging in research. It has demonstrated the elements of the process through a discussion of an exploratory research project carried out in three European countries.

Conclusion

As the aim of the study was to explore alternative practices to illuminate one's own, it is important to stress that the case studies cannot be taken as typical of either the region or country in which they took place. However, the findings of the ERS may have had resonance for you with topics you have encountered on your initial teaching programme and in school such as Early Years education, teacher training, working with parents, homework or assessment. For example, it may have alerted you to the significance of 'shadow education' in other countries, not a common term but its meaning will be known to you as denoting extra tuition outside the school context. Chapter 8 identified the value of teachers engaging in the study of comparative education. You may feel that this is not something you could undertake now by carrying out primary research but it will hopefully make you aware of the benefits of finding out about alternative practices of teachers working under different statutory regulation, particularly at a time when less centralised intervention in schools is indicated by our own government.

It is important to consider not just the content and findings of this study in relation to your role as a teacher but also the research practice discussed. If you were carrying out research as a student teacher on either a QTS or CPD programme it would be completed under the auspices of the awarding organisation and would be governed by the guidelines on good research practice of that organisation. It is unlikely that the research you carry out will be sponsored by outside bodies but you may find that your research as part of a CPD programme is sponsored by your school. Research sponsors cannot be prescriptive about individual approaches taken by researchers to solving particular research problems. However, sponsors can expect an awarding organisation to ensure that an adequate policy framework exists that promotes good research practice in terms of ethics, integrity, accountability and adherence to relevant legislation. If you do carry out research independently, then guidance can be found on the British Education Research Association (BERA) website (http://www.bera.ac.uk/).

Review questions

1. What research could you carry out as an individual or with colleagues?
2. Share ideas for possible contacts and how you could plan research required for your initial teaching programme or a personal or school-based objective.

References

Askew, M., Hodgen, J., Hossain, S. and Bretscher, N. (2010) *Values and Variables: Mathematics Education in High-Performing Countries*, Nuffield Foundation Report. Available online at: http://www.nuffieldfoundation.org (accessed 12 November 2011).

Bassey, M. (1999) *Case Study Research in Educational Settings*. Buckingham: Open University Press.

BERA (2011) *Revised Ethical Guidelines for Educational Research*. Southwell: BERA.

Brause, R. S. and Mayher, J. (eds) (1991) *Search and Research: What the Inquiring Teacher Needs to Know.* London: Falmer Press.

DfE (2010) *The Importance of Teaching: The Schools White Paper.* London: DfE. Available online at: http://www.education.gov.uk/publications/eorderingDownload/CM-7980.pdf (accessed 7 March 2012).

Hopkins, D. (1993) *A Teacher's Guide to Classroom Research*, 2nd edn. Milton Keynes: Open University Press.

Opie, C. (2004) *Doing Educational Research*. London: Sage.

Websites

Information on Education Systems and Policies in Europe (EURYDICE): http://eacea.ec.europa.eu/education/eurydice/index_en.php (accessed 15 October 2011).

International Review of Curriculum and Assessment (INCA): http://www.inca.org.uk (accessed 15 October 2011).

Further reading

Denscombe, M. (2010) *The Good Research Guide*, 4th edn. Buckingham: Open University Press.

Denzin, N. and Lincoln, Y. (2011) *Handbook of Qualitative Research*, 4th edn. Thousand Oaks: Sage.

Dowling, P. and Brown, A. (2009) *Doing Research, Reading Research*, 2nd edn. Abingdon: Routledge.

Flick, U. (2009) *An Introduction to Qualitative Research*, 4th edn. London: Sage.

Fraser, S., Lewis, V., Ding, S., Kellett, M. and Robinson, C. (2003) *Doing Research with Children and Young People*. London: Sage/Open University Press.

Ghaye, A. and Ghaye, K. (1998) *Teaching and Learning Through Critical Reflective Practice*. London: David Fulton.

Lewis, V., Kellett, M., Robinson, C., Fraser, S. and Ding, S. (2003) *The Reality of Research with Children and Young People*. London: Sage/Open University Press.

Macintyre, C. (2000) *The Art of Action Research in the Classroom*. London: David Fulton.

Silverman, D. (2010) *Doing Qualitative Research*, 3rd edn. London: Sage.

Comparative research

Bryant, P. and Nunes, I. (ed.) (1997) *Learning and Teaching: An International Perspective*. London: Taylor & Francis.

Italian education

Abbott, L. and Nutbrown, C. (2001) *Experiencing Reggio Emilia: Implications for Preschool Provision*. Buckingham: Open University Press.

Edwards, C., Gandini, L. and Forman, G. (eds) (1998) *Hundred Languages of Children*. London: Ablex.

Loris Malaguzzi International Centre (English language version): http://www.thewonderoflearning.com/about/malaguzzi/?lang=en (accessed 2 October 2011).

Ministero della Pubblica Istruzione (2007) *Indicazioni per il curricolo per la scuola dell'infanzia e per il primo ciclo d'istruzione.* Rome: Ministero della Pubblica Istruzione. Available online at: http://www.indire.it/indicazioni/templates/monitoraggio/dir_310707.pdf (accessed 24 October 2001).

Thornton, L. and Brunton, P. (2005) *Understanding the Reggio Approach.* David Fulton.

Spain

Curriculum documents.

Noticias Juridicicas: http://noticias.juridicas.com/base_datos/Admin/lo2-2006.html (accessed 20 October 2011).

Republic of Ireland

Curriculum documents.

National Council for Curriculum and Assessment (NCCA): http://www.curriculumonline.ie/en/Primary_School_Curriculum/ (accessed 20 November 2011).

Journals

Educational Action Research
British Educational Research Journal
Reflective Practice

Educational review

Sage Research Methods Online (SRMO) – available as e-books. Available online at: http://srmo.sagepub.com/ (accessed 6 March 2012).

CHAPTER 10

CONCLUSION

Aims

By the end of this chapter you should:

- be aware of the importance of creating a philosophical landscape in devising national curricula for education;
- be aware of the societal, personal and child-related factors that affect practice in the teaching of mathematics;
- understand the role of the teacher in meeting the evolving needs of society and the child within the bounds of mathematics;
- have a knowledge of strategies for self-empowerment.

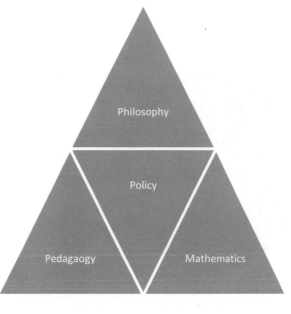

Introduction

There is an extensive body of research evidence available concerning curriculum changes in England in the Early Years and at primary level. Some evidence specifically concerns mathematics (Williams, 2008; Ofsted, 2009; Askew et al., 2010; Vorderman et al., 2011) while other evidence is more generic (Rose, 2009, Alexander, 2009, Tickell, 2011). Although there are those that would suggest that the situation is not as negative in international terms as has been indicated by government (Bradshaw et al., 2007) there is evidence that there is much to be done in to improve mathematical confidence and competence across the population. These recent reviews have indicated a number of evidence-based steps that can be taken. As with any process, teaching primary mathematics is underpinned by a range of philosophical, pedagogical and mathematical perspectives that can place differing emphasis on how that process is put in place. Difference in emphasis evolves from the roles of those involved:

- children and their families
- teachers and their schools
- governments and politicians representing the electorate and their advisers within an international and global perspective.

These groups have a vested interest in education and are commonly referred to in business jargon as 'stakeholders'. They will also have a multiplicity

Children and
their familes

Teachers and
their schools

Government –
politicians and
their advisers

Global
perspective

of roles. For example, politicians and teachers are often parents and they form a sub-group of the electorate. Such interests can present challenges as to who devises policy and the decisions that are made. However, if a model of education for the benefit of society is accepted, then we are all stakeholders, not just those who directly engage in the system. There have been significant challenges in making such ideals acceptable to all strata of society as well as making them viable. This chapter will consider these challenges set against emerging government policy.

Teaching primary mathematics

Philosophy

Philosophy is fundamental to education policy and is based upon beliefs that form principles which, in turn, are used to devise policy. As such, philosophy and pedagogy are intertwined. Mathematics education is just one element of education policy as a whole. Education policy emanates from government and, in recent years, government has taken a strong steer in how policy has been put into practice, a role formerly that was the province of teachers and schools. A challenge for any government and its people is whether the philosophy underpinning the provision of education is shared by all its stakeholders.

As discussed in Chapter 3 it is important to be clear about the purpose of education. The attitude of seeing education as of benefit to society has supported change just as it did in the later 1870s when factory workers were needed to have basic literacy and numeracy. Such views make a subtle move away from ideas of egalitarian principles of social cohesion to a more economic business model whereby investment in education needs to be seen as 'value for money' in terms of its benefits to society as a whole (Every Child a Chance Trust, 2009; OECD, 2010). Such thinking can lead to a business model approach devoid of philosophical principles.

Government perspective

Policy change is challenging for government. Government needs to ensure adequate funding to prepare children for the global marketplace and so make them capable citizens. However, political expediency fuelled by the media can overthrow policy and lead to a reduction in the explicit identification of research-based action. For example, investment in programmes like Sure Start Children's Centres for parents and children under statutory school age is neither designed nor likely to show significant benefits over the period of a government to justify the expense yet its efficacy is supported through a wide range of data (EURYDICE, 2009: OECD, 2010).

As governments change so do philosophies based upon political ideology. Although it is not possible to know the current Coalition government's educational philosophy explicitly as there have been no statutory changes to the National Curriculum at the time of writing (November 2011) interpretations can be made from the White Paper (DfE, 2010, online) and the Teachers' Standards (DfE, 2011). The current government has voiced the wish to return the decision-making process to schools and teachers by giving them more autonomy, with decentralisation and a less prescriptive curriculum, reduced roles for local councils and encouragement for new providers of schools in the form of free schools and academies. The challenge will be enabling teachers to make decisions that will not be directly influenced by prescriptive accountability systems.

Investment in education could be thought to be a mutually beneficial right for the individual and society yet challenges emerge as the philosophical stance taken on education may be fundamentally different. Basing policy on practice that has emerged from successful practice in other countries is potentially problematic as it does not necessarily represent the historical background and context from which policy has emerged. However, it would seem that government policy is in the process of evolving. The rhetoric of the early days of the current government about traditional values and academic rigour is being replaced by a range of reports and speeches that encompass research-informed evidence. For example, a speech given by Michael Gove, Secretary of State for Education, on 28 October 2011 referred to different perspectives on learning and advances in understanding learning through neurological research (Gove, 2011).

- How do you interpret the government's philosophy on mathematics education?
- How does it relate to your philosophy of mathematics education?

Teachers and their schools

Teachers and schools must convert policies into practice but in recent years there has been significant direction in how to practice in terms of teaching approaches, assessment and Ofsted inspection. As we have seen, Boaler (2009) believes that many of the problems in English classrooms stem from the level of accountability required by government and the labelling of children in terms of their mathematical attainment from an early age. Such structures can lead to a particular style of teaching which emphasises procedural knowledge rather than the conceptual, intuitive learning that encourages children to be active thinkers. Any school-based policy will have to receive the support of government, and parents should understand the changes and be able to see the value and tangible benefits of change.

Changing mathematics education is highly complex. As discussed in earlier chapters, it cannot be solved by generic ideas about teaching and learning but involves understanding and participation by all stakeholders. The teacher voice has been limited in terms of identifying philosophical beliefs about education and turning them into policy and practice. In order for that voice to be heard, teachers must regain their confidence and act in schools and within professional bodies to make sure that their perspective is taken into consideration along with the government agenda.

- Are you able to articulate your ideas about mathematics education to inform debate within your school?
- Can you support your ideas with reference to theory and practice based upon research evidence?

Children and their families

As has been outlined in Chapter 1 the philosophy behind statutory education has changed as society has evolved over the last 140 years in terms of greater social cohesion and an individual right to educational opportunity for personal development as well as that of society. The danger is that practice is put in place without developing a shared philosophy with parents, a significant group within society. Adults tend to understand and filter new initiatives through their own experience of the process which may be far removed from current practice. Although it is probably unlikely that groups other than parents and those actively interested in education will become involved, it is important that as many members of society as possible take responsibility for what happens within schools. Comparative data from such countries as Italy and Spain (EURYDICE, 2011) suggest that parents across all strata of society generally perceive their involvement more directly than their counterparts in England. Parent–teacher associations and governing bodies are the vehicles that are in place to allow such engagement. Sure Start Centres have shown that with the appropriate support more parents can develop the confidence and will to become involved in policy at a local level (Brodie, 2003).

- How can schools foster active parental engagement with policies that support mathematics education?
- How can a school enable parents to articulate a philosophy of education?
- How can parental anxiety about mathematics be supported by schools?
- How can schools support a positive image of mathematics with parents and children?

Mathematics – the curriculum of the future

Chapter 2 discussed the distinctive features of mathematics and considered a broad view of the subject. How a subject is perceived by a child will depend upon the interpretation given. Boaler (2009) believes that children are gaining a both narrow and unrealistic interpretation of the subject and this is affecting both their perception and competence in the subject. Politicians have been actively involved in obtaining advice about mathematics education in recent years. Although much has been written about the importance of mathematics and how it should be taught in recent reports, there has been less discussion about what should be included within the curriculum.

The Williams Review (2008)

In 2007, the Labour government of the time commissioned the report on Early Years and Primary mathematics teaching chaired by Sir Peter Williams, the current Chancellor of the University of Leicester. The report was wide-ranging but as its full title suggests the emphasis was on teaching rather than the curriculum and no significant changes to the mathematics curriculum were advocated.

Summary of recommendations of the Williams Review (2008)

Recommendation 1	When GCSE mathematics I and II are firmly established, the Government should review whether attainment of a minimum of grade C GCSE in both subjects should become a requirement for entry into ITT. For students who have taken or will take GCSEs before then, a grade C in single award mathematics should remain the requirement.
Recommendation 2	Local authorities should upskill their field force of mathematics consultants. The National Strategies, in partnership with the National Centre for Excellence in the Teaching of Mathematics, should develop 'refresher' CPD for all local authority mathematics consultants.
Recommendation 3	There should be at least one Mathematics Specialist in each primary school, in post within 10 years, with deep mathematical subject and pedagogical knowledge, making appropriate arrangements for small and rural schools. Implementation should commence in 2009 and be targeted initially to maximise impact on standards and to narrow attainment gaps.
Recommendation 4	That the DCSF commissions a set of materials on mathematical mark making and children's mathematical development which can be used to support early years practitioners' CPD.
Recommendation 5	That the forthcoming review of the EYFS in 2010 considers the inclusion of time and capacity within the early learning goals.

Recommendation 6	That the DCSF continues to increase the proportion of graduate practitioners in early years settings, recognising the respective contributions of the Qualified Teacher (QTS) and the Graduate Early Years Practitioner (graduate EYP). The review supports the goals which are currently in place.
Recommendation 7	Before any intervention programme is implemented, it is important that the child is committed to it and that the parents or carers are involved and understand the nature of the programme. These issues, and the question of the integration of intervention teaching and classroom teaching, should be considered in the development phase of Every Child Counts.
Recommendation 8	*Intervention* The programme for intensive wave 3 intervention in 'Every Child Counts' should be based on the following characteristics: (i) It should be led by a qualified teacher and should generally involve one child. (ii) However, the development phase of Every Child Counts should give adequate attention to assessing the benefits of small-group working, particularly in pairs. (iii) In assessing the child for intervention, the teacher with direct contact with the child must take the lead in shaping the decision to intervene; the use of video techniques in this and in training should be investigated further. (iv) Appropriate diagnostic tools should be developed to assist in assessment and in measuring progress on exit from intervention. (v) Intervention in mathematics should be complete by the end of Key Stage 1; where a child needs intervention in both literacy and numeracy, both must be given equal priority over the course of Key Stage 1. (vi) A wide range of multi-sensory resources should be available to enable the child and the intervention specialist to select those appropriate to the specific circumstances. (vii) CPD programmes should be developed for both the intervention specialist and the LA intervention teacher leader. (viii) Consideration should be given to combining the roles of intervention specialist and Mathematics Specialist, depending on the size and circumstances of the school. (ix) Less intensive wave 3 and wave 2 interventions could be led by appropriately trained Teaching Assistants; consideration should be given to the training required and the use of interventions, with a robust evidence base of impact on learning and progress. (x) A longitudinal study should be commissioned to assess the long-term benefits of intervention both at Key Stage 2 and, eventually, at GCSE level.

Recommendation 9	The Primary National Curriculum in Mathematics should continue as currently prescribed, subject to any changes which may result from Sir Jim Rose's forthcoming review of the Primary Curriculum; the latter should examine the concept of 'use and application' more generally across subjects to assess whether mathematical or other aspects of the curriculum need amendment.
Recommendation 10	This review recommends a renewed focus by practitioners on 'oral and mental mathematics'. Providers of ITT and CPD should ensure that this practice receives careful attention, both during ITT and in CPD programmes.

The Independent Review of the Primary Curriculum (Rose, 2009)

The Independent Review of the Primary Curriculum was commissioned by the Labour government in 2008 and chaired by Sir Jim Rose, a former director of Ofsted until 1999 and then a consultant to the government. Although the recommendations did not advocate significant content changes to the mathematics curriculum, it proposed that there should be more emphasis on problem-solving and cross-curricular work.

Recommendations of the Rose Report (2009)

Recommendation 1	A National Curriculum should be retained as a statutory entitlement for all children.
Recommendation 2	Consideration should be given to making the historically reactive response to curriculum review a proactive strategy whereby the EYFS and the statutory curriculum for primary and secondary schools are reviewed at agreed intervals as a whole, rather than as separate phases reviewed out of sequence. This would impose a discipline on the process of review such that schools could be assured of a period of stability in which to achieve agreed curricular goals.
Recommendation 3	The aims for a revised primary curriculum derived from the 2002 Education Act, the Children's Plan and Every Child Matters should be underpinned by a unified statement of values that is fit for all stages of statutory education. The aims and values established as part of the recent secondary curriculum review should be extended to the primary curriculum.
Recommendation 4	In preparing for a revised curriculum in 2011, the QCA should provide examples of how successful schools manage time in order to achieve a broad and balanced curriculum.

Recommendation 5	The content of the primary curriculum should be organised as it is now under knowledge, skills and understanding but structured as six areas of learning to enable children to benefit fully from high-quality subject teaching and equally challenging cross-curricular studies, and to improve the continuity of learning from the EYFS to Key Stage 3.
Recommendation 6	(i) To help primary schools sustain curricular continuity and secure pupils' progress from reception class to Year 7, the QCA should work closely with the National Strategies to assist schools to plan the new curriculum. (ii) Web-based guidance should be made available drawing upon the experience of that for the secondary curriculum. This should include refreshing the primary literacy and numeracy frameworks. (iii) In line with arrangements for implementing the new secondary curriculum, the DCSF should provide primary schools with one extra training day in 2010 to enable the workforce in each school to understand the new primary curriculum and start planning how it will work in their school.
Recommendation 7	The DCSF should commission a plain language guide to the curriculum for parents to help them understand how it will change to match children's developing abilities and how they can best support their children's learning at school.
Recommendation 8	(i) Literacy, numeracy and ICT should form the new core of the primary curriculum. (ii) Schools should continue to prioritise literacy, numeracy and ICT as the foundational knowledge, skills and understanding of the primary curriculum, the content of which should be clearly defined, taught discretely, and used and applied extensively in each area of learning. (iii) The DCSF expert group on assessment should give consideration to how the new core of literacy, numeracy and ICT should be assessed and these aspects of children's performance reported to parents.
Recommendation 9	Primary schools should make sure that children's spoken communication is developed intensively within all subjects and for learning across the curriculum. In so doing, schools should capitalise on the powerful contributions of the performing and visual arts, especially role play and drama.

Recommendation 10	(i)	Primary schools should continue to build on the commendable progress many have made in teaching decoding and encoding skills for reading and spelling through high-quality, systematic phonic work as advocated by the 2006 reading review as the prime approach for teaching beginner readers.
	(ii)	Similar priorities and principles should apply to numeracy in keeping with the recommendations of the Williams Review.
Recommendation 11	(i)	The two early learning goals for writing should be retained as valid, aspirational goals for the end of the EYFS.
	(ii)	The DCSF should consider producing additional guidance for practitioners on supporting children's early writing and should offer practical examples of how this can work.
Recommendation 12		The DCSF, working with the QCA and Becta, should consider what additional support teachers will need to meet the raised expectations of children's ICT capabilities and use of technology to enrich learning across the curriculum and set in train adequate support.
Recommendation 13	(i)	The QCA, in consultation with representative groups, should exemplify and promote the range of learning envisioned in the new framework for personal development with the firm intention of helping schools to plan for balanced coverage and avoid piecemeal treatment of this central aspect of the curriculum.
	(ii)	Personal development together with literacy, numeracy and ICT constitute the essentials for learning and life. The DCSF should work with the QCA to find appropriate and innovative ways of assessing pupils' progress in this area.
Recommendation 14	(i)	The preferred pattern of entry to reception classes should be the September immediately following a child's fourth birthday. However, this should be subject to well informed discussion with parents, taking into account their views of a child's maturity and readiness to enter reception class. Arrangements should be such as to make entry to reception class an exciting and enjoyable experience for all children, with opportunities for flexible arrangements such as a period of part-time attendance if judged appropriate.
	(ii)	The DCSF should provide information to parents and local authorities about the optimum conditions, flexibilities and benefits to children of entering reception class in the September immediately after their fourth birthday.

Recommendation 15	The QCA should make sure that guidance on the revised primary curriculum includes clear advice on how best to support those children who need to continue to work towards the early learning goals and build on the learning that has taken place in the EYFS.
Recommendation 16	What constitutes high-quality, play-based learning and how this benefits young children, especially those entering the early primary stage, should be made explicit in QCA guidance. Because parents, too, need to understand the importance of play, this guidance should be routed through schools to parents.
Recommendation 17	Key Stage 1 teachers should be involved in the moderation of Early Years Foundation Stage Profile (EYFSP) assessments within schools, to increase their understanding of the EYFSP and their confidence in the judgements of reception class teachers.
Recommendation 18	Major central initiatives, such as Assessment for Learning and Assessing Pupils' Progress, have huge potential for strengthening the transition of children from primary to secondary schools. The DCSF should develop these initiatives to keep pace with the fast-growing appetite in primary schools to take them on board.
Recommendation 19	With their local authorities, primary and secondary schools should agree a joint policy for bridging children's transition from Key Stage 2 to Key Stage 3. Five interdependent transition bridges are suggested for this purpose: administrative; social and personal; curriculum; pedagogy; and autonomy and managing learning. This should involve extended studies across Year 6 and Year 7, and draw upon the support of personal tutors.
Recommendation 20	When the National Strategies next review their materials they should look to further strengthen curricular continuity between Key Stage 2 and Key Stage 3.
Recommendation 21	The knowledge, skills and understanding that children need to acquire in languages should be situated within the area of learning entitled 'Understanding English, communication and languages'. This will enable teachers and pupils to exploit the links between English and the chosen language(s).
Recommendation 22	Schools should focus on teaching only one or two languages. This should not preclude providing pupils with experiences in other languages as opportunities arise in cross-curricular studies, as long as sustained learning is secured in one or two languages to ensure that children are able to achieve progression over four years in line with the expectations of the Key Stage 2 framework for languages.

Recommendation 23	Primary schools should be free to choose the language(s) that they wish to teach; however, as far as possible the languages offered should be those which children will be taught in Key Stage 3.
Recommendation 24	The commendable work that is taking place to support the delivery of language teaching through workforce development programmes should continue at current levels of funding.
Recommendation 25	A survey by Ofsted of how well primary schools are managing the introduction of languages as a compulsory subject should take place no later than 2014.

The Cambridge Primary Review (Alexander, 2009)

Later in 2009, an independent review of primary education was published. It was based at the University of Cambridge Faculty of Education and directed by Professor Robin Alexander and supported by the Esmée Fairbairn Foundation. The focus of the Cambridge Primary Review was far more wide-ranging than that of the Rose Review which focused on the curriculum. Mathematics was one of the eight curriculum 'domains'. Changes advocated were a broadening of the curriculum, the use of specialist teachers and giving control back to teachers.

The Cambridge Primary Review (Alexander, 2009) – overview of mathematics-related recommendations

Related themes	
School starting age	New structures. Strengthen early years provision; extend foundation stage to age six; replace KS 1 and 2 by a single primary phase; examine feasibility of raising school starting age to six in line with these changes and international research and practice.
Empowerment	End the 'state theory of learning' embodied in post-1997 strategies and policies. Support teaching grounded in repertoire, evidence and principle rather than recipe. Strengthen what separates expert teachers from the rest: their depth of engagement with what is to be taught, quality of classroom interaction and skill in assessing and providing feedback on pupils' learning.
Generalist/specialist roles of primary teachers	Extend teaching roles to include specialists and semi-specialists as well as generalist class teachers, especially for older children.

Research-informed practice	Replace current TDA professional standards by a framework properly validated by research on expertise, professional development and pupil learning. Reform CPD so that it balances support for less secure teachers with freedom for the experienced and talented.
ICT	Protect/expand school libraries. ICT and books are not alternatives: books remain fundamental to children's lives and education.

Values and Variables: Mathematics Education in High-Performing Countries (Askew et al., 2010)

This review was discussed in Chapter 8 and is part of the recent body of evidence which highlights the international perspective evident in emerging government policy.

The review identified that there were a number of key features that are thought to attribute to attainment in mathematics such as funding, use of interactive whiteboards and specific lesson structures. However, the review found that of the high performing countries, such features do not appear to make a difference to attainment. Askew and his team identified further research was needed in the following areas:

- Comparative studies of mathematics education from 'culturally near neigbours'
- Studies into pedagogies that lead to high attainment for all children in order to understand the relationship between beliefs about high attainment and individual progress in children.
- The relationship between high attainment and 'shadow education', particularly in relation to its limited access for children from low socio-economic backgrounds.

Additionally, Askew and his team advocated the following action should take place.

- Improvement in textbooks and e-resources in terms of
  - mathematical coherence
  - connections and variation
  - support for teachers
  - support for pupils to encourage independent learning.
- Development of strategies to reduce the 'opportunity gap' in terms of mathematical qualifications of teachers of pupils from different socio-economic background.
- Engagement of parents and pupils from all socio-economic backgrounds in establishing challenging yet realistic expectations for learning.

- Analysis of tasks that can lead to the development of deep understanding about mathematical concepts as well as competency in procedural methods.

Tickell Review (2011)

In 2010, the Children's Minister, Sarah Teather, asked Dame Clare Tickell, Chief Executive of Action for Children, to carry out a review of the EYFS with a focus on regulation, learning and development, assessment and welfare. The review was published in 2011 with the aim to implement its recommendations from September 2012.

Summary of Tickell Review of EYFS (2011)

Related themes	The Tickell Review of EYFS – overview of mathematics related recommendations
Early Years' qualifications	All early years practitioners to have at least a level 3 qualification (which is equivalent to A level) and the Government should consider applying the 'teaching schools' model to the early years.
Redefinition of areas of learning	(a) Personal, social and emotional development, communication and language and physical development identified as prime areas of learning (b) Four specific areas in which the prime skills are applied: literacy, mathematics, expressive arts and design, and understanding the world.

A World-Class Mathematics Education for All Our Young People (Vorderman et al., 2011)

In 2009, while still in opposition, David Cameron and Michael Gove commissioned a taskforce to improve mathematics teaching chaired by Carol Vorderman, the television personality, who became well-known for the long-running quiz programme *Countdown*. The result was the report *A World-Class Mathematics Education for All Our Young People* published in summer 2011. It concluded that urgent action should be taken as financial numeracy is important both for individuals and for the economy. The position of England in relation to international comparisons was discussed but caution erred against introducing any successful system from a 'culturally different society'. As far as the mathematics curriculum was concerned, it identified that mathematics education was different from other subjects and had to be treated so in terms of policies. It also raised the problem of micro-management and a tick-box approach to assessment in placing barriers to good teaching. It advocated that a National Curriculum should not prescribe teaching methods or the order in which mathematics is taught and emphasised that at primary level mathematics should be used both discretely and across the curriculum each day in the same way that English was practised.

Recommendations (pertaining to primary education) of Vorderman et al. (2011)

Section 1: Mathematics: a subject of critical importance	
1.1	Mathematics should be declared a subject of critical importance. Mathematics should be exempted from general regulations when they are incompatible with the best possible mathematics provision for our young people.
1.2	Mathematics has different requirements from other subjects. A wide community, including employers, should be empowered to take more ownership of all aspects of the mathematics curriculum.
Section 2: Overarching themes	
2.1	The micro-management which has been occurring at local, regional and national level results in barriers to good teaching and learning of mathematics. New styles of management are needed.
2.2	Much greater attention should be paid to the needs of the large number of students who currently learn very little useful mathematics.
2.3	Major innovation is needed to develop a provision that meets the diverse needs of all our students and not just the most talented. Current barriers to such innovation need to be identified and removed.
2.4	Accountability is an integral part of all professional activity but the methods currently in use are restricting the quality of mathematics in our schools and colleges. Different approaches are urgently needed.
Section 3: International comparisons	
3	The attainment of students in top-performing countries presents a target that we should aspire to reach. However, lessons from international comparisons must be applied in the context of this country.
Section 4: Primary Education	
4.1	Urgent steps should be taken to improve the mathematics background of teachers in primary schools.
4.2	Primary teachers should continue to provide a daily mathematics lesson and find appropriate opportunities for using mathematics at other times of the day.

4.3	The National Curriculum for mathematics should be expressed as end-of-primary school outcomes which do not predetermine teaching methods or chronology.
4.4	Each school should have the responsibility for adopting or creating its own mathematics programme.
4.5	Pupils' learning must be reported to parents in relation to the school's curriculum and their progress towards the statutory outcomes for the end of primary schooling.
4.6	The current end of Key Stage 2 National Test (SAT) has outlived its usefulness. The remit of a review should include transition arrangements from Year 6 to Year 7.

Similar sentiments concerning the importance of mathematics to the economy were identified by the Every Child a Chance Trust, an organisation that is a collaboration of the business sector, charitable trusts and government which considers the educational potential of socially disadvantaged children. It commissioned research which has highlighted that around seven million adults in the UK have the mathematics ability of a nine-year-old and that as a result they are more likely to have poor employment opportunities throughout life leading either to low income or to unemployment with all the negative implications in terms of the economy and social cohesion (Every Child a Chance Trust, 2009).

Ofsted Review (2011)

The Ofsted Review (2011, online) considered the work of ten maintained and ten independent schools that had good track records of high achievement in mathematics. The focus was on identifying the characteristics of effective practice.

Key findings of the Ofsted Review (2011)

The following key findings, taken together, reflect the 'what' and 'how' that underpin effective learning through which pupils become fluent in calculating, solving problems and reasoning about number.

- Practical, hands-on experiences of using, comparing and calculating with numbers and quantities and the development of mental methods are of crucial importance in establishing the best mathematical start in the Early Years Foundation Stage and Key Stage 1. The schools visited couple this with plenty of opportunities for developing mathematical language so that pupils learn to express their thinking using the correct vocabulary.

- Understanding of place value, fluency in mental methods, and good recall of number facts such as multiplication tables and number bonds are considered by the schools to be essential precursors for learning traditional vertical algorithms (methods) for addition, subtraction, multiplication and division.[1]
- Subtraction is generally introduced alongside its inverse operation, addition, and division alongside its inverse, multiplication. Pupils' fluency and understanding of this concept of inverse operations are aided by practice in rewriting 'number sentences' like $3 + 5 = 8$ as $8 - 3 = 5$ and $8 - 5 = 3$ and solving 'missing number' questions like $\square - 4 = 5$ by thinking $5 + 4 = 9$ or $9 - 4 = 5$.
- High-quality teaching secures pupils' understanding of structure and relationships in number, for instance place value and the effect of multiplying or dividing by 10, and progress in developing increasingly sophisticated mental and written methods.
- In lessons and in interviews with inspectors, pupils often chose the traditional algorithms over other methods. When encouraged, most showed flexibility in their thinking and approaches, enabling them to solve a variety of problems as well as calculate accurately.
- Pupils' confidence, fluency and versatility are nurtured through a strong emphasis on problem-solving as an integral part of learning within each topic. Skills in calculation are strengthened through solving a wide range of problems, exploiting links with work on measures and data handling, and meaningful application to cross-curricular themes and work in other subjects.
- The schools are quick to recognise and intervene in a focused way when pupils encounter difficulties. Thus ensures misconceptions do not impede the next steps in learning.
- Many of the schools have reduced the use of 'expanded methods' and 'chunking' in moving towards efficient methods because they find that too many steps in methods confuse pupils, especially the less able. Several of the schools do not teach the traditional long division algorithm by the end of Year 6 (age 11) and most of those that do say that a large proportion of pupils do not become fluent in it.
- A feature of strong practice in the maintained schools is their clear, coherent calculation policies and guidance, which are tailored to the particular school's context. They ensure consistent approaches and use of visual images and models that secure progression in pupils' skills and knowledge lesson by lesson and year by year.
- These schools recognise the importance of good subject knowledge and subject-specific teaching skills and seek to enhance these aspects of subject expertise. Some of the schools benefit from senior or subject leaders who have high levels of mathematical expertise. Several schools adopt whole-school approaches to developing the subject expertise of teachers and teaching assistants. This supports effective planning, teaching and intervention. Most of the larger independent preparatory schools provide specialist mathematics teaching from Year 4 or 5 onwards.

Note
1. Place value is determined by the position of a digit within a number, for instance in 6135, the value of the 3 is three tens, and the 6 is six thousands. Number bonds include useful pairs of numbers, such as 1 and 9 or 3 and 7, both pairs of which add up to 10.

Stakeholders

Government perspectives

It can be seen that the government has a considerable body of evidence on which to draw which has identified the imperative of changing primary mathematics teaching and learning to a more problem-based approach grounded in school-based policies and practices. Additionally, there is evidence to suggest that a subject specialist emphasis would be valuable in our primary education system rather than one based on generic teaching and learning strategies.

- Look at the report summaries. Can you identify any common themes related to the age group which you teach?
- What do you believe are the priorities in mathematics education?

Teachers and their schools

The government has made clear recommendations about schools becoming more autonomous in the way that teaching and learning takes place.

- How will schools manage greater autonomy following a period of significantly reduced autonomy?
- What do you believe should take place in schools where you have taught or currently teach?

Children and their families

When policies change, the evidence for the change is not always clear or disseminated among 'stakeholders'.

- How do you believe children and their families can access the evidence to understand any changes that may be made?

Pedagogy

As has been highlighted in the reviews of mathematics primary education, there are specific differences in mathematical pedagogy compared to general pedagogy. Teacher confidence and competence – hence empowerment – comes from having good knowledge. As discussed in Chapter 4, subject knowledge includes not only knowledge of mathematics but beliefs about and attitudes towards the curriculum and pedagogy. If teachers are equipped with such knowledge they can design a teaching and learning approach that is well-researched and contextually relevant to the children in their care. The recent micro-management of the education system by the government can be seen to have effects beyond just disempowering teachers. Apart from limited reference being given to the research basis for new initiatives, it has the potential to confuse the fundamental process of assessment as a teaching and learning strategy with the accountability of teachers and their schools. Teachers have been expected to implement rather than evaluate such initiatives and in so doing are being trained rather than educated. However, teaching is not a skill that produces a product by defined processes. Teaching is a dynamic process that relates to an evolving relationship between the learner, the teacher and the curriculum. Many practising teachers are likely to be challenged when given more autonomy over decision-making within this process now they have become used to having defined processes to deliver.

At the heart of changing practice is the way we view 'teacher training' from 0–11. In terms of the 5–11 teaching age range, simply selecting candidates with a higher level of entry qualifications has been shown not to be necessarily a solution (Askew et al., 1997). What did support teachers was continuing professional development.

Government

In his speech at the Pimlico Academy in October 2011 the Secretary of State for Education, Michael Gove, discussed the importance of Early Years education and highlighted the issue of differences in qualifications between the workforces in the early years and statutory sector. Also, he discussed pedagogy and the impact of nurture in the Early Years on a child's brain as well as the different perspectives on how children learn.

- How can the differences in recruitment and qualifications of the Early Years workforce be managed?
- Do you think there are strategies the government could provide to support teachers and schools in the transition to greater autonomy in teaching and learning?

Teachers and their schools

The government White Paper (DfE, 2010, online) has identified a shift from training in universities to a more decentralised model with more training taking place in schools with an emphasis on recruiting graduates with at least an upper second degree.

- How do you view the changes in relation to your teacher education?
- How can schools enable teachers to engage in CPD outside a centralised module that includes CPD providers such as local authorities and universities?
- What types of CPD in mathematics teaching could be made available to all teachers?

Children and their families

A significant challenge in the micro-management of teaching and learning in school has been relating it to the individual children and their families within the school. Education is a process not a product and equal input does not mean equal output. The range of variables that confront any classroom teacher is enormous and can be compounded in schools where more than one chronological age group is taught together. Changes that are currently evolving may mean that parents more actively choose a school based upon specific teaching and learning approaches and the strategies for supporting individual learners.

- How can the views of parents and their children be taken into account when deciding on teaching and learning strategies in mathematics?

Summary

This chapter has looked at the roles of mathematics, pedagogy and philosophy that inform policy. It has considered how the influence of the stakeholders in mathematics education can influence how policy is defined.

Conclusion

An old adage has been that history is a record of the past, a guide to the present and a forecast of the future. Initially this may not seem appropriate to the focus of this book: teaching primary mathematics. However, just as the Industrial Revolution heralded a change in the demand on society in the form of mass education, so the technological revolution is putting a new set of demands on society. Education, in whatever form, must meet these demands to function effectively. There is much talk about education for the twenty-first century but little agreement about what this means in practice. The level of autonomy in organising and implementing the curriculum is yet unknown. School autonomy will only have any real meaning if schools are enabled to act as part of a professional body, accountable, but not at the level of minutiae currently expected. However, unless as a society we know where we are aiming in education then little will change. Chapter 3 discussed the curriculum as what Mick Waters called the 'Big Picture'. We are all stakeholders in the 'Big Picture'. Educational reviews encourage participation by stakeholders but do not necessarily transfer to genuine understanding and engagement at school level. It would seem now is the time for schools to take on this role.

For ITE students going into primary education, the challenge is meeting all the requirements of a fast-changing educational field together with personal challenges across a variety of subject areas that bring different demands. Such challenges require time and patience and the setting of goals and priorities that are realistic. One teacher cannot change the world but one teacher can change the world of the children in a class. Working in a school that fosters learning for all its stakeholders – teachers, teaching assistants, children, their families and communities – would be an ideal. To be the teacher of a class that is enthusiastic about mathematics and respect and hopefully love it would seem a worthy aim.

Review questions

1. What do you think are the challenges that face you with the new proposals?
2. How does your personal experience of the education system relate to the practice you know today? What is similar and what is different? You may be able to use these reflective thoughts to extend the pen portrait started in Chapter 1.
3. Can you match your personal perspectives with national and local agenda?

References

Alexander, R. (ed.) (2009) *Children, Their World, Their Education: Final Report and Recommendations of the Cambridge Primary Review*. London: Routledge. Available online at: http://www.primaryreview.org.uk/ (accessed 12 November 2011).

Askew, M., Brown, M., Rhodes, V., Wiliam, D. and Johnson, D. (1997) *Effective Teachers of Numeracy: Report of a Study Carried Out for the Teacher Training Agency*. London: King's College, University of London.

Askew, M., Hodgen, J., Hossain, S. and Bretscher, N. (2010) *Values and Variables: Mathematics Education in High-Performing Countries*, Nuffield Foundation Report. Available online at: http://www.nuffieldfoundation.org (accessed 12 November 2011).

Boaler, J. (2009) *The Elephant in the Classroom. Helping Children Learn and Love Maths*. London: Souvenir Press.

Bradshaw, J., Sturman, L., Vappula, H., Ager, R. and Wheater, R. (2007) *Achievement of 15-year-olds in England: PISA 2006 National Report*, OECD Programme for International Student Assessment. Slough: NFER. Available online at: http://www.nfer.ac.uk/nfer/publications/NPC02/NPC02_home.cfm?publicationID=2 98&title=Achievement of 15-year-olds in England: PISA 2006 National Report (accessed 7 March 2012).

Brodie, I. (2003) *The Involvement of Parents and Carers in Sure Start Local Evaluations*. London: National Evaluation of Sure Start.

DfE (2010) *The Importance of Teaching: Schools White Paper*. Available online at: https://www.education.gov.uk/publications/eOrderingDownload/CM-7980.pdf (accessed 7 March 2012).

DfE (2011) *Teachers' Standards in England from September 2012*.

EURYDICE (2011) *Information on Education Systems and Policies in Europe*. Available online at: http://eacea.ec.europa.eu/education/eurydice/index_php (accessed 15 October 2011).

Every Child a Chance Trust (2009) *Long-Term Costs of Numeracy Difficulties*. Available online at: http://www.everychildachancetrust.org/downloads/ecc/Long%20term%20costs%20of%20numeracy%20difficulties.pdf.

Gove, M. (2011) Speech, 28 October. Available online at: http://www.education.gov.uk/a00199946/michael-gove-speaks-at-pimlico-academy-about-the-importance-of-early-years (accessed 10 November 2011).

Information on Education Systems and Policies in Europe (EURYDICE) (2009) Available online at: http://eacea.ec.europa.eu/education/eurydice/index_en.php (accessed 15 October 2011).

OECD (2010) *PISA 2009 Results: What Students Know and Can Do – Student Performance in Reading, Mathematics and Science*. Available online at: http://www.oecd.org/edu/pisa/2009 (accessed 6 March 2012).

Ofsted (2009) *Mathematics: Understanding the Score: Improving Practice in Mathematics Teaching at Primary Level*. London: Ofsted.

Ofsted (2011) *Good Practice in Primary Mathematics: Evidence from 20 Successful Schools*. Ofsted. Available online at: http://www.ofsted.gov.uk/resources/good-practice-primary-mathematics-evidence-20-successful-schools (accessed 7 March 2012).

Rose, J. (2009) *Independent Review of the Primary Curriculum: Final Report*. London: DCFS.

Tickell, C. (2010) *The Tickell Review of the Early Years Foundation Stage*. London: HM Government.

Vorderman, C., Budd, C., Dunne, R., Hart, M. and Porkess, R. (2011) *A World-Class Mathematics Education for All Our Young People*. DfE. Available online at: http://www.conservatives.com/News/News_stories/2011/08/~/media/Files/Downloadable%20Files/Vorderman%20maths%20report.ashx (accessed 16 November 2011).

Williams, Sir P. (2008) *Independent Review of Mathematics Teaching in Early Years Settings and Primary Schools*. London: DCSF.

Further reading

Bolam, R., McMahon, A., Stoll, L., Thomas, S. and Wallace, M. (2005) *Creating and Sustaining Effective Professional Learning Communities*, Research Report 637. London: Department for Education and Skills.

Cordingley, P., Bell, M., Rundell, B. and Evans, D. (2003) 'The impact of collaborative CPD on classroom teaching and learning: how does collaborative continuing professional development (CPD) for teachers of the 5–16 age range affect teaching and learning?', in *Research Evidence in Education Library*. London: EPPI-Centre, Social Research Unit, Institute of Education.

Goodson, I. F. (2003) *Professional Knowledge, Professional Lives: Studies in Education and Change*. Maidenhead: Open University Press.

Hodgen, J. and Askew, M. (2007) 'Emotion, identity and teacher learning: becoming a primary mathematics teacher', *Oxford Review of Education*, 33 (4): 469–87.

Jones, K. (2004) 'A new past, an old future', cited in T. Locke, G. Vulliamy, R. Webb and M. Hill (2005) 'Being a professional primary school teacher at the beginning of the 21st century: a comparative analysis of primary teacher professionalism in New Zealand and England', *Journal of Education Policy*, 20 (5): 555–81.

NUT (2005) 'Professionalism today', special issue of *Education Review*, 18 (2).

EUROPEAN RESEARCH STUDY

Secondary data

INCA database: http://www.inca.org
Eurydice database: http://www.eurydice.org

Primary data – contextual information

I. Italy

(a) Research took place in Gambolò, a small town near Vigevano in Lombardy, approximately 60 kilometres to the south-west of Milan. It is a semi-urban location in an agricultural area which produces rice. Schools from the baby 'nest' to the secondary school are grouped together and serve the local community. Two teachers and their classes of 9–10-year-old children were observed and this process was followed by a semi-structured interview.

(b) Research took place in Reggio Emilia, a prosperous city in northern Italy, in the Emilia-Romagna region. The economy of the area is based upon agriculture and one product it is famous for is the Parmigiano-Reggiano (Parmesan) cheese. The name Reggio Emilia has become synonymous with Early Years education on an international basis.

A meeting was arranged with a pedagogue (teacher) for the Infant Toddler Centre and Infant School Institutions. The discussion took place in the Loris Malaguzzi International Centre. The location afforded the opportunity of looking at the exhibits of children's work and the facilities for professional development and research for teachers, families and researchers.

2. Ireland

(a)   The Church of Ireland College of Education and Kildare Place National School (on site), Rathmines, Dublin, Republic of Ireland. The College is 200 years old, and as such is one of the oldest teacher training colleges in Ireland. A meeting was arranged with the Lecturer in Mathematics. The meeting was followed by observation in the school of two teachers and their classes of 9–10-year-old children and a semi-structured interview with the teachers and head teacher of the school.
(b)   Malahide County Dublin. Originally a village, Malahide is a coastal suburban, generally affluent town on the outskirts of Dublin. Two schools were visited and semi-structured interviews took place with staff in each school.
(c)   England-born teacher on a CPD course in England but living and teaching in the Republic of Ireland.

3. Spain

Jerez de la Frontera (Jerez) is a city of approximately 200,000 people in the region of Andalucía in a fertile area in south-west Spain. It is famous worldwide for sherry, Flamenco festivals and the riding school, the Royal Andalusian School of Equestrian Art. Southern Spain has suffered from high unemployment for a number of years. This has had an effect on the population. Staff at the Teachers' Centre cited personal situations identifying family incomes being significantly reduced as only one parent is able to gain employment.

(a)   Primary School, Jerez – two-year entry from 3 to 12 years divided into three years of pre-primary and six years of primary. There are approximately 25 children per class. Parents were identified socio-economically as lower middle class. Parents actively involved in their children's education going to every meeting and participating in every activity that the school organises. They help their children to do homework. Two teachers and their classes of 9–10-year-old children were observed followed by semi-structured interviews.

(b) Teaching Centre Jerez – semi-structured interview with advisers at the Centre.

International comparisons

While international comparisons have been discussed in Chapter 8, it is thought useful to contextualise the data in relation to international comparisons. There is little published data on PISA and TIMSS by countries other than the UK, USA and Ireland. Neither Spain or Ireland has participated in TIMSS. In the PISA OECD Executive Summary (2010) it was noted that Italy was one of the countries where:

> Students in urban schools perform better than students in other schools, even after accounting for differences in socioeconomic background the performance gap between students in urban schools and those in rural schools is more than 45 score. As in Italy there are significant differences between the industrial north and rural south it is particularly difficult to analyse PISA rankings in Italy.

	PISA 2009	**TIMSS**
England	34th	7th
Italy	32nd	19th
Republic of Ireland	32nd	n/a
Spain	35th	n/a

Research in Italy

Key topics

As stated, the themes come from a subjective basis in terms of the researcher and the interpretation of information expressed by teachers.

Enjoyment of mathematics

The response by teachers was that some children found it hard but it was important that it was made meaningful to them and it was important that they valued mathematics. As far as the teachers were concerned, they appeared to have a respect for the subject and did not see it as a matter of dislike or not.

Curriculum

Although the curriculum is updated nationally, it did not appear that the changes were significant. For example, the pre-schools run by the city of Reggio Emilia are not state schools. They are fee-paying but the fee is based upon parental income. Such schools follow the same curriculum as all pre-schools in Italy. The fact that the curriculum is the basis for education whether private or state did not appear to be an issue of contention. This may be because it is written in the form of coverage and general guidance rather than being prescriptive. For example, a competence at the end of pre-school is:

> The child gathers and sorts according to different criteria, compares and evaluates quantity; uses simple symbols to record; accomplished by simple measurements tools. (Ministero della Pubblica Istruzione, 2007: 39)

and at the end of primary school:

> The student develops a positive attitude with respect to mathematics . . . moves confidently in written and mental calculations with whole numbers . . . (Ministero della Pubblica Istruzione, 2007: 94)

School planning documents and textbooks exemplify the curriculum in detail. As textbooks are chosen by the Teachers Assembly, along with other resources in consultation with parents, they have ownership of teaching. The Teachers Assembly is composed of all the permanent and temporary teachers of each primary school group or of an individual primary school. It is responsible for teaching and planning for each school year. It must follow national legislation and guidelines and take note of community needs and concerns, i.e. school hours. As such, teachers have ownership along with parents and hence more autonomy about what it is being taught and how it is taught.

Textbook coverage showed content very similar to the UK but explanatory information was evident. For example, children were given examples of how calculations could be solved using knowledge of the associative, commutative and distributive laws. When teachers were asked about the curriculum one stated:

We have the booklet which our planning is based on. We don't look at it that much but the textbooks are based on it so we know we cover it. We plan each subject for the year and then break it down in three-month cycles. Each week we meet to plan for two hours.

When asked how teachers incorporated the curriculum stress on proof and discussion into their teaching one teacher stated:

Well maths is about proof – finding truth – you know the great mathematicians – that is what they did. Children must try to think like that.

The response in Gambolò was very similar to the discussion in Reggio Emilia. Although the focus in Reggio Emilia was pre-primary education, the philosophy behind mathematics was similar – searching for truth in different forms, making sense of it and finding out together.

Teaching and learning/differentiation/resources

Classroom organisation with the teacher at the front and children sitting in rows with a textbook placed on their desk gave the impression of a didactic model of teaching and learning but such an initial impression from observing in classrooms was misleading. The style of teaching was such that the teacher did not control learning in terms of prescribing procedures, but enabled children to 'discover' the mathematics by structured questions and the teaching points made, a style of teaching that would be classed probably as 'interactive' in England. In this way the teacher facilitated understanding by bridging new learning into existing knowledge through encouraging children to think and make links. For example, the children were finding out how to work out the area of a rhombus. The teaching focus was eliciting information from the children by asking for ideas on how to find the area, proof, using previous knowledge, i.e. area of square, perpendiculars, right angles, diagonals. At no time were the children told how to work out the area of the rhombus. If they offered an idea they had to say why. Although the learning outcome was the same for all children and it was hard to identify the level of differentiation, it appeared that some children who needed additional help were targeted with more detailed questions. Using the knowledge of the solution to the worked example, the same interactive technique was used to work out a formula using the diameters of the rhombus – $D \times d/2$. The children were given a small rhombus on squared paper to stick in their books. They drew in the diagonals and wrote their bisected lengths. They then made the four triangles into squares to show the method of proof and then wrote down the formula. The teacher then dictated the method of how to work out the area of a regular rhombus and they wrote it under their diagram.

The lesson concluded with the children being directed back to the textbook and told to start the exercise of finding areas of rhombi which they were to complete for homework.

Teacher training/subject knowledge

Teachers found questions about how their initial training supported their understanding of teaching mathematics confusing. They seemed quite clear that it had done so and as teachers it was their responsibility to know how to teach mathematics. Although both teachers observed displayed excellent subject knowledge, no judgements can be drawn other than stating they were chosen to be observed purely based on time available, not as having any specialism in mathematics.

Assessment

Children are assessed regularly in the class and at the end of each year. This was seen as supporting both the children and their parents in understanding mathematical progress. When the subject of accountability was broached, teachers did not seem to have a concept of their teaching being judged beyond the school or within the school. The only related response obtained was that it was their duty to do the best for the children.

Resources

The concept of resources was hard to define but appeared to come back to the idea of making learning meaningful. In Reggio Emilia, the environment is seen as the third teacher so it could be said that resources were a significant element in teaching but this would be misleading. There was a lack of purpose-made mathematical resources. With younger children there were 'real' resources such as paving stones and plants and with older children there appeared to be more use of diagrams and language related to real objects rather than the objects themselves. ICT but was not in use regularly in the classrooms, i.e. there was no interactive whiteboards. It appeared to be used by teachers as a teaching aid rather than a learning aid. The key resource appeared to be the teachers working with the children, and with older children, the textbook appeared to structure learning and support the link between involvement with parents at home. ICT in the form of interactive whiteboards and software was available but not in all classes.

Textbooks were easy to follow for a non-Italian speaker due to the nature of the Italian language and the similarity of the mathematics vocabulary in

English and Italian coupled with the extensive use of visual representations of mathematics on the blackboard and in textbooks.

Emerging issues

The role of teachers

One of the topics often discussed in literature about the Reggio Emilia system is the fact that staffing levels are high, with two teachers per class as well as an artist (*atelier*) and care staff. Although not all schools have artists, staffing ratios in all Italian schools are high. In the school visited there were two teachers attached to each class. When they were not taking their class they could be taking another class to cover for that teacher, participating in a group planning meeting or free to mark books. As the maximum number of taught hours per week is 27, class contact hours are much less. Additionally there are staff who, like teachers, hold civil service jobs called 'bidella' and 'bidello'. They are literally 'caretakers' – they look after the children as well as the building. Although teachers were 'caring' of children and some were demonstrative in their affection for the children they taught it was quite clear that the teachers were there to teach, not do ancillary jobs.

The role of homework

It was expected that when children went home they completed homework from the textbook. Hours at school ranged between 24 and 27 with sometimes additional activities in the afternoon for those who wished to participate and when their parents were working. These activities were not seen as part of the main curriculum.

Class size

The fact that the classes were no more than 24 meant there could be active participation on the part of the children. Questions were answered by a 'hands-up' routine but teachers selected children so they were involved and any that did not volunteer were asked questions.

Research in the Republic of Ireland

Key topics

Enjoyment of mathematics

Discussions indicated that there were similar issues concerning mathematics in terms of dislike of the subject within the country. One teacher was aware of literature concerning mathematics and the research carried out by Buxton (1981) and was aware of research in the USA.

The curriculum

There is evidence from both secondary and primary data that there are significant similarities between the Early Years and Primary School systems in terms of curriculum content and the way Early Years education has evolved in recent years. This is not surprising given their proximity and shared use of English. It does mean that the differences in the systems appear more striking and are not always evident from documentation. Textbooks make a significant contribution to the teaching approach and act as a form of planning.

Teaching and learning strategies, differentiation and textbooks

Observations initially indicated a didactic style of teaching with either a textbook or workbook being the key resource. However, the difference in lessons observed depended on the teacher. It was the teacher who enabled learning to involve thinking rather than following procedures and completing textbook examples. Questioning was fundamental to this approach and was the basis for structuring children's thinking. Although there was a set book per class, there was a range of books called 'shadow' books that supported both the most and the least able. One concern raised by a teacher was that the shadow books for the able gave more of the same rather than developing the child's understanding. Additionally, there were other textbooks that were used to support the range of abilities within a class. For those less able children, they might attend Learning Support for additional maths. Occasionally a child would remain with his or her year group but work on books for either the year above or below.

Teacher training and subject knowledge

Theoretical subjects of philosophy, psychology and sociology are studied as well as the more practiced-based subjects. Issues of mathematics competence and confidence were raised in discussion.

Assessment

Assessment is carried out regularly in class and at the end of each year and shared with parents. Assessment has been introduced at the end of the primary years but did not seem to be of significant concern in terms of accountability. Teachers were aware of Ofsted and those I spoke to had a very negative opinion of such a form of accountability.

Resources

There was a range of structural resources in classrooms and ICT was used to some extent but as a teaching aid rather than an aid to learning. Some classrooms had interactive whiteboards but they were not used each day for teaching. The key resource was the teacher working with either workbooks or textbooks. Textbooks are used across the whole curriculum and it is the responsibility of parents to buy the textbooks. Schools do not consult parents about which book schemes to use. Although there is a means-tested school clothing allowance, in the present economic climate there have been complaints about the cost of 'free' education as it is expected that parents buy the school uniform, books and make a school contribution.

Publishers often update books every year which makes it difficult to pass on books if a school decides to go with latest edition. Some schools have book rental schemes where the textbooks are hired from the schools and only workbooks need to be bought. A few secondary schools are now using e-books and the child rents a laptop to gain access to the e-books.

Emerging issues

The role of teachers

The role of teachers in terms of expectations of the job beyond teaching was significant. Overall teachers are paid better than their counterparts in England and work significantly less hours. Additionally the majority of schools are rural. As such, the school is the centre of the community and relationships between parents, teachers and children appear strong. It was not thought strange to be on first name terms with parents and children saw teachers at social occasions.

Shadow education

Askew et al. (2010) identified the significance in attainment of what is termed 'shadow education', education that is additional to that which takes place in school. Shadow education appeared to be a major feature of education in Ireland. Denoted as 'Grinds', according to a survey carried out by Student Enrichment Services (2011) 61 per cent of Leaving Certificate students did Grinds on a regular basis in 2010 in response to poor Leaving Certificate results. As a result there had been a drive to find good mathematics teachers.

Language teaching

Teachers must be fluent in Irish and must attend the Gaeltacht (Irish-speaking regions) as part of their programme. Irish is taught throughout primary school. Teachers interviewed believed that if it was possible for children to be competent in two languages in Ireland, the same was possible in England.

Research in Spain

Key topics

Enjoyment of mathematics

Advisory teachers were very aware of concerns about mathematics attainment in Spain. Some blamed traditional approaches and what they believed to be rote learning while others thought the issue was to do with variable teacher training. Their concern focused around attainment rather than enjoyment. Due to the high level of English language competency in the class it was possible to ask the children about their attitude to mathematics. The response was mixed, some saying it was boring whereas others were very positive. According to the teacher their response was not based on their attainment in the subject.

Curriculum

The curriculum (Sala de Comisiones, 2006) includes legislation and teacher training as well as the pre-school and statutory curriculum. It gives general principles and overviews of subjects. For example, in the primary phase Article 7, Objectives for Primary Education, it states:

> Develop basic math skills and initiative in solving problems that require the elementary operations of calculus, geometry and estimates and be able to apply them to everyday life situations.

Teaching and learning/differentiation/resources

Teachers were generalists but tended to specialise in a subject. One teacher observed stated that her special subject was English but it was fine teaching mathematics. She used the textbook as a basis to research lessons before she taught them. Considering she did not believe mathematics to be her specialism her style was very lively and engaged the children. Teaching was very interactive and all children were actively involved. At the end of the lesson the children started on their homework task. One child was struggling and asked for help and was called to the front to work with the teacher. Class sizes were no more than 24 per class.

Teacher training and subject knowledge

As discussed subject knowledge is identified in general terms in *La ley orgánica de educación* (Sala de Comisiones, 2006). Concerns were raised by some advisory teachers about the standard of teacher training. Teachers who were interviewed did not support this view but felt it was up to them to improve their knowledge.

Assessment

Children are assessed regularly in class and at the end of the year. At one time it was common to hold children back until they had passed the end-of-year tests but this rarely happens now. One adviser was concerned that although it was agreed it is not good for a child socially and emotionally to be held back, no clear structure was in place to support or differentiate work.

Accountability was not understood in the way it is meant in England. When asked if the head teacher checked a teacher's planning the teacher was shocked and said 'No, it is written in *my* book!' This may in part be due to the fact that head teachers do not have the same authority as in the UK. Head teachers are elected from the senior members of staff and have a reduced teaching timetable.

Resources

Textbooks are the key resource along with some use of ICT. Some advisers blame textbooks for poor results and believe they lead teaching and do not meet the needs of the child. The challenge has been that textbooks are such an implicit part of teaching and learning strategies in Spain that it would be seen as unacceptable to remove them. Additionally, they represent a significant financial commitment to education as Andalucía decided to give textbooks free of charge to children. This initiative increases the incentive to use them.

Emerging issues

Relationship between teachers and children

Teachers did not appear to rely on their status to manage children. They dressed casually and teachers and children addressed each other by first names. A lesson observed taken by a young teacher contained an element of banter, including light jokes. Another teacher observed had taken semi-retirement and so worked a reduced timetable. His style was very different to the younger teacher but equally relaxed. Again the teacher made jokes which amused the children but there was never an issue of negative behaviour.

Language

Surprisingly, the children were able to converse with me well and explain what they were doing. Andalucía has a bilingual language programme running in schools and in the 10–12 age group the children were taught science through English. Their workbooks were fairly formal, i.e. the next lesson was to be about the water cycle and included a written description in English with explanatory diagrams. What was surprising was the level of English of all children in the class. Although there were differences, all children could speak in sentences about their mathematics work.

Discussion of ERS

I. Textbooks

Askew et al. (2010) raised the issue of textbooks in their comparative review in 2010. The ERS identified the significance of textbooks as a resource for teaching and learning mathematics and the relationship between home and school. The textbooks were very easy to understand for a non-speaker of the language concerned.

* *Should textbooks be a significant part of teaching and learning mathematics?*
* *How can the quality of textbooks be judged?*

2. ICT

Although ICT was evident in schools it was not as evident as in English schools. In some cases it was more an aid to teaching rather than learning.

* *What is the role of ICT in teaching and learning mathematics?*
* *Is the use of ICT equated with preparing children for the future?*
* *Could the strengths of textbook use be combined with the ICT structure in place in England?*

3. The role of teachers

The teachers visited were not under so much scrutiny as those in England.

* *Should teachers govern and regulate themselves?*
* *What would have to change to allow this to happen?*

With regard to expectations of the teacher's role, the teachers visited did not have such a wide range of expectations beyond teaching as in England.

* *What should teachers be expected to do beyond teaching?*

- *What should be the role of assistants in classrooms, i.e. should they be involved in more care and less teaching?*
- *Does the way classes are organised make teaching require the support of assistants who teach?*
- *Should teachers be expected to run clubs and activities?*

The relationship between children and teachers was found to be different to that found in England.

- *Are the differences in relationships purely cultural?*
- *Are certain types of behaviour demonstrated by teachers and children, i.e. first name terms seen as lack of respect, and if so, why?*
- *Would more informal relationships between children and teachers support teaching and learning as well as behaviour management?*

With regard to teacher training and subject knowledge, mixed views were found. The approach to mathematics in Italy raised a different perspective on the subject of mathematics.

- *Should a view of mathematics as a subject to be respected be promoted?*
- *Could this come from greater understanding of historical development?*

With regard to pre-school education, compared to England and the Republic of Ireland pre-school education is firmly embedded in society in Italy and Spain. The role of the state and the family would appear to be perceived differently in these countries, with them both complementing each other in the care and education of children, neither being seen as more responsible than others.

- *How is the responsibility of pre-school children understood in England?*
- *How can state and family mutually support each other in the care and education of children?*

With regard to language teaching, although Modern Foreign Languages is taught in England it is not a fundamental aspect of the curriculum.

- *Could second language teaching support the development of children's language skills across the whole curriculum?*

References

Askew, M., Hodgen, J., Hossain, S. and Bretscher, N. (2010) *Values and Variables: Mathematics Education in High-Performing Countries.* Nuffield Foundation Report. Available online at: http://www.nuffieldfoundation.org (accessed 12 November 2011).

Buxton, J. (1981) *Do You Panic About Maths? Coping with Maths Anxiety.* London: Heinemann.

Ministero della Pubblica Istruzione (2007) *Indicazioni per il curricolo per la scuola dell'infanzia e per il primo ciclo d'istruzione.* Rome: Ministero della Pubblica Istruzione. Available online at: http://www.indire.it/indicazioni/templates/monitoraggio/dir_310707.pdf (accessed 24 October 2001).

Sala de Comisiones (2006) *La ley orgánica de educación* (Education Law). Available online at: http://www.me.gov.ar/doc_pdf/ley_de_educ_nac.pdf (accessed 6 March 2012).

Student Enrichment Services (2011) Available online at: http://www.studentenrichment.ie/ (accessed 19 October 2011).

REFLECTION AND 'WRITING' A REFLECTIVE JOURNAL

Reflection is a term that is used frequently in academic circles. Students are expected to 'reflect' on their learning. In the context of teaching, emphasis is placed on becoming a reflective practitioner. Students may initially reject this idea as they find it hard work to develop skills that are not clearly defined. Modelling reflective writing has its drawbacks as, by its very nature, reflection is distinctly personal. However, there is the danger of surrounding the process of reflection in mystique. At its simplest form reflection is learning from experience. It is useful to record your reflective thoughts and ideas in a journal.

The journal *could* include any or all of the following:

- research notes;
- personal comments on your previous experience, studies or teaching;
- notes/images from visits to school or other related educational settings;
- extracts from lectures, tutorials, books, journals, newspapers;
- photos/diagrams;
- mind maps.

Reflective writing is evidence of looking back at an experience (event, idea or process) and it usually involves:

- analysing and commenting on the experience from different points of view using current ideas and theories;
- exploring and explaining the importance or relevance of the experience;
- considering what went well and why;
- considering what could have been improved and why;
- saying what the experience means to you;
- saying how your learning will affect your future practice.

It helps to structure your reflection. Whatever form you decide to use, sometimes it is helpful to have a 'toolbox' of language to help write reflectively. You will see some examples below.

- Brief description:
  - what it is
  - what happened
  - why I am reflecting upon it.

Language

The significant / important / relevant / useful aspect(s) / element(s) / experience(s) / issue(s) was / were . . .

Previously/ at the time / initially / subsequently / later I thought / felt / noticed / realised . . .

This could be / is probably because of / due to / explained by / related to . . .

This reveals / demonstrates / is different from / is similar to . . .

The consensus between the finding of x and y puts a strong case for . . .

There appears to be agreement/tension between . . .

- Interpretation – what is:
  - important
  - relevant
  - interesting
  - useful
  - how similar to or different from others
  and how can it be:
  - explored
  - explained using contemporary theories?

- Outcome:
  - What have I learned from this?
  - How will it influence my future work?

Having read / experienced / analysed / compared I now / feel / think / realise / wonder / know . . .

I have significantly developed / improved my knowledge of / understanding / ability to . . .

In the light of x's argument I have considered . . .

This reveals / demonstrates / is different from / is similar to . . .

The implications for my research/teaching are . . .

X's findings have shed light on my experience because . . .

Given x, it could be argued . . .

INDEX